THE DAILY STUDY BIBLE

(OLD TESTAMENT)

General Editor: John C. L. Gibson

EZRA, NEHEMIAH, AND ESTHER

EZRA, NEHEMIAH, AND ESTHER

J. G. McCONVILLE

WESTMINSTER JOHN KNOX PRESS
LOUISVILLE, KENTUCKY

Published by
The Saint Andrew Press
Edinburgh, Scotland
and
Westminster John Knox Press
Louisville, Kentucky

PRINTED IN THE UNITED STATES OF AMERICA

6 8 10 12 11 9 7

Library of Congress Cataloging in Publication Data

McConville, J. G. (J. Gordon)
Ezra, Nehemiah, and Esther.

(The Daily study Bible series)
Bibliography: p.
1. Bible. O.T. Ezra—Commentaries. 2. Bible. O.T. Nehemiah—Commentaries. 3. Bible. O.T. Esther—Commentaries. I. Title. II. Series: Daily study Bible series (Westminster Press)
BS1355.3.M29 1985   222   84-25825
ISBN 0-664-21814-8
ISBN 0-664-24583-8 (pbk.)

GENERAL PREFACE

This series of commentaries on the Old Testament, to which Dr McConville's volume on *Ezra, Nehemiah and Esther* belongs, has been planned as a companion series to the much-acclaimed New Testament series of the late Professor William Barclay. As with that series, each volume is arranged in successive headed portions suitable for daily study. The Biblical text followed is that of the Revised Standard Version or Common Bible. Eleven contributors share the work, each being responsible for from one to three volumes. The series is issued in the hope that it will do for the Old Testament what Professor Barclay's series succeeded so splendidly in doing for the New Testament—make it come alive for the Christian believer in the twentieth century.

Its two-fold aim is the same as his. Firstly, it is intended to introduce the reader to some of the more important results and fascinating insights of modern Old Testament scholarship. Most of the contributors are already established experts in the field with many publications to their credit. Some are younger scholars who have yet to make their names but who in my judgment as General Editor are now ready to be tested. I can assure those who use these commentaries that they are in the hands of competent teachers who know what is of real consequence in their subject and are able to present it in a form that will appeal to the general public.

The primary purpose of the series, however, is *not* an academic one. Professor Barclay summed it up for his New Testament series in the words of Richard of Chichester's prayer—to enable men and women "to know Jesus Christ more clearly, to love Him more dearly, and to follow Him more nearly." In the case of the Old Testament we have to be a little more circumspect than that. The Old Testament was completed long before the time of Our Lord, and it was (as it still is) the sole Bible of the Jews, God's first people, before it became part of the Christian Bible. We must take this fact seriously.

Yet in its strangely compelling way, sometimes dimly and sometimes directly, sometimes charmingly and sometimes embarrassingly, it holds up before us the things of Christ. It should not be forgotten that Jesus Himself was raised on this Book, that He based His whole ministry on what it says, and that He approached His death with its words on His lips. Christian men and women have in this ancient collection of Jewish writings a uniquely illuminating avenue not only into the will and purposes of God the Father, but into the mind and heart of Him who is named God's Son, who was Himself born a Jew but went on through the Cross and Resurrection to become the Saviour of the world. Read reverently and imaginatively the Old Testament can become a living and relevant force in their everyday lives.

It is the prayer of myself and my colleagues that this series may be used by its readers and blessed by God to that end.

New College   JOHN C. L. GIBSON
Edinburgh   General Editor

AUTHOR'S PREFACE

The assistance of my wife Helen has been indispensable in the production of this volume, mainly because she undertook the lion's share of the typing at the same time as keeping numerous bodies and souls together. My thanks are also due to my sister-in-law Jane for her contribution. The book is dedicated to my wife.

CONTENTS

Chronological Table xi
Jerusalem in Nehemiah's day......................... xii
Introduction to Ezra and Nehemiah 1

EZRA

Return (1:1–11) 6
Return! (1:1–11) (*cont'd*) 8
Who's Who—I (2:1–70) 11
Who's Who—II (2:1–70) (*cont'd*) 15
Mixed Feelings—I (3:1–13) 18
Mixed Feelings—II (3:1–13) (*cont'd*) 21
Flaming Darts (4:1–24)............................... 23
How to Get Things Done? (4:1–24) (*cont'd*)............. 27
Sharper than a Two-edged Sword (5:1–17) 30
An Emblem of Grace—and Response to the Word (5:1–17)
    (*cont'd*) 34
By Decrees (6:1–12) 37
It is Finished (6:13–22) 40
Enter Ezra (7:1–10).................................. 44
Ezra's Mission (7:11–26) 48
Ezra and Co. (7:27–8:20)............................. 51
"Journeying Mercies" (8:21–36) 55
A Fly in the Ointment (9:1–4) 59
If We Say We Have No Sin . . . (9:5–15) 62
A Desperate Remedy—I (10:1–44) 66
A Desperate Remedy—II (10:1–44) (*cont'd*).............. 69

NEHEMIAH

Trouble and Shame (1:1–11) 73
Give Success (1:1–11) (*cont'd*) 75
Wise as Serpents (2:1–8).............................. 77
The Fight (2:9–20)................................... 81
Building Together (3:1–32)............................ 85
The Pressure On (4:1–23)............................. 89

Dry Powder (4:1–23) (*cont'd*)   92
Strife Within (5:1–13)   95
True Love (5:14–19)   99
Death Throes? (6:1–19)   102
Triumph (6:1–19) (*cont'd*)   106
Priorities (7:1–73*a*)   109
The Need to Know (7:73*b*–8:8)   113
A Time to Dance (8:9–18)   118
A Time to Mourn (9:1–38)   121
The Sure Mercies (9:1–38) (*cont'd*)   124
*An Oath—*I (10:1–39)   128
*An Oath—*II (10:1–39) (*cont'd*)   131
Settlement (11:1–36)   134
Dedication (12:1–13:3)   137
The Joy of Jerusalem (12:1–13:3) (*cont'd*)   141
*Epilogue—*I (13:4–31)   144
*Epilogue—*II (13:4–31) (*cont'd*)   148

ESTHER
Introduction   152
King's Opening (1:1–11)   154
Queen's Defence (1:12–22)   156
A Funny Thing Happened (2:1–23)   159
*Dilemma—*I: *Mordecai* (3:1–15)   164
*Dilemma—*I: *A Final Solution?* (3:1–15) (*cont'd*)   166
*Dilemma—*II: *Esther . . .* (4:1–17)   169
*Dilemma—*II: *. . . and God* (4:1–17) (*cont'd*)   171
Half My Kingdom (5:1–14)   174
Decline . . . (6:1–14)   178
. . . and Fall (7:1–10)   181
Turnabout (8:1–17)   185
Purim (9:1–28)   190
Finale (9:29–10:3)   195

Further Reading   198

CHRONOLOGICAL TABLE

Year (B.C.)
- 539—Cyrus comes to power in Babylon
- 538—Cyrus' decree; first returnees to Jerusalem under Zerubbabel
- 530—Accession of Cambyses II to throne
- 522—Accession of Darius I
- 516—Completion of Temple
- 486—Accession of Xerxes I
- *c.* 486–480—Events of Book of Esther
- 465—Accession of Artaxerxes I
- 458—Ezra's arrival in Jerusalem
- 445—Nehemiah's arrival in Jerusalem
- 444—Completion of walls of Jerusalem
- 433—Nehemiah returns to Babylon
- ? —Nehemiah makes subsequent, undated visit to Jerusalem

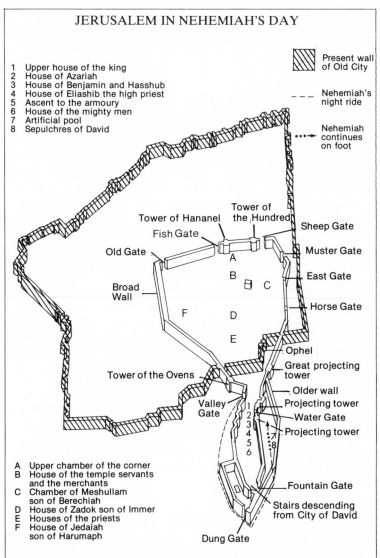

JERUSALEM IN NEHEMIAH'S DAY

1 Upper house of the king
2 House of Azariah
3 House of Benjamin and Hasshub
4 House of Eliashib the high priest
5 Ascent to the armoury
6 House of the mighty men
7 Artificial pool
8 Sepulchres of David

Present wall of Old City

--- Nehemiah's night ride

••••► Nehemiah continues on foot

Tower of the Hundred
Tower of Hananel
Fish Gate
Sheep Gate
Old Gate
Muster Gate
Broad Wall
East Gate
Horse Gate
Ophel
Great projecting tower
Tower of the Ovens
Older wall
Valley Gate
Projecting tower
Water Gate
Projecting tower
Fountain Gate
Stairs descending from City of David
Dung Gate

A Upper chamber of the corner
B House of the temple servants and the merchants
C Chamber of Meshullam son of Berechiah
D House of Zadok son of Immer
E Houses of the priests
F House of Jedaiah son of Harumaph

The diagram above is adapted from *Illustrated Bible Dictionary*, N Hillyer (Ed), Inter-Varsity Press and redrawn by David Simon, Edinburgh.

INTRODUCTION TO EZRA AND NEHEMIAH

HISTORICAL BACKGROUND

The Books of Chronicles, which immediately precede Ezra–Nehemiah in our English Bibles, related how the people of Judah, because of their disobedience to God, had seen their country laid waste, and their capital city, Jerusalem, with its Temple, destroyed at the hands of Nebuchadnezzar king of Babylon (587 B.C.). The people themselves had been taken into exile. In due course, however, and in fulfilment of God's word by Jeremiah (25:11–12), a new imperial power arose in Mesopotamia which saw fit to allow the Jewish exiles to return to their ancestral land, 538 B.C. (2 Chr. 36). The Books of Ezra–Nehemiah explicitly take their cue from 2 Chronicles by repeating almost verbatim (in Ezra 1:1–3) the final two verses of that book. If Chronicles in its last chapter tells us that God acted in mercy by restoring his people Judah, Ezra–Nehemiah will reveal to us how they fared upon their return, privileged with a new opportunity to be God's people in their own land.

Behind the account in Ezra–Nehemiah of the theological significance of the things that befell Judah in those days lie events which were and are of more general historical interest and about which, therefore, we have a certain amount of non-biblical information. We know that in the succession of powers which dominated the Middle East in the first millennium B.C. Babylon gave way to Persia, following a period of uneasy alliance between the eccentric last Babylonian king Nabonidus and the politically far more astute Cyrus of Persia. The latter took advantage of Nabonidus' incapacity to stage what appears to have been a bloodless coup, leaving him sole heir to the huge Babylonian territories. A decade or so later Cyrus' successor Cambyses conquered Egypt. The Persian Empire against which most of our story is set, therefore, was one of the greatest that the world had yet seen.

Cyrus himself is the most significant of the Persian kings in our story. This is because the biblical portrayal of the restoration from exile as prophecy fulfilment has as its counterpart the historical fact that Cyrus adopted a policy *vis-à-vis* his subject peoples which was in direct contrast to that of Babylon. His "Cyrus Cylinder" (see further on Ezra 1) proclaims that he returned numerous peoples to their homelands and indeed gods to their temples. Even his taking of Babylon had been associated with the restoration of the god Marduk, neglected by Nabonidus, to supremacy there. Everywhere in the Empire, then, Cyrus sought popular support by appealing to traditional religious sentiments. Historically speaking, Judah benefited from this policy.

However, it was as difficult for kings then as for governments now to please all the people all of the time. Resettling Jews in their former homeland meant upsetting others who saw their ascendancy in wider Palestine threatened. The scene is thus set for the local conflicts experienced first by Zerubbabel and later by Nehemiah. And Persian kings evidently did not pursue a consistently pro-Judean policy as they arbitrated (see Ezra 4:23–24, where Artaxerxes I sides with the adversaries of Judah), showing that their only ultimate interest was the security of the Empire itself.

MINISTRIES OF EZRA AND NEHEMIAH

If the year 538 B.C. is of crucial significance for our books, their interest extends, nevertheless, to more than a hundred years of history. Indeed the characters in the title roles do not appear until the middle of the 5th century, with the early struggles to rebuild the Temple long past, and decades of intermittent aggression from rivals passed over more or less in silence.

Controversy surrounds the relative dating of the ministries of Ezra and Nehemiah. Following the dates supplied in our books

Ezra arrived in Jerusalem in 458 B.C. and was followed thirteen years later (445 B.C.) by Nehemiah. Both men participated in the great act of covenant renewal in Neh. 8–10 and in the dedication of the newly-built walls (Neh. 12). For various reasons, however (chief among them being the paucity of allusions in each man's memoir to the other and the different order of events in the apocryphal book, 1 Esdras, which covers much the same ground as Ezra–Nehemiah), many scholars have taken the view that Nehemiah preceded Ezra and indeed that the ministries of the two did not overlap at all. Ezra's arrival in Jerusalem is thus sometimes dated to 398 B.C. and his activity placed in the reign of Artaxerxes II, not I.

The debate cannot be engaged in a commentary of the present dimensions and purpose. Suffice it to say that the author believes that the order of events as suggested by our books themselves can be sustained by historical research and it is therefore adopted for the purposes of the exposition. (The reader who wishes to enquire further into the matter should see the contrasting views taken in the commentaries of Kidner and Brockington; see Further Reading).

SOURCES AND AUTHORSHIP

The chief sources in our books are the so-called "memoirs" of Ezra (Ezra 7–10) and Nehemiah (largely Neh. 1–7, with fragments in chs. 11–13). Both within and outside these, however, there are a number of others, consisting largely of letters passing between the centre of Empire and the provinces (both Judah and Samaria) and of official lists and inventories. These will be noticed in the course of the exposition. Ezra and Nehemiah themselves evidently had access to various official documents (not surprisingly, in view of the exalted status of each in the imperial organization) and the final author of the books may have had independent access to others (especially those in Ezra 1–6). One effect of the ready recourse to official documents is that parts of the Book of Ezra (4:8–6:18; 7:12–26) are written in Aramaic, the official language of Persian diplomacy, rather than in

Hebrew, the dominant language of our books as of the Old Testament in general.

The identity of the final author of Ezra–Nehemiah is not known. Many scholars hold him to be none other than the author of Chronicles—himself known only as "the Chronicler"! The contrary view—that the two authors should *not* be identified—is currently gaining strength, however. For the purposes of our exposition, common authorship of the two works is not assumed. However, the reader should not miss the clear link that is made between them, perhaps by an editor (2 Chr. 36:22–23; Ezra 1:1–3), the appropriateness of regarding Ezra–Nehemiah as a sequel to Chronicles, and their sharing of a number of central themes (e.g. the importance of the building of the Temple for the right constitution of the people).

THEOLOGY

Our books are dominated by the idea of the restoration of God's people to the land promised long ago (cf. Exod. 23:23ff.), in fulfilment of the prophecy of Jeremiah. Each new achievement of the community (the rebuilding of the Temple, the building and the dedication of the walls, with attendant victories over enemies) is celebrated with worship and thanksgiving as an act of God on behalf of his people. Following all the doubts to which the exile had given rise, the community in Judah is re-established as the covenant people, possession of the historic land—or at least the part of it that contained Jerusalem—constituting the sign and seal of their recovered status. The covenant renewal ceremony in Neh. 9–10 is not only the latest in a long line of such recommitments (cf. Josh. 24; 2 Kings 22–23), but has as its specific background the dismay which the exile had produced because it had appeared to spell the end of Israel's special relationship with God. The joy in Nehemiah is that of recovered confidence in God's promises, occasioned by a favourable turn in the nation's fortunes that remains, on any account of the matter, highly remarkable. The influence of the exile stamps itself on the whole work through the consistent reference to the community in Judah as the *Gola*, or "exiles". The term at once draws attention to the fact that the people of God has now undergone a chastening and should therefore be more disposed to being faithful, and to the mercy of God in continuing to deal with a people that had formerly been determined in its rebellion.

Without in any sense diminishing the greatness of the deliverance from Babylon or its demonstration of God's commitment to Judah, there is nevertheless a strong feeling throughout our books that the full potential for a relationship between God and his people has not yet been realized. This is related, no doubt, to the fact that the community, *though* chastened, falls again and yet again into sin (see on Ezra 9–10). The events that occur under Zerubbabel, Ezra and Nehemiah are not God's last word. The "restoration" is nothing in itself, but—in terms of a wider biblical theology—merely a necessary setting of the stage for a far greater act of God in which his search for human obedience within the covenant is finally gratified in the life of Jesus of Nazareth—at once himself God and, in his humanity, representative "Israel".

It is this intermediate status of the post-exilic restoration which makes it possible for *Christians*—who have no interest in Jewish temple, walls or nationhood *as such*—to take the Books of Ezra and Nehemiah profitably to themselves. Their real significance neither begins nor ends with bricks and mortar, but lies rather in the fact that God has acted again, and *will* act, on behalf of his people.

EZRA

RETURN

Ezra 1:1–11

[1]In the first year of Cyrus king of Persia, that the word of the Lord by the mouth of Jeremiah might be accomplished, the Lord stirred up the spirit of Cyrus king of Persia so that he made a proclamation throughout all his kingdom and also put it in writing:

[2]"Thus says Cyrus king of Persia: The Lord, the God of heaven, has given me all the kingdoms of the earth, and he has charged me to build him a house at Jerusalem, which is in Judah. [3]Whoever is among you of all his people, may his God be with him, and let him go up to Jerusalem, which is in Judah, and rebuild the house of the Lord, the God of Israel—he is the God who is in Jerusalem; [4]and let each survivor, in whatever place he sojourns, be assisted by the men of his place with silver and gold, with goods and with beasts, besides freewill offerings for the house of God which is in Jerusalem."

[5]Then rose up the heads of the fathers' houses of Judah and Benjamin, and the priests and the Levites, every one whose spirit God had stirred to go up to rebuild the house of the Lord which is in Jerusalem; [6]and all who were about them aided them with vessels of silver, with gold, with goods, with beasts, and with costly wares, besides all that was freely offered. [7]Cyrus the king also brought out the vessels of the house of the Lord which Nebuchadnezzar had carried away from Jerusalem and placed in the house of his gods. [8]Cyrus king of Persia brought these out in charge of Mithredath the treasurer, who counted them out to Shesh-bazzar the prince of Judah. [9]And this was the number of them: a thousand basins of gold, a thousand basins of silver, twenty-nine censers, [10]thirty bowls of gold, two thousand four hundred and ten bowls of silver, and a thousand other vessels; [11]all the vessels of gold and of silver were five thousand four hundred and sixty-nine. All these did Shesh-bazzar bring up, when the exiles were brought up from Babylonia to Jerusalem.

(i)

The Book of Ezra opens (as the Books of Chronicles had closed) with one of the great saving events of the Old Testament, the restoration from Babylon of those who had been in exile there since Jerusalem was ravaged by Nebuchadnezzar. The first verse makes a mighty claim for the lordship of Israel's God in human history.

In 539 B.C. the observer of world events would have had little hesitation in naming Cyrus' Media as the "super-power" of the east. In a decade and a half Cyrus had risen from the status of vassal within an empire that was junior ally to Babylon to be master of Babylon itself and heir to all its territories. The new power must have seemed far more formidable than the shaky state that Babylon had been in its last years. Soon Egypt too (under a successor of Cyrus) would fall under its sway. Cyrus comes on to the biblical stage, therefore, with all the thrusting impressiveness of human political power.

In its quiet way, however, Ezra 1:1 shows not only that this mighty king was subject, whether he knew it or not, to the promptings of God (who "stirred up his spirit"), but also that God had brought him to pre-eminence for the very purpose of the salvation of his people. Cyrus' proclamation was made "that the word of the Lord by the mouth of Jeremiah might be accomplished" (cf. Jer. 29:10), viz. that the exiles would be restored to their own land. Even more strikingly, prophecies occur in the Book of Isaiah (41:2; 44:28; 45:1, 13; cf. Jer. 51:11) which refer expressly to this "stirring up" of Cyrus to overthrow Babylon and restore God's people. Behind this opening verse, then, lies the affirmation that all the might of the ancient world was in subjection to God, and put at the disposal of his people for their salvation.

(ii)

Cyrus will hardly have seen things quite in this way. True, he says in his proclamation (v. 2): "The Lord, the God of heaven [i.e. Israel's God], has given me all the kingdoms of the earth ..." This is hardly more than the conventional language of diplomacy as far as Cyrus is concerned, however; its correspondence with the truth is simply one of the great ironies of the Book of Ezra. On the political level, the return of Judeans to Jerusalem, together with their cultic accoutrements (vv. 7ff.) and with a commission to rebuild their temple, was purely a matter of foreign policy. Whereas the Babylonians saw their security in deporting potentially rebellious peoples, Cyrus and his successors preferred to court their loyalty by permitting a measure of self-determination and by respecting their religions. In the famous Cyrus Cylinder (a lengthy inscription on a cylindrical tablet now in the British Museum) the king claims, regarding the gods of peoples who had been brought to Babylon: "I returned [them] to their places and housed them in lasting abodes." This text furnishes the precise historical background to Ezra 1, showing that Cyrus repatriated all exiled communities in Babylon without distinction, and provided for the restoration of their deities to their temples. If a religious motivation was mingled with his political cunning it was entirely in terms of his own polytheism: "Let all gods," Cyrus further decreed, "which I have brought to their cities pray daily to Bel and Nabu for my length of days."

The prophecies of Isaiah, therefore, do not lead the author of Ezra into a naïve romanticism about Cyrus (nor were they themselves romantic). Cyrus is the real successor not only of Babylon but of Assyria (cf. Ezra 6:22). As such he is merely a puppet, whose motivation, and indeed comprehension of events, are fundamentally at variance with those of the Lord (cf. Isa. 10:5–11). When Cyrus had his proclamation put in writing (v. 1) that symbolized, for him, an authority which was beyond challenge; it was literally a "law of the Medes and Persians". Yet the real source of authority in these events is not a king's official seal, but the Lord, who raises kings and pulls them down (Isa. 40:23–24).

RETURN!

Ezra 1:1–11 (*cont'd*)

(iii)

Perhaps the most surprising feature of Ezra 1 is the fact that so *little* is made of the prophecies referred to above in the Book of Isaiah. Why is it that only a couple of verses in Jeremiah are explicitly indicated by the author of Ezra, when an array of other texts would have confirmed his case that the events he recorded were the fulfilment of prophecy, telling not only of the restoration from exile, but of the rebuilding of Jerusalem and of a glorious future for the people (cf. e.g. Isa. 2:2–4; 56; 60; 61:1–7; 62 etc.)?

Here we sense how delicate was the task of the author of Ezra. On the one hand he had to depict the power of God over the nations and especially in the salvation of Judah. To this end he refers to Jeremiah's prophecy. To this end also he hints at an analogy between the release from Babylon and that earlier release from captivity which was to become central to Israel's faith in God, namely the exodus from Egypt. (The latter parallel is suggested in verses 4 and 6 and in the idea that the captors themselves ensured that the captives went away liberally supplied with all they needed both for their return and for the establishment of their worship; cf. Exod. 12:35–36. The precise meaning of verse 4—obscured in RSV—is probably that those Jews who were *not* returning to Judah should assist those who were. The term "survivor" simply means "one who is left", and in this context one who is left behind in Babylon. It is, however, Cyrus who presides over this, and therefore the parallel with the exodus holds good.)

On the other hand the author of Ezra has to guard against complacency on the part of those for whom he writes. If he slips into triumphalism he may give the impression that the return from exile is God's final act, ushering in a Messianic age in which the people of Judah enjoy pre-eminence in the world and even the servitude of the nations (Isa. 60:10). To do so would in any case be unrealistic for, as the events of Ezra show, life was hard for the returned community. His account of the return, therefore, does not omit to show the need for obedient response on the part of God's people.

As God had "stirred" Cyrus, so also he stirs the returnees "to go up to rebuild the house of the Lord" (v. 5). God's "stirring" does not diminish the required obedience; rather it draws attention to it, and shows that it proceeds ultimately from his own prompting. Obedience, nevertheless, it is. And when, in verse 4, reference is made to those who opt to remain in Babylon, a value judgment is implied by the author. A similar idea is contained in verse 11, where the technical term *Gola*—frequent in Ezra— refers not to the exiles in general but expressly to those who heard God's call and returned. Here Ezra depends in a new way upon Jeremiah, who showed that God's plans for his people beyond exile would focus upon the community that was to be chastened by the exile (rather than those who had remained in Judah); see Jer. 24. However, the mere fact of belonging to the exiles is, in Ezra's view, no guarantee of God's continuing favour. With the return of the exiles, prophecy was indeed fulfilled. But the return was itself an act of obedience. And in Ezra obedience is a necessary ongoing concomitant of prophecy fulfilment. It is because our author knows of failures on the part of the exiles (see chs. 9–10) that he refrains from marshalling the full armoury of prophetic texts relating to restoration. His restraint is a way of saying: "There is still some way to go"; and it becomes part of his challenge.

(iv)

We can only speculate whether the Jews who chose to remain in Babylon gave willingly to the returnees, or whether they did so only under duress. A contemporary analogy to this situation may exist in the relationship between the Jewish Diaspora and those Jews who choose to make *aliya* (a term that is related to the idea of "going up" in verse 3) to the state of Israel. In our day many of the Diaspora have been more than generous to the immigrants, while others have been dubious about the whole enterprise. It must be stressed that the modern situation can only provide psychological and historical analogies, not theological ones. From a Christian point of view the Book of Ezra cannot be seen as a blueprint for a modern Jewish return to "the land".

(v)

The action of Cyrus makes exact restitution for the depredations of Nebuchadnezzar. As it was the two southern tribes (Judah and Benjamin), together with the priestly tribe of Levi, which had constituted the remnant of Israel prior to the exile, so it is with these tribes still that the post-exilic future of God's people lies. As the treasures of the Temple were carried off by Nebuchadnezzar (2 Chr. 36:18), so now they are returned (the list here is probably based on the official document authorizing their return). In a sense the standing of the furnished Temple of God symbolizes the existence of his covenant with his people. This is why the rebuilding of the Temple occupies so central a place in the Book of Ezra. If there had been a question mark beside God's willingness to continue with his people, it is dramatically set aside when the Empire willingly surrenders what it once confiscated (v. 7). The covenant stands; the Lord will not cast off his people for ever.

Notes
(1) *The officials*, v. 8. Mithredath appears to have been a Persian official charged with the task of returning temple treasures to the various peoples who were restored by Cyrus' decree to their homelands. Sheshbazzar, who has sometimes been equated, wrongly, with Zerubbabel, was probably a Babylonian governor whom Cyrus left in office, and who was in due course, perhaps on his death, succeeded by Zerubbabel (cf. Hag. 1:1).
(2) *The figures*, vv. 9–11. Basing itself on 1 Esdras, RSV has corrected a Hebrew text which, presumably due to textual corruption, fails to add up.

WHO'S WHO—I

Ezra 2:1–70

¹Now these were the people of the province who came up out of the captivity of those exiles whom Nebuchadnezzar the king of Babylon had carried captive to Babylonia; they returned to Jerusalem and Judah, each to his own town. ²They came with Zerubbabel, Jeshua, Nehemiah, Seraiah, Re-el-aiah, Mordecai, Bilshan, Mispar, Bigvai, Rehum, and Baanah.

The number of the men of the people of Israel: ³the sons of Parosh, two thousand one hundred and seventy-two. ⁴The sons of Shephatiah, three hundred and seventy-two. [5]The sons of Arah, seven hundred and seventy-five. [6]The sons of Pahath-moab, namely the sons of Jeshua and Joab, two thousand eight hundred and twelve. [7]The sons of Elam, one thousand two hundred and fifty-four. [8]The sons of Zattu, nine hundred and forty-five. [9]The sons of Zaccai, seven hundred and sixty. [10]The sons of Bani, six hundred and forty-two. [11]The sons of Bebai, six hundred and twenty-three. [12]The sons of Azgad, one thousand two hundred and twenty-two. [13]The sons of Adonikam, six hundred and sixty-six. [14]The sons of Bigvai, two thousand and fifty-six. [15]The sons of Adin, four hundred and fifty-four. [16]The sons of Ater, namely of Hezekiah, ninety-eight. [17]The sons of Bezai, three hundred and twenty-three. [18]The sons of Jorah, one hundred and twelve. [19]The sons of Hashum, two hundred and twenty-three. [20]The sons of Gibbar, ninety-five. [21]The sons of Bethlehem, one hundred and twenty-three. [22]The men of Netophah, fifty-six. [23]The men of Anathoth, one hundred and twenty-eight. [24]The sons of Azmaveth, forty-two. [25]The sons of Kiriatharim, Chephirah, and Be-eroth, seven hundred and forty-three. [26]The sons of Ramah and Geba, six hundred and twenty-one. [27]The men of Michmas, one hundred and twenty-two. [28]The men of Bethel and Ai, two hundred and twenty-three. [29]The sons of Nebo, fifty-two. [30]The sons of Magbish, one hundred and fifty-six. [31]The sons of the other Elam, one thousand two hundred and fifty-four. [32]The sons of Harim, three hundred and twenty. [33]The sons of Lod, Hadid, and Ono, seven hundred and twenty-five. [34]The sons of Jericho, three hundred and forty-five. [35]The sons of Senaah, three thousand six hundred and thirty.

[36]The priests: the sons of Jedaiah, of the house of Jeshua, nine hundred and seventy-three. [37]The sons of Immer, one thousand and fifty-two. [38]The sons of Pashhur, one thousand two hundred and forty-seven. [39]The sons of Harim, one thousand and seventeen.

[40]The Levites: the sons of Jeshua and Kadmi-el, of the sons of Hodaviah, seventy-four. [41]The singers: the sons of Asaph, one hundred and twenty-eight. [42]The sons of the gatekeepers: the sons of Shallum, the sons of Ater, the sons of Talmon, the sons of Akkub, the sons of Hatita, and the sons of Shobai, in all one hundred and thirty-nine.

[43]The temple servants: the sons of Ziha, the sons of Hasupha, the sons of Tabbaoth, [44]the sons of Keros, the sons of Siaha, the sons of Padon, [45]the sons of Lebanah, the sons of Hagabah, the sons of Akkub, [46]the sons of Hagab, the sons of Shamlai, the sons of Hanan, [47]the sons of Giddel, the sons of Gahar, the sons of Re-aiah, [48]the sons

of Rezin, the sons of Nekoda, the sons of Gazzam, ⁴⁹the sons of Uzza, the sons of Paseah, the sons of Besai, ⁵⁰the sons of Asnah, the sons of Me-unim, the sons of Nephisim, ⁵¹the sons of Bakbuk, the sons of Hakupha, the sons of Harhur, ⁵²the sons of Bazluth, the sons of Mehida, the sons of Harsha, ⁵³the sons of Barkos, the sons of Sisera, the sons of Temah, ⁵⁴the sons of Neziah, and the sons of Hatipha.

⁵⁵The sons of Solomon's servants: the sons of Sotai, the sons of Hassophereth, the sons of Peruda, ⁵⁶the sons of Jaalah, the sons of Darkon, the sons of Giddel, ⁵⁷the sons of Shephatiah, the sons of Hattil, the sons of Pochereth-hazzebaim, and the sons of Ami.

⁵⁸All the temple servants and the sons of Solomon's servants were three hundred and ninety-two.

⁵⁹The following were those who came up from Tel-melah, Tel-harsha, Cherub, Addan, and Immer, though they could not prove their fathers' houses or their descent, whether they belonged to Israel: ⁶⁰the sons of Delaiah, the sons of Tobiah, and the sons of Nekoda, six hundred and fifty-two. ⁶¹Also, of the sons of the priests: the sons of Habaiah, the sons of Hakkoz, and the sons of Barzillai (who had taken a wife from the daughters of Barzillai the Gileadite, and was called by their name). ⁶²These sought their registration among those enrolled in the genealogies, but they were not found there, and so they were excluded from the priesthood as unclean; ⁶³the governor told them that they were not to partake of the most holy food, until there should be a priest to consult Urim and Thummim.

⁶⁴The whole assembly together was forty-two thousand three hundred and sixty, ⁶⁵besides their menservants and maidservants, of whom there were seven thousand three hundred and thirty-seven; and they had two hundred male and female singers. ⁶⁶Their horses were seven hundred and thirty-six, their mules were two hundred and forty-five, ⁶⁷their camels were four hundred and thirty-five, and their asses were six thousand seven hundred and twenty.

⁶⁸Some of the heads of families, when they came to the house of the Lord which is in Jerusalem, made free-will offerings for the house of God, to erect it on its site; ⁶⁹according to their ability they gave to the treasury of the work sixty-one thousand darics of gold, five thousand minas of silver, and one hundred priests' garments.

⁷⁰The priests, the Levites, and some of the people lived in Jerusalem and its vicinity; and the singers, the gatekeepers, and the temple servants lived in their towns, and all Israel in their towns.

(i)

Having recorded Cyrus' decree permitting the Jewish exiles to return home, our author now furnishes a list of those who returned. The same list, with a few differences, appears in Neh. 7:6–73 (where it is used on the occasion of a solemn assembly following the completion of the city walls). The list's repeated use in this way shows that it entered the archives of the returned community and became an important factor in establishing its sense of identity. Neh. 7:5 calls it "the book of the genealogy of those who came up at the first". The people named here, therefore, were the first to respond to the call to return. There is reason to think that others followed over the ensuing decades. And indeed we find Ezra himself leading another significant wave of returnees on his arrival in Jerusalem almost a century after Cyrus' decree (cf. 8:1).

The leaders of this first wave, however, are Zerubbabel and Jeshua (v. 2). Zerubbabel was of the Davidic line (1 Chr. 3:19). This led to his association with a messianic hope in Zechariah, but nothing is made of it in Ezra. The two leaders are named along with a number of other notable men, from whom nevertheless they are distinguished in the subsequent record by their pre-eminence in the initiation, and ultimate completion, of the new Temple (3:2; 4:3; 5:2). From this time, the pattern of the community is set, with the new arrivals taking up residence again in the towns of Judah which had been laid waste by Nebuchadnezzar, and presumably been largely uninhabited since. The lapse of one or two generations in Babylon had evidently not dimmed families' memories of their exact provenance in Judah. It is interesting to notice that some of these memories have been preserved by reference to places (e.g. the sons of Bethlehem, simply meaning those who traced their origins to that place, v. 21) and others by family descent (mainly in vv. 3–20). Since people and places were so closely linked, this distinction may not be so hard and fast. In any case, we have no evidence of difficulty or rivalry in relation to the resettlement. The careful search for continuity with the past, which our list itself represents, may have procured smoothness in this operation.

WHO'S WHO—II

Ezra 2:1–70 (*cont'd*)

(ii)

If there was harmony initially among the returning exiles, it does not follow that the return was free from controversy and friction of other sorts. As subsequent events show, there was no shortage, in Judah and further afield, of those who would have been happier if Cyrus had never issued his decree at all. It may be, indeed, that there were those who had designs on the territory which Nebuchadnezzar had so conveniently depopulated. We know that *some* poorer people were not deported (Jer. 52:16). These may have improved their lot in the interim. And the theology which appeared to exclude them from a future interest in the promises of God (cf. Jer. 24:8–10) will not have encouraged them to welcome the returning exiles with open arms. Our list, therefore, probably aims to distinguish "the people of the province who came up out of the captivity" (v. 1) from *other* people in the province (namely the imperial province Beyond the River, which included Judah and Samaria, cf. 4:16), making the point that it was only those of the *Gola* (i.e. the "exiles") who properly constituted "Israel" (v. 2). The list may have had the additional legal function of re-establishing the rights of individual families to their ancient inheritances.

(iii)

It follows from the foregoing that the central question in the present chapter is: who belongs to "Israel"? In one sense the use of this term is archaic. Properly, "Israel" applies either to the fully constituted twelve tribes, or more narrowly to the old northern kingdom. Historically, neither of these had existed since 721 B.C. when the northern kingdom was destroyed and its inhabitants dispersed. Yet here (vv. 2, 59), as in the Books of Chronicles (e.g. 1 Chr. 2:1–2), the idea of Israel is preserved in order to make the point that the returning exiles are the legitimate descendants of old Israel, and therefore the covenant community and heirs to God's promises. "Israel" may no longer have its classical outward expression. Yet it continues to exist in a way that is more subtle and profound. In a political world in which Israel as a power is no more than a memory, God is awakening something infinitely more significant, because it is spiritual.

The need to define Israel explains many of the details in the chapter. Verses 59–60 show that the system may have broken down in some cases. Some groups could not prove their heritage in Israel. There was possible danger to the community here, because, as we know from 4:2, there were attempts to infiltrate it by those who did not truly belong. Since those who are named in verses 59–60 appear to have been accepted into their community, we must suppose that there were some who could vouch for them. But for a community whose power did not consist in armies but in the knowledge and service of God it was impossible to be too careful in ascertaining who truly stood with it.

The issue is most pointed in relation to the officials of the cult. These are listed (vv. 36–58) according to categories laid down in 1 Chr. 23–26. The priests (v. 36) are the descendants of Aaron who, with his sons, was ordained to be responsible for altar sacrifice (Exod. 28–29). The Levites (v. 40) are those members of the tribe of Levi who are not descended from Aaron, and who assist the priests (cf. Num. 3:5ff). The singers (v. 41) and gatekeepers (v. 42) are taken from families among the Levites to whom David apportioned these special tasks (1 Chr. 25–26). The "temple servants" (or Nethinim), v. 43 and the "sons of Solomon's servants" (v. 55) are probably descendants of peoples conquered in war and put to menial duties related to the worship.

Verses 61–63 tell of a claim to priestly status which could not be proven. The danger of contamination of the community is here compounded by the great fear of committing a grave cultic offence. (For the seriousness of false claims to priestly status, cf. Num. 16.) Even Sheshbazzar, the Babylonian governor now in the service of the Persians, is drawn into this issue, and settles it by requiring a *bona fide* priest to employ Urim and Thummim, the ancient Israelite method of discovering God's will in any matter (cf. 1 Sam. 14:41. The exact sense of Urim and Thummim is obscure, but it seems to be similar to drawing lots.)

The ancient constitution of Israel is thus in every way respected. The first Jews to return from exile were evidently determined to keep the community pure as "Israel" enters upon this new phase, with new opportunities to know the blessing of God.

(iv)

The impression of a community that is motivated by the noblest intentions is borne out by the generosity of at least *some* of the heads of families in providing for the building of the Temple (v. 68). There is an echo of the exodus account here (as there was in 1:4, 6), for the people of that generation were also asked to make large contributions to the building of the first sanctuary (Exod. 25:2–9), and they responded willingly (Exod. 35:21ff.). The granting of the outward symbol of God's presence is accompanied from the start, therefore, by a spirit of willing self-sacrifice.

To balance this side of the picture, the point is also made (vv. 64–67) that the first community was by no means impoverished. These are the trappings of wealth. The people that seeks its God knows blessing. This the Old Testament affirms as a principle (though it voices perplexity at times, e.g. in the Book of Job, Ps. 73; and the Christian will spiritualize the idea in the light of the New Testament, e.g. Matt. 5:1ff.). In Ezra, the point of bringing together the community's early concern for purity, and its corresponding enjoyment of blessing, is to affirm again that there is in this new situation a new opportunity. There is irony when this passage (vv. 64–67) is placed alongside Hag. 1:7–11, which pictures the people, only a few years after this, impoverished because it has ceased to care for precisely those things which mark it out as God's (represented by the Temple). There may be a hint of the disappointing performance that is to come in the notice that only *some* of the heads of families gave willingly. Our author continues to make it clear that the fulfilment of prophecy and the enjoyment of God's blessing are always provisional, and need to be fed by whole-hearted obedience. Otherwise gain can so easily turn to loss.

The chapter is dominated in the end, however, by a sense of excitement at a new opportunity—an opportunity which exists because God's mercies are "new every morning" (Lam. 3:23).

MIXED FEELINGS—I

Ezra 3:1–13

¹When the seventh month came, and the sons of Israel were in the towns, the people gathered as one man to Jerusalem. ²Then arose Jeshua the son of Jozadak, with his fellow priests, and Zerubbabel the son of She-alti-el with his kinsmen, and they built the altar of the God of Israel, to offer burnt offerings upon it, as it is written in the law of Moses the man of God. ³They set the altar in its place, for fear was upon them because of the peoples of the lands, and they offered burnt offerings upon it to the Lord, burnt offerings morning and evening. ⁴And they kept the feast of booths, as it is written, and offered the daily burnt offerings by number according to the ordinance, as each day required, ⁵and after that the continual burnt offerings, the offerings at the new moon and at all the appointed feasts of the Lord, and the offerings of every one who made a freewill offering to the Lord. ⁶From the first day of the seventh month they began to offer burnt offerings to the Lord. But the foundation of the temple of the Lord was not yet laid. ⁷So they gave money to the masons and the carpenters, and food, drink, and oil to the Sidonians and the Tyrians to bring cedar trees from Lebanon to the sea, to Joppa, according to the grant which they had from Cyrus king of Persia.

⁸Now in the second year of their coming to the house of God at Jerusalem, in the second month, Zerubbabel the son of She-alti-el and Jeshua the son of Jozadak made a beginning, together with the rest of their brethren, the priests and the Levites and all who had come to Jerusalem from the captivity. They appointed the Levites, from twenty years old and upward, to have the oversight of the work of the house of the Lord. ⁹And Jeshua with his sons and his kinsmen, and Kadmi-el and his sons, the sons of Judah, together took the oversight of the workmen in the house of God, along with the sons of Henadad and the Levites, their sons and kinsmen.

¹⁰And when the builders laid the foundation of the temple of the Lord, the priests in their vestments came forward with trumpets, and the Levites, the sons of Asaph, with cymbals, to praise the Lord, according to the directions of David king of Israel; ¹¹and they sang responsively, praising and giving thanks to the Lord,

"For he is good,
    for his steadfast love endures for ever toward Israel."

And all the people shouted with a great shout, when they praised the Lord, because the foundation of the house of the Lord was laid. ¹²But many of the priests and Levites and heads of fathers' houses, old men who had seen the first house, wept with a loud voice when they saw the foundation of this house being laid, though many shouted aloud for joy; ¹³so that the people could not distinguish the sound of the joyful shout from the sound of the people's weeping, for the people shouted with a great shout, and the sound was heard afar.

(i)

While Ezra 2 enables us to picture the threads of normal life being picked up once more in the hillsides of Judah, we are now reminded that the people that have been redeemed cannot dissolve into isolated groups, however much the remoteness of their localities, the difficulty of the terrain separating them, and the demands of settling to a new and independent life might tempt them to do just that. When in the seventh month of the first year of their return (September/October 537 B.C.) they "gathered as one man to Jerusalem" (v. 1), they were obeying the law of God as laid down in Exod. 23:16. (The "feast of ingathering" in that place is the same as the "feast of booths" here, v. 4; cf. Lev. 23:34–36.)

Beyond the simple matter of obedience to a command, however, they were doing two things.

(a) They were signifying their unity. Their gathering together from all parts of the land three times in the year (cf. Exod. 23:14) was a necessary counter-balance to the long months of living in small groups. The faith of the "exiles", like that of modern Christians, depended on the perception that each individual or group belonged to a much larger body, confessionally united, and expressing both unity and faith in worship together.

(b) In the Feast of Booths the exiles were remembering in a special way the deliverance of their forefathers from Egypt centuries before (Lev. 23:42–43). This was appropriate for the community that had so recently been delivered from its own bondage to an imperial overlord. They went, therefore, primarily to rejoice in the goodness of their God. This motive underlies all the activities which take place in this seventh month. The altar is rebuilt (vv. 2–3), not only for the feast which must be celebrated so imminently, but for all the offerings of the regular cult, namely the daily sacrifice and the various feasts (vv. 2, 5; cf. Exod. 29:38–42; Lev. 23). The song that accompanied the laying of the foundation of the Temple some months later (v. 11) shows that the people were well aware that their very existence depended on the "steadfast love" of God. We may suppose, therefore, that their worship on both occasions marked their gratitude to him for his deliverance. Recent events confirmed for them what perhaps the exile had caused some to doubt, namely that "his steadfast love endures for ever". (With this song in v. 11, cf. that which was sung at the dedication of Solomon's temple over four centuries earlier, 2 Chr. 7:3.)

The character of the Feast of Booths, furthermore, was well designed to throw them back upon God's mercy. In it, the worshippers did actually live for a week in makeshift accommodation, perhaps tents, in the environs of Jerusalem (Lev. 23:42). This style of living was in deliberate contrast to their permanent homes, to remind them not only that God had delivered them, but that their continuing existence was more fragile than the security of a regular pattern of life could suggest. How readily the returned exiles would appreciate this point may be imagined from the fact that they can scarcely have had time to establish a routine, perhaps even rebuild derelict houses, before the call to worship supervened. It is far more difficult to hear the message of fragility of life and the fact of dependence upon God for each succeeding breath amid the settled affluence and long life-expectancy that so many in the modern western world enjoy. Yet all our securities are ultimately illusory. Any attempt to peel them away, whether by temporary abstention from some of the good things of life, or whether by deliberate exposure to and sharing of the hard realities experienced by the poor and disadvantaged, can only be salutary.

MIXED FEELINGS—II

Ezra 3:1–13 (*cont'd*)

(ii)

The exiles' sense of precariousness is illustrated also by the fact that "fear was upon them because of the peoples of the lands" (v. 3). The phrase is somewhat obscure, as we are not told quite how their fear relates to the building of the altar. It is clear enough what *kind* of fear it was. It was not, in itself, religious fear, no "fear of the Lord" (for which a different Hebrew word would have been necessary), but a terror of the exiles' human foes. We noticed in connection with the preceding chapter that there were many in Judah and Samaria who were disenchanted with the exiles' return.

The question then remains whether we are to imagine the exiles rushing to erect the altar in an act of frantic piety born of terror, or whether the act itself is something which for some reason *produces* fear of their enemies. The former picture hardly fits either with the fact that the authority of Cyrus himself underwrites the exiles' presence in Judah or with the boldness of Zerubbabel and the other leaders in resisting the overtures of the same enemies in 4:2. More probably, their fear arises from the fact that their building of the altar actually involves the dismantling of a rough altar which had stood on the spot of Solomon's original, and which had been used not only by those Jews who had not been deported but also by groups which had been settled in Samaria by the Assyrians, and which by now had percolated south into the open spaces of Judah (cf. Ezra 4:10 and Jer. 41:5). The sense of verse 3, then, may be that they rebuilt the altar *despite* their fear, and the statement testifies to the determination of the exiles to set their worship on a right basis, come what may, from the beginning.

(iii)

At both the building of the altar and the laying of foundations for
the new Temple, there were bound to be comparisons with the
magnificent former edifice of Solomon. Comparisons are invited
in the first instance in verse 7 where we read that the exiles were
able to finance not only the actual building but the importation of
cedars from Lebanon in the manner of Solomon (2 Chr. 2:3ff.).
The analogy implies that the wealth of the nations is put at the
disposal of God's people. If the new community does not have
Solomon's wealth in its own right, it can nevertheless command it
because the authority of Cyrus guarantees it. Other hints of an
analogy with Solomon's Temple consist in the fact that the work
begins in the second month (cf. 1 Kings 6:1—though it may only
be coincidence, since this is the appropriate time of the year,
early spring, to begin building work), and in the appointment,
before the Temple has been built, of priests and Levites to do the
work in it. (cf. 1 Chr. 23:4ff., and notice vv. 26f. for the change
of the Levites' age of service from thirty to twenty years, as in our
v. 8.)

Together with these intimations of Solomon there is in addition
more than a suggestion of the prophecy contained in Isa. 60:10–
14, where there is reference not only to the wealth of Lebanon,
but also to "foreigners" rebuilding Jerusalem. The chief "for-
eigner" here is Cyrus, who thus appears not merely as the unwit-
ting servant of the Lord, but of the exiles themselves. Both the
past grandeur of Solomon's Israel and a future grandeur pre-
dicted in the Book of Isaiah are brought to bear on the foundation
of the new Temple of Zerubbabel and Jeshua.

However, the effect of the comparison is to introduce a hollow
note into the account of the proceedings. Verses 10–11 relate the
great joy which attended the laying of the foundation. This
is typical of comparable events in Old Testament history (cf.
1 Chr. 15:2ff., on the occasion of David's bringing the ark to
Jerusalem), and reminds us that the worship of Israel was no dull
affair, nor any model for dry formality in Christian worship
today. The exiles will perhaps have been still in the first flush of
their enthusiasm for their new life in Judah, particularly grateful,

no doubt, to have survived the best part of the first year back, apparently without mishap despite earlier fears. The hollow note is struck, however, when we are told that many of the older exiles, who had seen the first Temple, wept at the laying of the foundation of the new.

It is usually supposed that this was because the foundations showed that the new Temple would be much smaller than the old. We do not know the dimensions of Zerubbabel's temple, however. (Cyrus appears to have intended that it should be at least as grand as the one destroyed by the Babylonians; 6:3; cf. 1 Kings 6:2. It is, unfortunately, impossible to be sure, as the text of 6:3 gives only two dimensions and may be incomplete or corrupt.) It is possible that part of the cause of the old men's sadness was simply the painful memories that were evoked. That the new Temple was inferior in some respects, however, perhaps in the richness of the materials available for its beautification, is apparent from Hag. 2:3. Whatever the nature of the new Temple's inferiority, it is clear that the author of Ezra has made a considerable point of the fact that the old men's weeping was mingled with the shouts of joy (v. 13). The effect is to suggest, once again, that there is but a partial fulfilment of the hopes of Israel here. The joy at the deliverance and the new opportunity is tempered by the feeling that the people have seen greater blessing from God in the past.

It may also be implied that the possibility of greater blessing in the future still exists. This would explain the somewhat muted allusion to Isa. 60:10–14 noted above (in keeping with the approach to prophecy fulfilment found in ch. 1). Once again joyful affirmation of the re-establishment of God's covenant with Israel is not permitted to overshadow the fact that full blessing depends on the ongoing obedience of the people.

FLAMING DARTS

Ezra 4:1–24

[1]Now when the adversaries of Judah and Benjamin heard that the returned exiles were building a temple to the Lord, the God of Israel,

²they approached Zerubbabel and the heads of fathers' houses and said to them, "Let us build with you; for we worship your God as you do, and we have been sacrificing to him ever since the days of Esarhaddon king of Assyria who brought us here." ³But Zerubbabel, Jeshua, and the rest of the heads of fathers' houses in Israel said to them, "You have nothing to do with us in building a house to our God; but we alone will build to the Lord, the God of Israel, as King Cyrus the king of Persia has commanded us."

⁴Then the people of the land discouraged the people of Judah, and made them afraid to build, ⁵and hired counsellors against them to frustrate their purpose, all the days of Cyrus king of Persia, even until the reign of Darius king of Persia.

⁶And in the reign of Ahasuerus, in the beginning of his reign, they wrote an accusation against the inhabitants of Judah and Jerusalem.

⁷And in the days of Artaxerxes, Bishlam and Mithredath and Tabeel and the rest of their associates wrote to Artaxerxes king of Persia; the letter was written in Aramaic and translated. ⁸Rehum the commander and Shimshai the scribe wrote a letter against Jerusalem to Artaxerxes the king as follows— ⁹then wrote Rehum the commander, Shimshai the scribe, and the rest of their associates, the judges, the governors, the officials, the Persians, the men of Erech, the Babylonians, the men of Susa, that is, the Elamites, ¹⁰and the rest of the nations whom the great and noble Osnappar deported and settled in the cities of Samaria and in the rest of the province Beyond the River, and now ¹¹this is a copy of the letter that they sent—"To Artaxerxes the king: Your servants, the men of the province Beyond the River, send greeting. And now ¹²be it known to the king that the Jews who came up from you to us have gone to Jerusalem. They are rebuiding that rebellious and wicked city; they are finishing the walls and repairing the foundations. ¹³Now be it known to the king that, if this city is rebuilt and the walls finished, they will not pay tribute, custom, or toll, and the royal revenue will be impaired. ¹⁴Now because we eat the salt of the palace and it is not fitting for us to witness the king's dishonour, therefore we send and inform the king, ¹⁵in order that search may be made in the book of the records of your fathers. You will find in the book of the records and learn that this city is a rebellious city, hurtful to kings and provinces, and that sedition was stirred up in it from of old. That was why this city was laid waste. ¹⁶We make known to the king that, if this city is rebuilt and its walls finished, you will then have no possession in the province Beyond the River."

¹⁷The king sent an answer: "To Rehum the commander and

Shimshai the scribe and the rest of their associates who live in Samaria and in the rest of the province Beyond the River, greeting. And now [18]the letter which you sent to us has been plainly read before me. [19]And I made a decree, and search has been made, and it has been found that this city from of old has risen against kings, and that rebellion and sedition have been made in it. [20]And mighty kings have been over Jerusalem, who ruled over the whole province Beyond the River, to whom tribute, custom, and toll were paid. [21]Therefore make a decree that these men be made to cease, and that this city be not rebuilt, until a decree is made by me. [22]And take care not to be slack in this matter; why should damage grow to the hurt of the king?"

[23]Then, when the copy of King Artaxerxes' letter was read before Rehum and Shimshai the scribe and their associates, they went in haste to the Jews at Jerusalem and by force and power made them cease. [24]Then the work on the house of God which is in Jerusalem stopped; and it ceased until the second year of the reign of Darius king of Persia.

(i)

Chapters 4–6 tell of the completion of the Temple despite the opposition of the inhabitants of the land. In the present chapter we learn of their initial success in hindering the work.

The structure of chapter 4 is at first glance a little confusing. While verses 1–5, 24 are concerned with the relatively short period following the exiles' return, viz. 538 B.C. down to 520 B.C. (the second year of Darius, v. 24), verses 6–23 picture opposition to the exiles also in the reigns of Xerxes (= Ahasuerus), 486–465 B.C., and Artaxerxes I, 465–425 B.C. The logic of the chapter is particularly difficult to follow if verse 24 is read as a sequel to verse 23 (since Darius precedes Artaxerxes by a considerable period). In fact, however, verses 6–23 should be seen as a kind of extended parenthesis. Following a known practice in ancient writing, verse 24 marks the fact that the main thread of the discourse has now resumed by repeating the last thing that was said before the parenthesis.

The effect is similar to one that is produced in many modern stories and films by a "flashback"—except that here we have a "flash-forward". The events which are chiefly under scrutiny are illuminated by similar events from different periods. Opposition to the exiles, we are told, occurred not only when they first resettled in Judah, but was a factor in their lives throughout the period of a century or so to which the Books of Ezra and Nehemiah relate. The impression of unremitting antagonism is given not only by the "flash-forward", but by verses 4–5, where the verbs "discouraged", "made ... afraid", "hired" are in a tense which shows that these activities were habitual. This says something about the nature of the opposition. Whenever God initiates a spiritual work it follows that there will be resistance. It is interesting that the word for "accusation" in verse 6 is *sitna*, closely related to "Satan". It is not clear whether the point is merely semantic. Yet for the exiles the opposition they experienced was nothing other than "the flaming darts of the evil one" (Eph. 6:16).

(ii)

The enemies of the exiles tried various ploys. The first approach, made to Zerubbabel himself, is an attempt to destroy by assimilation. The opponents point out the important similarities between the exiles and themselves (v. 2). To do so they refer to their origins. The reference to Esarhaddon, king of Assyria, who had brought them there, reminds us that the population of the north, or large parts of it, consisted of people who had been planted there by the Assyrians in place of the genuine Israelite inhabitants who were deported elsewhere following the fall of Samaria in 721 B.C. (The story is told in 2 Kings 17:1–6. The king of Assyria in that place is Sargon, 722–705. That Esarhaddon, 681–669, is mentioned here suggests that the Assyrian planting of the region of Samaria continued over an extended period.) Our passage is further illuminated by 2 Kings 17:24ff. In that place we learn that, in response to early difficulties on the part of settlers, the Assyrians provided an Israelite priest to teach them the ways of the Lord (v. 28). This is the basis for the claim made by Zerubbabel's antagonists that they worshipped the Lord. The Kings passage makes it very clear, however, that this allegiance was shallow. Rather "every nation [that had been brought to Samaria] still made gods of its own"; 2 Kings 17:29.

Here, then, is the first danger to the exiles from the people of the land. They appeared to be similar to them in essential respects. The activities described in verses 4–5, moreover, may be a kind of wheedling that encouraged the exiles to abandon what was dearest to them by throwing in their lot with their neighbours. Verse 5, read more literally than RSV, means that they hired "counsellors" to frustrate their "counsel". That is to say that, under the guise of advice and interest, they sought to seduce the exiles from following the mind of God to follow a different mind. After their first rebuttal (v. 3) the tactic may have changed (i.e. from offering to help build to discouraging from building at all). But the point was consistent. The peoples of the land wished the exiles to be entirely like them. But these were people whose allegiance was fundamentally not to Yahweh. For the exiles to have assimilated would have meant destruction. Zerubbabel's resistance, therefore (v. 3), was informed by a spiritual insight. In a similar way, the apostle Paul warns Christians to avoid conformity to the world's standards and thinking. Only by "*transformation*" and a renewed mind can one do the will of God (Rom. 12:2).

HOW TO GET THINGS DONE?

Ezra 4:1–24 (*cont'd*)

(iii)

The real colours of the adversaries appear in the letter written by Rehum and his associates in the time of Artaxerxes (vv. 8ff. Notice that this is the second of two letters written to Artaxerxes, cf. v. 7, besides the one that was written to Xerxes, v. 6.) Here the tactics have changed. Now that the adversaries (albeit a new generation of them) are addressing the seat of empire rather than the exiles themselves, their concern, far from stressing the similarities, is to show how different they are. This they do by presenting themselves as good and loyal imperial subjects. Features of the letter itself help evoke the background to their activity. First, it is written in Aramaic, a language which has affinities with

Hebrew. It was spoken originally by the Aramaeans, a Semitic
people which had links with the Israelites going back to patri-
archal times. Isaac's wife Rebekah and Jacob's wives, Rachel and
Leah, were Aramaeans. Jacob himself is called an Aramaean in
Deut. 26:5. By the Persian period, Aramaic had become the
official language of the Empire. It was, therefore, the correct
medium for Rehum and his associates to adopt in addressing the
king.

Secondly the letter pictures for us the diversity of the Empire.
Verse 9 lists not only people who occupied important imperial
positions in Samaria, but different nationalities (represented presumably by their leaders) who made up the population of the
province following generations of the policy of deportation.
Osnappar (v. 10) is better known as Ashurbanipal, the last of the
great Assyrian kings (669–626). The fulsome manner of reference
to the Assyrian Osnappar in a letter to the Persian Artaxerxes
shows how little the realities of life had changed for the imperial
provinces in all the convulsions at the centre of things. Osnappar
is quite simply one of Artaxerxes' predecessors.

The allusion to Osnappar, therefore, is of the same order as the
more obvious obsequiousness of verses 14–16, where Rehum
expresses his horror at the thought that the king's interests should
suffer any detriment in Samaria. The ingenuity of the tactic is
only fully appreciated when we realize that the Persian Empire in
the 5th century B.C. was troubled by rebellions, notably that of
the satrap Megabyzus in the province of Trans-Euphrates. It was
also a period when Persia's treasuries may have been at a low ebb,
following the costly and disastrous wars against the Greeks
known to us from names like Marathon and Thermopylae. This in
turn increased the likelihood of rebellions because of the necessarily heavier tax burdens imposed on the provinces. Artaxerxes
was understandably uneasy. Rehum, therefore, paints a picture
of a province (Beyond the River) whose many constituent
peoples are zealously loyal, with the one glaring exception of the
Jewish exiles. The historical justification for the claim that
Jerusalem is a chronically rebellious city will have consisted in
such events as Hezekiah's withholding of tribute from Assyria (2

Kings 18:7, c. 724 B.C.) and Zedekiah's abortive bid for freedom from the Babylonians, which led to the cataclysm of 587 (2 Kings 24:20ff.). The Assyrian and Babylonian annals were evidently available to the Persian kings. And it is clear that a nerve is touched.

(iv)

The reply to Rehum (vv. 17ff.) appears to have taken the bait entirely. Artaxerxes is evidently much troubled by the thought of lost revenue (vv. 20, 22), and has perhaps been even more impressed by the potential of Judah for self-aggrandizement than either Rehum could have hoped or historical actuality can have warranted. (Verse 20 is an exaggeration even if it has in mind the largest extent of the Davidic-Solomonic realm.) It may be that Assyro-Babylonian records exaggerated the extent of Israelite-Judean influence in order to magnify their own achievements in subduing it, and that these exaggerations have informed Artaxerxes. The Old Testament does, of course, picture Solomon receiving tribute from his neighbours (2 Chr. 9:22–28). In any case, Artaxerxes is convinced, and orders work to stop on the rebuilding (v. 23). (This rebuilding is not mentioned elsewhere in Ezra–Nehemiah. It clearly occurred prior to that of Nehemiah, which was successfully completed, Neh. 6:15. Nevertheless the fact that a start was made on the work, v. 12, may be one explanation for the speed with which Nehemiah was subsequently able to finish it. This verse, incidentally, may be better translated: "they are beginning the work of rebuilding the walls and repairing the foundations." It is impossible to imagine the walls near to completion prior to Nehemiah.)

Perhaps the most notable feature of the chapter as a whole is the underlying misconception as to the nature of causation. In general both the adversaries and the king subscribe to the view that the will of the king is paramount (vv. 15, 22) and that power consists in royal decrees (vv. 19, 21). We have already noticed in chapter 1 the difference between Cyrus' conception of what he was doing and that of the biblical writer. More specifically, the adversaries condemn themselves out of their own mouths. In trying to show the common ground they share with the exiles they blunder out the damning fact that they have no true heritage in Israel (v. 2). Most ironically, though the opposition to the exiles had success in the times of both Zerubbabel and Artaxerxes (vv. 23f.), the sequel to this chapter will show that it ultimately had the opposite effect to that which was desired. It may even be that the fears aroused in Artaxerxes by Rehum's letter were instrumental in his decision to send Nehemiah to Jerusalem, known for his loyalty to Persia, yet with a commission very distasteful to those who shared the concerns of Rehum! Rehum evidently did not know the proverb: "A man's mind plans his way, but the Lord directs his steps" (Prov. 16:9, cf. v. 25). And even if the king perceived, and perhaps enjoyed, the folly of Rehum, he will hardly have guessed at his own role in the re-establishment of the people from whom in time a true king would come. When the Psalmist exclaimed:

> What is man that thou dost regard him,
>   or the son of man that thou dost think of him?
> Man is like a breath,
>   his days are like a passing shadow (Ps. 144:3–4)

he might have had in mind just such self-deluding human pretensions as pervade the present chapter, pretensions which are conveyed from one passing generation to the next and are ultimately nothing.

SHARPER THAN A TWO-EDGED SWORD

Ezra 5:1–17

[1]Now the prophets, Haggai and Zechariah the son of Iddo, prophesied to the Jews who were in Judah and Jerusalem, in the name of the God of Israel who was over them. [2]Then Zerubbabel the son of She-alti-el and Jeshua the son of Jozadak arose and began to rebuild the house of God which is in Jerusalem; and with them were the prophets of God, helping them.
    [3]At the same time Tattenai the governor of the province Beyond the River and Shethar-bozenai and their associates came to them and

spoke to them thus, "Who gave you a decree to build this house and to finish the structure?" [4]They also asked them this, "What are the names of the men who are building this building?" [5]But the eye of their God was upon the elders of the Jews, and they did not stop them till a report should reach Darius and then answer be returned by letter concerning it.

[6]The copy of the letter which Tattenai the governor of the province Beyond the River and Shethar-bozenai and his associates the governors who were in the province Beyond the River sent to Darius the king; [7]they sent him a report, in which was written as follows: "To Darius the king, all peace. [8]Be it known to the king that we went to the province of Judah, to the house of the great God. It is being built with huge stones, and timber is laid in the walls; this work goes on diligently and prospers in their hands. [9]Then we asked those elders and spoke to them thus, 'Who gave you a decree to build this house and to finish this structure?' [10]We also asked them their names, for your information, that we might write down the names of the men at their head. [11]And this was their reply to us: 'We are the servants of the God of heaven and earth, and we are rebuilding the house that was built many years ago, which a great king of Israel built and finished. [12]But because our fathers had angered the God of heaven, he gave them into the hand of Nebuchadnezzar king of Babylon, the Chaldean, who destroyed this house and carried away the people to Babylonia. [13]However in the first year of Cyrus king of Babylon, Cyrus the king made a decree that this house of God should be rebuilt. [14]And the gold and silver vessels of the house of God, which Nebuchadnezzar had taken out of the temple that was in Jerusalem and brought into the temple of Babylon, these Cyrus the king took out of the temple of Babylon, and they were delivered to one whose name was Shesh-bazzar, whom he had made governor; [15]and he said to him, "Take these vessels, go and put them in the temple which is in Jerusalem, and let the house of God be rebuilt on its site." [16]Then this Shesh-bazzar came and laid the foundations of the house of God which is in Jerusalem; and from that time until now it has been in building, and it is not yet finished.' [17]Therefore, if it seem good to the king, let search be made in the royal archives there in Babylon, to see whether a decree was issued by Cyrus the king for the rebuilding of this house of God in Jerusalem. And let the king send us his pleasure in this matter."

(i)

The previous chapter evoked the discouragement and counsels of despair which weakened the Jewish community's resolve in the century after the return. Now we see the effect, like a hammer blow, of that kind of influence: the empowering word of God which shows up the debilitating word of man for what it is. The catalogue of discouragements in chapter 4 has no doubt been brought together thematically partly so that this report of the activity of Haggai and Zechariah should reflect on them all. Historically speaking, that activity bore only upon the inertia that prevailed up to the time of Darius. But as the material is arranged the point is made that there is always an effective answer to discouragement in the bold proclamation of the word of God— not simply as propositions to be assented to, but as a call to action. This sequence—word and action—is well illustrated by the first two verses: "Haggai and Zechariah prophesied . . . Then Zerubbabel and Jeshua arose . . ."

The prophecies of Haggai and Zechariah are recorded for us in the Old Testament. That of Haggai refers wholly to the period under discussion; that of Zechariah partly so. Broadly, they can be said to contain two elements, viz. *rebuke* and *promise*. The rebuke comes mainly from Haggai, who deplores the people's greater concern for their own comfort than for the house of the Lord (Hag. 1:4), a concern which is misguided and actually issues in their impoverishment (Hag. 1:9–11). Haggai shows us that there was more to the abandonment of work on the Temple than external opposition alone. Somehow, in the short time since the return, that opposition had combined with a self-regarding decline from the initial determination to do God's will, evidenced by Zerubbabel at Ezra 4:3. Presumably even Zerubbabel had lost his early resolve, so that he had to be stirred up again by the preaching of the prophets.

Zechariah (in chs. 1–8) majors rather on the glorious future that awaits Judah. His burden is: "the Lord will again comfort Zion and again choose Jerusalem" (Zech. 1:17), and he pictures the city enjoying prosperity and peace (Zech. 8:1–13). Joshua (Jeshua) and Zerubbabel, furthermore, are not only the addressees of the prophecy, but figure in it, representing respectively the priestly (3:1–8) and royal (6:10–14) aspects of messianic hope. (6:10–14 probably refers in fact to Zerubbabel and not to Joshua, textual corruption having produced the present confusion.) That hope was not finally to be fulfilled in either man. Nevertheless each was shown to stand for a dimension of the Jewish heritage which would one day reassert itself in an entirely new way.

Promise and rebuke belong equally, therefore, to the preaching which galvanized the exiles into fresh action. It is always so. When God's word comes to us in a convincing way it both awakens us to our deficiencies in life and faith and holds out a vision of what we might be. The rebuke, though searching, does not crush. The prophets do not simply accuse while remaining detached. Rather we find them standing alongside the builders helping them (v. 2*b*; this may include others besides Haggai and Zechariah). Here we have a fine picture of how the Lord "wounds and heals" (cf. Hos. 6:1). He makes the right path clear, then walks it with us.

(ii)

There is, at first glance, something faintly curious about this exhortation of the prophets to rebuild the Temple. In their preaching, Haggai and Zechariah stand aside from some of the great biblical prophets who saw the Temple as a positive danger to piety (cf. Amos 5:21ff.; Isa. 1:11–17; Jer. 7:1–15). This temple, begun by Zerubbabel, was the same (though much extended by Herod) whose curtain would be torn at the death of Jesus (Matt. 27:51) and which would be destroyed according to his word (Luke 21:6).

The Temple had its place, however, in the Lord's purposes for his people. The return from exile was a time of great potential discouragement to the Jews. The first euphoria following Cyrus' decree quickly evaporated when they found themselves in a homeland which was now disputed territory, which yielded no easy living and which was, apparently, under the immediate political ascendancy of Samaritan rivals who were more worldly-wise in their ability to "handle" the Empire. The temptation to believe the age-old lie, "the Lord is not with us" (cf. Exod. 17:7),

must have been strong indeed. This will have had as its consequence the belief that the gods of the stronger peoples must be
stronger gods, and hence the downward spiral of religious apathy
and assimilation to the peoples of the land (through marriage)
which Ezra would find some years later.

In this situation a symbol of God's presence was all-important.
The insistence of Haggai and Zechariah that the people build the
Temple is ultimately inspired by the same concern which had led
Jeremiah to announce its imminent destruction because it had
become a fetish. In both cases the danger was that the people
would assimilate to the surrounding nations and there would
cease to be a people of God. Prophecy in the modern Church too
is that which counsels against becoming indistinguishable from
the world, and against the submersion of a clear witness that there
is a living God dwelling and working among a people today.

AN EMBLEM OF GRACE—AND RESPONSE TO THE
WORD

Ezra 5:1–17 (*cont'd*)

(iii)

The Temple, as already suggested, had no eternal or absolute
significance. It came to its moment. More accurately, it came
again to its moment, having once, under Solomon, served to
parade before the world the splendour of the God of all the earth
(see e.g. 2 Chr. 9:1–4). Now, under Zerubbabel, it served as an
emblem to a people that was stripped of all else. Every group—
from nation to scout troupe—needs emblems of its identity. The
need exists even where the group perceives itself to have real
power (the American flag!). But it is perhaps more important still
where no such power exists, and perhaps especially where it has
been lost. God's gift of the Temple to his people, then, was an act
of his compassion, by which he gave them something that they
really needed in order to keep them faithful. It is more than any
mere group emblem, of course, because there is a sense in which
God was truly present in this Temple. Yet there was nothing

permanent or essential about that, as the Cross and the New Testament's theology of the Lord dwelling spiritually among his people (John 14:23) would show. Rather, this was a case of the Lord meeting his people at the point of their need and providing for them to be faithful.

The people's response to the word of God consists not only in the resumption of work on the Temple but in their reply to the Persian officials' enquiry of verse 4. The approach by Tattenai, Shethar-bozenai and their associates is distinct, of course, from the discouragements of "the adversaries" (4:1), coming some years later, and after the people have been fortified by the preaching of Haggai and Zechariah. It is clearly also an official deputation, different in character from the underhand attacks recorded in chapter 4. The officials give the impression of being about their regular business, reporting on possibly significant developments in the territory under their jurisdiction, and having no axe to grind in local disputes between Judeans and Samaritans. Their enquiry (vv. 3, 9) is not charged with any antagonism.

The report of Tattenai to Darius incorporates an account of Cyrus' decree as given, for the first time, by the exiles themselves (vv. 11–16). In the course of it they furnish not merely the bare historical facts, but their understanding of their exile and return. This has two elements:

(a) *Confession* (v. 12). There are no excuses here. The exile had happened as a result of generations of disobedience to God. Yet the exiles are not blaming their forefathers in order to exonerate *themselves*. Rather the tone of their words shows that they have taken to heart the rebuke of Haggai and include themselves in the punishment. The recognition of guilt is the first step in their rediscovery of their identity as the people of God.

(b) *God's love*. The exiles' words also testify to a recovered belief that they are the special objects of God's love. The reference to the great king who first built the Temple (Solomon) (v. 11), and to the reversal of the action of Nebuchadnezzar in despoiling it (notice how exact that reversal is, vv. 14–15) shows a recaptured sense of the activity of God among them now, as in ages past. Their reply to Tattenai, while in every sense proper, contains a hint of determination that the earlier completion of a temple by Solomon (v. 11) would be matched by the completion of a new one in their day (v. 16). That determination derived from a conviction that God was among them again. The faith pictured here is healthy. It does not idly wait for God to manifest himself. It embarks upon the course of action which is perceived to be one of God, and expects vindication.

(iv)

Success attends the exiles' response to the preaching of Haggai and Zechariah. The very atmosphere suggests it. With Tattenai we have no longer the spirit of "the adversaries" but of Cyrus who had first authorized the exiles' present activity. Tattenai's report shows that the work is proceeding rapidly and impressively (v. 8) and the reason for the progress is contained in verse 5, where we see that no human agency is to be allowed to prevent the building this time. There is a wry touch, furthermore, in the exiles' reference, in their reply to Tattenai, to the "great king" who had built a temple in the past. It was precisely Judah's glorious past which, on another occasion, led to imperial resistance to the rebuilding of Jerusalem (4:20). Yet now it becomes part of an approach which produces a favourable response.

There could hardly be a better illustration of the ultimate impotence and whimsicality of human power, and of the fact that *all* powers are subject to God's timing. The confidence of the exiles here might be summed up in the words of Ps. 146, especially verses 3–5:

> Put not your trust in princes,
>   in a son of man, in whom there is no help.
> When his breath departs he returns to his earth;
>   on that very day his plans perish.
> Happy is he whose help is the God of Jacob,
>   whose hope is in the Lord his God.

BY DECREES

Ezra 6:1–12

¹Then Darius the king made a decree, and search was made in Babylonia, in the house of the archives where the documents were stored. ²And in Ecbatana, the capital which is in the province of Media, a scroll was found on which this was written: "A record. ³In the first year of Cyrus the king, Cyrus the king issued a decree: Concerning the house of God at Jerusalem, let the house be rebuilt, the place where sacrifices are offered and burnt offerings are brought; its height shall be sixty cubits and its breadth sixty cubits, ⁴with three courses of great stones and one course of timber; let the cost be paid from the royal treasury. ⁵And also let the gold and silver vessels of the house of God, which Nebuchadnezzar took out of the temple that is in Jerusalem and brought to Babylon, be restored and brought back to the temple which is in Jerusalem, each to its place; you shall put them in the house of God."

⁶"Now therefore, Tattenai, governor of the province Beyond the River, Shethar-bozenai, and your associates the governors who are in the province Beyond the River, keep away; ⁷let the work on this house of God alone; let the governor of the Jews and the elders of the Jews rebuild this house of God on its site. ⁸Moreover I make a decree regarding what you shall do for these elders of the Jews for the rebuilding of this house of God; the cost is to be paid to these men in full and without delay from the royal revenue, the tribute of the province from Beyond the River. ⁹And whatever is needed—young bulls, rams, or sheep for burnt offerings to the God of heaven, wheat, salt, wine, or oil, as the priests at Jerusalem require—let that be given to them day by day without fail, ¹⁰that they may offer pleasing sacrifices to the God of heaven, and pray for the life of the king and his sons. ¹¹Also I make a decree that if any one alters this edict, a beam shall be pulled out of his house, and he shall be impaled upon it, and his house shall be made a dunghill. ¹²May the God who has caused his name to dwell there overthrow any king or people that shall put forth a hand to alter this, or to destroy this house of God which is in Jerusalem. I Darius make a decree; let it be done with all diligence."

(i)

Almost incidentally, the sequel to Tattenai's request for an authoritative word concerning the Jerusalem Temple permits us a glimpse of the flurry of activity in the Empire's corridors of power. Though search was made first in Babylon, according to Tattenai's suggestion (v. 1, cf. 5:17), it was at Ecbatana, capital of the former Median Empire, that the relevant documents came to light. The Empire which Cyrus had built afforded him a selection of majestic capitals viz. Babylon, Susa in Elam (cf. Esth. 1:5) and Ecbatana (modern Hamadan in Northern Iran), where he had first risen to power. We know from a non-biblical source that Cyrus regularly spent a season of the year in each of these capitals, choosing Ecbatana for the summer period. The discovery of the Aramaic version of his momentous decree in this city is consistent with his having spent the first summer of his reign over the whole Empire (538 B.C.) there.

Equally, the existence of an Aramaic memorandum of the decree, parallel to that which we have met in 1:2–4, has an air of authenticity. Cyrus' decree would have spanned a number of different documents, each with its own function. This memorandum (vv. 2b–5) may have belonged to treasury records designed to certify that the temple vessels from Jerusalem had been returned. This would explain the extra information that is contained here when compared with the version of the decree in chapter 1. Only here does Cyrus authorize the meeting of the cost of the rebuilding from the royal treasury, and indeed the return of the vessels. Similarly, it is only here that we have the measurements of the Temple (v. 3), together with directions about the manner of its building (v. 4). These latter details may be designed to set limits to royal expenditure on the project! (The dimensions in v. 3 seem to be incomplete, since there are only two rather than three. The text appears to have suffered in transmission, and we should probably read here the measurements given for Solomon's Temple in 1 Kings 6:2, viz. $60 \times 20 \times 30$ cubits.)

(ii)

Darius' own reply to Tattenai (vv. 6–12) follows immediately on the cited words of Cyrus with which his letter opens, and has the status of a new decree. Its effect is to confirm entirely the measures of his forerunner and reapply them to the new situation some eighteen years on. As an answer to the adversaries of Judah and Benjamin (4:1) it is complete and even savage. That it is calculated as such (at least by our author) appears from the term "without *delay*" (v. 8), which exactly reverses the state of affairs in 4:24 ("the work . . . *stopped*") by the use of a form of the identical verb. The order that much of the burden of the maintenance of the Jerusalem cult should be met from resources in the province of Beyond the River itself ensured that the rebuff of the "adversaries'" self-interested plans was costly.

Failure to comply would be costlier yet. The savagery of verse 11 reminds us that we are in a world in which kings used cruel measures as a calculated means to effect stability. We need not doubt Darius' will to eliminate dissent by measures such as those of verse 11. His ascent to the throne of Persia occurred in the midst of rebellion. He himself, in a text that has been preserved, cites numerous areas of the Empire in which he had to quell rebellions in the year 522–521 B.C. (including Persia—understood in the narrower sense—, Elam, Media, Assyria and Egypt). One source (Herodotus) tells how, in the subjugation of the Babylonian rebellion, Darius had three thousand of the leading citizens crucified. Impalement was also widely practised following sieges. The use of a beam from a man's own house shows that the punishment intends not only to inflict the death-penalty but to expunge his name from memory, the worst fate the ancient world could imagine.

Darius' policy, therefore, is very similar to that of Cyrus. Like him he comes to power with a victory over Babylon. Like him he pursues a policy of cult conservation. (That is to say, he "supports the local gods" throughout the Empire, thinking thus to keep the conservative majority on his side.) Like Cyrus, too, he must be seen not as an angel of light but as a ruthless monarch, labouring no doubt under the religious superstitions of the ancient world, but fundamentally a despot. (Hence the application to him of the title "king of Assyria", v. 22, aligning him with kings who had been openly hostile to Israel.)

The more remarkable, then, if full of irony, that his interests should, on the surface, coincide so exactly with those of the God of heaven. This is well illustrated by the language which Darius adopts—perhaps advised by a Jewish scribe—in verse 12, which is so redolent of Old Testament theology (especially in the idea of the *dwelling* of the *name* of God at Jerusalem; cf. Deut. 12:5). He thus takes some pains to "co-opt" the God of Israel, little thinking that the dwelling of God's name at Jerusalem was of a significance which would outlast him, or that the Name would one day in Jerusalem, by an act of self-sacrifice which Darius could not have understood, initiate an Empire which would know no end.

IT IS FINISHED

Ezra 6:13–22

[13]Then, according to the word sent by Darius the king, Tattenai, the governor of the province Beyond the River, Shethar-bozenai, and their associates did with all diligence what Darius the king had ordered. [14]And the elders of the Jews built and prospered, through the prophesying of Haggai the prophet and Zechariah the son of Iddo. They finished their building by command of the God of Israel and by decree of Cyrus and Darius and Artaxerxes king of Persia; [15]and this house was finished on the third day of the month of Adar, in the sixth year of the reign of Darius the king.

[16]And the people of Israel, the priests and the Levites, and the rest of the returned exiles, celebrated the dedication of this house of God with joy. [17]They offered at the dedication of this house of God one hundred bulls, two hundred rams, four hundred lambs, and as a sin offering for all Israel twelve he-goats, according to the number of the tribes of Israel. [18]And they set the priests in their divisions and the Levites in their courses, for the service of God at Jerusalem, as it is written in the book of Moses.

[19]On the fourteenth day of the first month the returned exiles kept the passover. [20]For the priests and the Levites had purified themselves together; all of them were clean. So they killed the passover lamb for all the returned exiles, for their fellow priests, and for themselves; [21]it was eaten by the people of Israel who had returned from exile, and also by every one who had joined them and separated himself from the pollutions of the peoples of the land to worship the Lord, the God of Israel. [22]And they kept the feast of unleavened bread seven days with

joy; for the Lord had made them joyful, and had turned the heart of the king of Assyria to them, so that he aided them in the work of the house of God, the God of Israel.

(i)

For the period from Cyrus to Darius, therefore, the "adversaries of Judah and Benjamin" are dealt a hefty blow. Their appeal (4:2) had based itself on the will of a king; with poetic justice it is the will of a king that frustrates them. If the reader is niggled by the thought that this victory was to be short-lived, as the catalogue of chapter 4 has already shown, our author has anticipated the problem (which he himself had deliberately created). The reference to Artaxerxes (v. 14) is surprising, since the narrative of chapter 6 pertains entirely to the reign of Darius. Both Cyrus and Darius are intelligible in the context. Artaxerxes, however, as we have already noticed, reigned much later than the events described here (viz. 465–425 B.C.). Nevertheless, the author's purpose is clear. Informed by a logic that did not necessarily share the patterns of our own, he slipped in a reference to the later period to show that the same victory which was won here would also be won then, in the time of Ezra and Nehemiah.

The author thus makes chapter 6 serve a deeper purpose than merely to announce the successful completion of the building of the Temple. The allusion to Artaxerxes transforms the account into a response to the whole gloomy catalogue of chapter 4. Just as there was perpetual opposition to the interests of the exiles, so the purposes of the Lord must ever and ultimately prevail. The history of restoration, in the hands of our author, is always an illustration of the principles that govern *all* history, and an intimation that its final outcome will be the vindication of the God who is over all, and of the people who belong to him.

(ii)

For the moment, a new Cyrus brings to completion the work that his illustrious predecessor had begun. The end of this section of the book (chs. 1–6) thus balances its beginning. The progress of the exiles is guaranteed by a benefactor, and opposition from without is swept aside with the tacit promise that when it re-appears it will meet a similar fate. So Judah prospers (v. 14) with a prosperity which, linked with the activity of the prophet, is made dependent upon her ability to grasp and have faith in the principles which the whole chapter unfolds. And she celebrates (vv. 16ff.).

The celebration falls into two parts: first, the dedication itself (vv. 16–18) and, second, the Passover, signalling the resumption of regular worship according to the most ancient of Israel's feasts (Exod. 23:15ff.).

The dedication is reminiscent of that of Solomon's Temple (2 Chr. 7), though the comparison throws up above all the glaring discrepancy between the wealth of the sacrifices on that occasion and the relative poverty here (with our v. 17 cf. 2 Chr. 7:5). That apart, the events are similar. With the positioning of the priests and Levites, our author evinces all the care that worship should be properly conducted that also characterizes the Books of Chronicles (cf. 1 Chr. 15:12–15). And there is joy (vv. 16, 22). The exiles might be in reduced circumstances (like the Church so often today). Yet they knew their God. And the re-establishment of the place where, centuries before, he had chosen to put his name was a token that greater things were in store for his faithful people.

The exiles' joy, like all godly joy, was solemn. That is not to say that it was inhibited; it means, rather, that it remained in touch with the deep-rooted cause of their recent sufferings. The sacrifices at the dedication thus took the form of a sin offering. The occasion of this kind of offering was, as its name suggests, the sinner's repentance and petition for forgiveness (cf. Lev. 4:13–21). The celebration thus looked both backwards and forwards: backwards to a past that had brought judgment and which was now remembered with sorrow; and forwards to an era of welfare in the care of the God who had delivered them. Such balance characterizes all healthy spirituality.

(iii)

There is a corresponding balance in the Passover celebration. There is a sense in which this is recorded simply because of the outstanding significance of the feast in ancient Israel, and especially because the deliverance from Babylon (only now complete by virtue of the erection of the Temple) had so much in common with the earlier deliverance from Egypt which the Passover remembered. We can look at it on another level, however. We have noticed already that there is a kind of exclusiveness about the exiles. They are carefully distinguished from all other inhabitants of the land (4:1ff.) and it is clear from the outset that God's purposes of salvation will be continued through them. We now find this idea taken a little further with the application of the term "Israel" to the exiles (v. 21; cf. v. 16). They alone can claim the title of people of God. Yet this is not narrow sectarianism, for the Passover was eaten in fact not only by those who had been through the Babylonian experience but also "by every one who had joined them and separated himself from the pollutions of the peoples of the land to worship the Lord, the God of Israel" (v. 21; cf. Neh. 10:28; Exod. 12:48). That is to say that those among the "pagan" population of Judah who were prepared to identify themselves with the exiles by sharing their commitment to the Lord were held in fact to belong to them.

There is a paradox here which is still true of the people of God. The Church only has an identity when it takes it from the events which constituted it centuries ago, viz. the Cross and Resurrection of Jesus Christ, and when it associates itself with all those who have proclaimed them ever since. In doing so it resembles the exiles' self-identification through the act of deliverance in Babylon. At every stage in its history, it seems, God's people must have a foundational experience of his disposition to deliver from bondage. Nevertheless, far from being "always the same", the Church is always changing, growing, composed of new generations and new kinds of people. Its very nature is to be open. And the only qualification for membership is a heartfelt commitment of mind and soul to the God who "was in Christ Jesus reconciling the world to himself" (2 Cor. 5:19).

ENTER EZRA

Ezra 7:1–10

> ¹Now after this, in the reign of Artaxerxes king of Persia, Ezra the son of Seraiah, son of Azariah, son of Hilkiah, ²son of Shallum, son of Zadok, son of Ahitub, ³son of Amariah, son of Azariah, son of Meraioth, ⁴son of Zerahiah, son of Uzzi, son of Bukki, ⁵son of Abishua, son of Phinehas, son of Eleazar, son of Aaron the chief priest— ⁶this Ezra went up from Babylonia. He was a scribe skilled in the law of Moses which the Lord the God of Israel had given; and the king granted him all that he asked, for the hand of the Lord his God was upon him.
> ⁷And there went up also to Jerusalem, in the seventh year of Artaxerxes the king, some of the people of Israel, and some of the priests and Levites, the singers and gatekeepers, and the temple servants. ⁸And he came to Jerusalem in the fifth month, which was in the seventh year of the king; ⁹for on the first day of the first month he began to go up from Babylonia, and on the first day of the fifth month he came to Jerusalem, for the good hand of his God was upon him. ¹⁰For Ezra had set his heart to study the law of the Lord, and to do it, and to teach his statutes and ordinances in Israel.

(i)

In these verses we have a brief account, soon to be filled out by his own memoir (8:15ff.), of Ezra's arrival in Jerusalem. Commentators often regard this as heralding a major new section of the book, since the action moves on some sixty years (to 458 B.C.; see Introduction) and the personality of Ezra now dominates the remaining chapters. This is true in a sense. Yet we have already seen that the author is not so much interested in strict chronological sequence as in the development of a theme. He has, indeed, already provided two glimpses of Artaxerxes' reign (4:7–23; 6:14), suggesting that the events now to be described will be in basic continuity with what we have seen in chapters 1–6.

There are, in fact, two important themes that continue here. The first is the Lord's disposal even over the mind and motives of the king. The reason why Ezra could undertake the mission to

Jerusalem with *the king's* favour was that "the hand of *the Lord* was upon him" (v. 6; cf. 6:22). The second theme is that of deliverance from captivity. Just as exiles returned from Babylon in 538 B.C., so now, eighty years on, a new wave, including priests and Levites and other temple personnel (v. 7), accompanies Ezra to the homeland. In both cases the power of the Lord's hand to achieve his will is in the foreground.

Verses 8–9 relate crisply that Ezra and his companions completed the arduous journey from Babylon in quick time. The dates are 8 April (= the first day of the first month) and 4 August (= the first day of the fifth month). The journey was undertaken, therefore, at the hottest time of the year, along a route which, though well-trodden and avoiding the desert, was not without its risks from banditry. The dangers involved emerge more explicitly in 8:22, in the account of the journey. Verses 1–10 anticipate that account, showing at the outset that in this connection also the Lord would overcome all barriers to the restoration and care of his people. The statement that "the good hand of his God was upon him [Ezra]" (v. 9) becomes a refrain in this chapter and the next (8:22, 31). If God seems to plot the minutiae of the lives of his servants, that should not prompt thoughts of men at the mercy of an arbitrary deity, in the spirit of Shakespeare's

> As flies to wanton boys, are we to the gods;
> They kill us for their sport. (King Lear)

The *good* hand of Ezra's God was upon him. Behind all his doings lies the desire, fundamental even to the Old Testament's creation theology, to bring about the good of all his creatures (see Gen. 1:28ff. for God's desire that his creatures should enjoy the "goodness" of what he has made; cf. also Rom. 8:28). It is well, furthermore, to be forearmed with this thought against any temptation to think of the religion of Ezra as a narrow and repressive thing.

(ii)

The real emphasis in our verses lies upon the personality of Ezra himself. We may consider this under three headings.

(a) *His lineage*. Ezra is presented to us first of all as a priest, by virtue of his descent from Aaron. (The genealogy is based on 1 Chr. 6, especially vv. 1–6, but is very compressed. This is not uncommon in biblical genealogy. The point here is not to give exhaustive detail, but simply to show the link between Ezra and Aaron.) In fact the subsequent account presents him hardly at all in a priestly role, though it is appropriate that a priest should have responsibility for the sanctification of vessels for the Temple offered by Artaxerxes (8:25–30). More important is the statement that Ezra was "a scribe skilled in the law of Moses" (v. 6). This places him in line of descent (figuratively speaking) from the great lawgiver himself. The priests had traditionally had a responsibility beyond their strictly cultic duties for teaching the law (cf. Deut. 31:10ff.). To this extent the occupation of the priest Ezra with the law is nothing new. During the exilic period, when priests were removed willy-nilly from their sacrificial duties, their responsibility for law teaching probably became their main official concern. They had no monopoly on it, however, for those who were traditionally called "wise men", Israel's third classical group of teachers alongside prophets and priests (cf. Jer. 18:18) had also come more and more to busy themselves with the law. And Ezra, in that he is called a "scribe" (v. 6), is also associated with these. (The word may also imply that he held an official Persian position, perhaps related to Jewish affairs. The point stands nonetheless.) It would be hard to imagine one better fitted to give Israel a new beginning, drawing together as he did the roles of priest, lawgiver (or prophet, cf. Deut. 18:15ff.) and wise man—roles to which Jesus Christ himself could be said to have succeeded. All of them focus on the law, in which Ezra is said to have been "skilled". The Lord had raised up a man for the hour, prepared by virtue of his whole prehistory for the task which lay before him.

(b) *His training*. Ezra, however, was no mere passive inheritor of the past. He had made himself highly competent in the area of his responsibility. The word translated "skilled" has at its root the idea of speed. He was so conversant with his material that he could make considered judgments rapidly. And this level of expertise had been achieved because "he had set his heart to study the law of the Lord". Preparation by heritage was not the only ingredient in Ezra's powerful character. Like the sportsman who, however talented, must discipline himself rigorously in order to succeed, Ezra had subjected himself to a régime which was designed to make him effective in God's service. This element in Ezra's make-up is perhaps even more important than his priestly background, for the quality of determination can compensate for actual disadvantages in circumstances, as has been the case with many who have been outstanding in Christian service. (One thinks of the celebrated Welsh girl, Mary Jones, who made a now legendary walk over miles of her country's rough terrain, in the days before transport was readily available, for the purpose of procuring a Bible.)

(c) *His desire.* Granted favourable circumstances, granted the will to be equipped, there remains yet the area of motivation. How readily the means can become the end! The business of study itself, or the mere mechanics of any area of Christian service, can be so attractive that it can cease to be subjected to the governing hand of God. Ezra, however, had not only "set his heart to study the law of the Lord", but also "to do it" (cf. Jas. 1:25) and "to teach his statutes and ordinances in Israel" (v. 10). For Ezra, to know the law of God was to know his mind, both in terms of promise and expectation, for his people. It was impossible, therefore, *merely* to study it. It had to be *lived.* A comparable New Testament idea is that of "doing the truth" (John 3:21). And it had to be lived not only by himself but by all the people of God. The model teacher in Ezra is a doer. And the doer can be no mere demonstrator. He must *be* what he would have his disciples be. This is what lies behind Ezra's readiness to leave his, probably comfortable, situation in Babylon for the perils of an arduous journey and the uncertainties of life in the small, ill-defended community in Judea: a desire that the people of God should walk with God. Such a desire also underlies the words "all that he asked" (v. 6). When his own will was directed to the service of God, it was not disappointed.

EZRA'S MISSION

Ezra 7:11–26

[11]This is a copy of the letter which King Artaxerxes gave to Ezra the priest, the scribe, learned in matters of the commandments of the Lord and his statutes for Israel: [12]"Artaxerxes, king of kings, to Ezra the priest, the scribe of the law of the God of heaven. And now [13]I make a decree that any one of the people of Israel or their priests or Levites in my kingdom, who freely offers to go to Jerusalem, may go with you. [14]For you are sent by the king and his seven counsellors to make inquiries about Judah and Jerusalem according to the law of your God, which is in your hand, [15]and also to convey the silver and gold which the king and his counsellors have freely offered to the God of Israel, whose dwelling is in Jerusalem, [16]with all the silver and gold which you shall find in the whole province of Babylonia, and with the freewill offerings of the people and the priests, vowed willingly for the house of their God which is in Jerusalem. [17]With this money, then, you shall with all diligence buy bulls, rams, and lambs, with their cereal offerings and their drink offerings, and you shall offer them upon the altar of the house of your God which is in Jerusalem. [18]Whatever seems good to you and your brethren to do with the rest of the silver and gold, you may do, according to the will of your God. [19]The vessels that have been given you for the service of the house of your God, you shall deliver before the God of Jerusalem. [20]And whatever else is required for the house of your God, which you have occasion to provide, you may provide it out of the king's treasury.

[21]"And I, Artaxerxes the king, make a decree to all the treasurers in the province Beyond the River: Whatever Ezra the priest, the scribe of the law of the God of heaven, requires of you, be it done with all diligence, [22]up to a hundred talents of silver, a hundred cors of wheat, a hundred baths of wine, a hundred baths of oil, and salt without prescribing how much. [23]Whatever is commanded by the God of heaven, let it be done in full for the house of the God of heaven, lest his wrath be against the realm of the king and his sons. [24]We also notify you that it shall not be lawful to impose tribute, custom, or toll upon any one of the priests, the Levites, the singers, the doorkeepers, the temple servants, or other servants of this house of God.

[25]"And you, Ezra, according to the wisdom of your God which is in your hand, appoint magistrates and judges who may judge all the

people in the province Beyond the River, all such as know the laws of your God; and those who do not know them, you shall teach. [26]Whoever will not obey the law of your God and the law of the king, let judgment be strictly executed upon him, whether for death or for banishment or for confiscation of his goods or for imprisonment."

(i)

These verses now contain the decree of Artaxerxes, who thus follows the lead of Cyrus and Darius in giving aid to the Jews in Jerusalem and any more who wished to return. Artaxerxes appears here, therefore, in a more favourable light than in 4:23. However, 5:14 gives an impression of a more benevolent disposition towards the Jews. In his long reign many things may have prompted changes of mind about them. His action here is intelligible in terms of established Persian policy, and may have been specifically intended to pre-empt the influence of a seditious Egyptian spirit upon Judah.

The terms of the decree both reflect its Persian provenance (note the king's seven counsellors, v. 14, a glimpse of the Persian power centre, cf. Esth. 1:14; the use of the term "God of heaven", v. 12; and the Persian practice of tax exemption for cult officials, v. 24) and a knowledge of Jewish interests and theology (e.g. in the sacrificial terminology, vv. 16–17, and the idea of Jews "freely offering" themselves, v. 13, cf. Judg. 5:2).

Artaxerxes' appointment of Ezra to the task prescribed here is consistent with Persian policy known from other accounts. Fensham in his Commentary draws a parallel with one Udjehar-resne, an Egyptian who was close to the Persian king Cambyses after Egypt had been brought within the Empire, and who was appointed by the king to carry out reforms in a sanctuary in Egypt. People from the provinces of the Empire were evidently used to keep the king and his counsellors advised about them. It is likely that Ezra held some such position in Persia. Indeed, he himself, or another Jew or Jews, may have drawn up the letter as we have it, on the authority of Artaxerxes. In it, once again, we see a strange harmony between the interests of the Empire and of the Lord. The establishment of the laws of God in Judah will serve Artaxerxes' purpose of maintaining stability, and he thus effectively makes them (i.e. the laws in the Pentateuch) his own for that part of the Empire, attaching to them his own sanctions (vv. 25–26). In a way that he does not suspect, however, his measure facilitates the theological purpose of bringing the Jews in Judah into a right relationship with their God.

(ii)

The purpose of Ezra's mission according to the king's decree is contained in verse 25: he was to appoint judges to judge on the basis of God's laws, and to ensure that all members of the community were conversant with them. The former task is reminiscent of Exod. 18:13ff., in which Moses agrees to delegate the business of judging to others. Each of these instances reflects the problem of applying law justly to a whole population. And how can there be justice, be the judges ever so fair, if the people themselves do not know what the law requires? Ezra's task was no slight one, therefore. The people of Israel and Judah had a history of burying what they knew of God so deep in their consciousness that it ceased to have any practical effect on how they lived. Nor was it the case that there had been no earlier attempts at reformation. The Books of Chronicles testify to numerous of these, from Asa (2 Chr. 14) to Josiah (2 Chr. 34–35).

Yet the decree of Artaxerxes was not simply in touch with the realities of Jewish history. As we have seen, it may well have been drawn up by Ezra himself, or someone in a similar position. It is, on the contrary, fully in the spirit of Jewish theology. From earliest times the religion of the Jews had openly depended upon instruction, with the family as the focus, and the father bearing the responsibility (cf. Deut. 6:4–9). And the Jews who followed Ezra would make the most sustained, and perhaps successful, attempt at bringing themselves under the influence of the law in a comprehensive way, an attempt which would issue ultimately in those secondary collections of law (Mishnah and Talmud) which still underlie Jewish belief and practice today.

Yet our passage invites comparison with another, which puts Ezra's task in a new perspective. That other is Jer. 31:31–34 (note especially v. 34), which our author undoubtedly knew. There Jeremiah speaks of a time when there will be no further need of teaching among God's people, "for they shall all know me . . . says the Lord". This is in the context of Jeremiah's famous New Covenant prophecy (v. 31), which holds out the hope of an immediate knowledge of God such as had not hitherto been common. We have seen before that the author of Ezra is hesitant to claim that the events which he relates are themselves the fulfilment of the prophecies made to Israel. Here again we have little more than a hint that a step is taken towards a grander fulfilment than the exiles were yet experiencing. The time of which Jeremiah speaks arrived only when Jesus Christ came to "make his home" with those who would believe in him, thus establishing a kind of intimacy between God and man which an outward law could only imperfectly achieve. For the time being, however, the Lord chose to be with his people through the teaching of law. His purpose of building a faithful community was taking a step further forward.

EZRA AND CO.

Ezra 7:27–8:20

27Blessed be the Lord, the God of our fathers, who put such a thing as this into the heart of the king, to beautify the house of the Lord which is in Jerusalem, 28and who extended to me his steadfast love before the king and his counsellors, and before all the king's mighty officers. I took courage, for the hand of the Lord my God was upon me, and I gathered leading men from Israel to go up with me.

1These are the heads of their fathers' houses, and this is the genealogy of those who went up with me from Babylonia, in the reign of Artaxerxes the king: 2Of the sons of Phinehas, Gershom. Of the sons of Ithamar, Daniel. Of the sons of David, Hattush, 3of the sons of Shecaniah. Of the sons of Parosh, Zechariah, with whom were registered one hundred and fifty men. 4Of the sons of Pahathmoab, Eliehoenai the son of Zerahiah, and with him two hundred men. 5Of the sons of Zattu, Shecaniah the son of Jahaziel, and with him three hundred men. 6Of the sons of Adin, Ebed the son of Jonathan, and with him fifty men. [7]Of the sons of Elam, Jeshaiah the son of Athaliah, and with him seventy men. [8]Of the sons of Shephatiah, Zebadiah the son of Michael, and with him eighty men. [9]Of the sons of Joab, Obadiah the son of Jehiel, and with him two hundred and eighteen men. [10]Of the sons of Bani, Shelomith the son of Josiphiah, and with him a hundred and sixty men. [11]Of the sons of Bebai, Zechariah, the son of Bebai, and with him twenty-eight men. [12]Of the sons of Azgad, Johanan the son of Hakkatan, and with him a hundred and ten men. [13]Of the sons of Adonikam, those who came later, their names being Eliphelet, Jeuel, and Shemaiah, and with them sixty men. [14]Of the sons of Bigvai, Uthai and Zaccur, and with them seventy men.

[15]I gathered them to the river that runs to Ahava, and there we encamped three days. As I reviewed the people and the priests, I found there none of the sons of Levi. [16]Then I sent for Eliezer, Ari-el, Shemaiah, Elnathan, Jarib, Elnathan, Nathan, Zechariah, and Meshullam, leading men, and for Joiarib and Elnathan, who were men of insight, [17]and sent them to Iddo, the leading man at the place Casiphia, telling them what to say to Iddo and his brethren the temple servants at the place Casiphia, namely, to send us ministers for the house of our God. [18]And by the good hand of our God upon us, they brought us a man of discretion, of the sons of Mahli the son of Levi, son of Israel, namely Sherebiah with his sons and kinsmen, eighteen; [19]also Hashabiah and with him Jeshaiah of the sons of Merari, with his kinsmen and their sons, twenty; [20]besides two hundred and twenty of the temple servants, whom David and his officials had set apart to attend the Levites. These were all mentioned by name.

(i)

Chapter 8 contains a fuller account of the journey of Ezra from Babylon to Jerusalem than that which appears in 7:8–9. The section 7:27–28 forms a bridge between the two chapters. It forms, in one sense, the climax of the accounts of Artaxerxes' decree, being Ezra's doxology for the goodness of God which was thus manifested (v. 27). Ezra was thus not merely the man of dogged faith and discipline, but also a man of worship, who recognized the hand of God in events, and gave him his due in praise.

The verses principally introduce what follows, however. On the most superficial level, they represent the beginning of the so-called "Ezra memoir" (7:27–9:15) in which events are related by Ezra in the first person. More importantly, they illustrate the link between the experience of God's help and the further practice of faith. Ezra observed what must have seemed marvellous to him, that a pagan king should not only restore but richly refurbish the Temple of the Lord, and so he "took courage" (v. 28), or more literally strengthened himself, in the knowledge that the project which lay on his mind was in reality God's, and would be attended with success. Faith feeds on seeing God at work. At the time of writing a major nationwide mission dominates the minds of Christians in England. Many are professing faith in Christ. But for many others who already stand within the Church, the experience has been almost as decisive. For they are seeing God at work changing lives, and thus belief in the value of prayer is reborn, as is a perception of faith as that which must issue in action and take risks. And so a dynamic is created which is *continuing* evidence of God at work in the world.

(ii)

Ezra did not return alone, but at the head of a substantial group who committed themselves to *aliya*. His mission is thus in the context of the waves of returning settlers which followed Cyrus' decree. There is a hint in verse 13—"those who came later"—that some of those who now accompanied Ezra belonged to a family (that of Adonikam) of which some members had come from Babylon earlier. This is confirmed by 2:13, where we find that a large number of that family accompanied Zerubbabel. Indeed, of the thirteen family names here (not counting those of the priests, Phinehas and Ithamar, v. 2), eleven occur, among others, in Ezra 2. It seems, then, that what is true of the family of Adonikam is true of all the others also. Even over the generations, it was particular families that were to the fore in making the journey back to the land. Reading between the lines, we may discern here an example of that faith-in-action (discussed above) transmitted from generation to generation by those families which took seriously their religious and educative duties.

One of the family names that occurs here but not in chapter 2 is that of David (v. 2). Our author thus notes explicitly what he had left unexpressed in the case of Zerubbabel (3:2), that the line of David was represented among those who had returned. He might have made much of this in the light of the prominence of David in messianic hopes expressed by some of the prophets. Once again, however, he chooses the path of reticence. God's hand is on this community indeed, but the full glories which are promised have not yet arrived.

(iii)

The expedition camped first by "the river that runs to Ahava" (v. 15), which may, more accurately, have been a canal linking the (unidentified) town of Ahava to the Euphrates. The location was probably a known and important departure point for caravans beginning the journey west.

Ezra's preliminary inspection of his company revealed that it contained no Levites—those temple officials who, while not actually priests, performed essential duties in the practice of worship. This might not have been a matter of urgent concern—since the actual initiation of worship in Jerusalem had already taken place under Zerubbabel and Jeshua, and therefore was not Ezra's task—had it not been typical of the whole resettlement ever since Cyrus' decree. The Levites had never been eager volunteers to return. (See again the huge discrepancy between the numbers of priests and Levites in 2:36–42.) Perhaps the removal from the scene of sacrificial activity had minimized in practice the differential between priests and Levites, and the latter were reluctant to resume a subordinate role, mundane in comparison with the possibilities which life in exile opened up. Babylon will have offered them, among other things, the opportunity to become people of substance for the first time, since they had been barred, under Israel's original charter of the occupation of the land, from possessing territory of their own (see e.g. Num. 18:24). Levites may well have been among those Jews who became wealthy in Babylon (e.g. in banking). On the other hand, the subsequent history of those who returned shows that they were often extremely badly treated—to the point of being deprived of their entitlement and in some cases starved to death—by their superiors the priests.

Who can blame them then for staying? The question, so reasonable, comes nevertheless from the apostle Paul's "natural" or "unspiritual" man (1 Cor. 2:14). It is clear to Ezra where the duty of the Levites lies. They are under a divine imperative to take up that role in the cult which had become possible once more, and which indeed was a token of salvation. He sends therefore to Casiphia (another location not certainly identified, but perhaps an important centre of Jewish population) "men of insight" (v. 16), who find a "man of discretion" (v. 18) prepared, with a number of his family, to leave all and go. Our author's emphasis on qualities akin to wisdom here reminds us once more of the line of thought in Paul to which the passage cited above belongs. The theme there, to state it rather simply, is the folly of human wisdom (1 Cor. 1:20) and the wisdom of divine "folly" (1 Cor. 1:25). The "discretion" (or better "shrewdness") of Sherebiah, son of Mahli, was no doubt in part great ability; it must also have had a dimension of spiritual insight, to see that the hard way was also the *right* way, and that it is also impossible to do better than do the will of God.

"JOURNEYING MERCIES"

Ezra 8:21–36

[21]Then I proclaimed a fast there, at the river Ahava, that we might humble ourselves before our God, to seek from him a straight way for ourselves, our children, and all our goods. [22]For I was ashamed to ask the king for a band of soldiers and horsemen to protect us against the enemy on our way; since we had told the king, "The hand of our God is for good upon all that seek him, and the power of his wrath is against all that forsake him." [23]So we fasted and besought our God for this, and he listened to our entreaty.

[24]Then I set apart twelve of the leading priests: Sherebiah, Hashabiah, and ten of their kinsmen with them. [25]And I weighed out to them the silver and the gold and the vessels, the offering for the

house of our God which the king and his counsellors and his lords and all Israel there present had offered; [26]I weighed out into their hand six hundred and fifty talents of silver, and silver vessels worth a hundred talents, and a hundred talents of gold, [27]twenty bowls of gold worth a thousand darics, and two vessels of fine bright bronze as precious as gold. [28]And I said to them, "You are holy to the Lord, and the vessels are holy; and the silver and the gold are a freewill offering to the Lord, the God of your fathers. [29]Guard them and keep them until you weigh them before the chief priests and the Levites and the heads of fathers' houses in Israel at Jerusalem, within the chambers of the house of the Lord." [30]So the priests and the Levites took over the weight of the silver and the gold and the vessels, to bring them to Jerusalem, to the house of our God.

[31]Then we departed from the river Ahava on the twelfth day of the first month, to go to Jerusalem; the hand of our God was upon us, and he delivered us from the hand of the enemy and from ambushes by the way. [32]We came to Jerusalem, and there we remained three days. [33]On the fourth day, within the house of our God, the silver and the gold and the vessels were weighed into the hands of Meremoth the priest, son of Uriah, and with him was Eleazar the son of Phinehas, and with them were the Levites, Jozabad the son of Jeshua and No-adiah the son of Binnui. [34]The whole was counted and weighed, and the weight of everything was recorded.

[35]At that time those who had come from captivity, the returned exiles, offered burnt offerings to the God of Israel, twelve bulls for all Israel, ninety-six rams, seventy-seven lambs, and as a sin offering twelve he-goats; all this was a burnt offering to the Lord. [36]They also delivered the king's commissions to the king's satraps and to the governors of the province Beyond the River; and they aided the people and the house of God.

(i)

On the river Ahava, Ezra proclaims a fast, for the purpose of praying for safe transit along the dangerous highways that lie ahead. A caravan so richly laden (as vv. 25ff. make very clear) yet so undefended—by Ezra's choice (v. 22)—would surely be easy prey for the bandits who haunted the route, and who must rarely have fallen easily upon so choice a morsel as this. The setting here, and the language, conjure up Isa. 40, the most celebrated proclamation of liberty to the Babylonian captives. Ezra's party is, more or less, "in the wilderness", praying for "a straight way" (Isa. 40:3, where the words "make straight . . . a highway" are closely related to our phrase). Most obviously, Ezra's "straight way" means a safe journey. Yet the overtones of the Book of Isaiah make the prayer into a statement of confidence that the release of which the prophet spoke is in train. Here as elsewhere, however, the note of fulfilment is muted, lest it should lead to false triumphalism. Ezra is well aware that real dangers lie ahead and that the circumstances require, first of all, uncompromising faith.

The passage contains several terms which speak of proper devotion to God. The people were to *humble themselves* (v. 21) and *seek* God (vv. 21–22). And when they had *fasted and prayed*, he *listened* (v. 23). The terms used are very similar to those of the well-known verse in 2 Chr. 7:14, which crystallizes the ideal of devotion in those books. Familiar in Chronicles also is the contrast between *seeking* and *forsaking* (v. 22); cf. 1 Chr. 28:9. Ezra, like the author of Chronicles and the biblical writers generally, is keenly aware that God, though full of love and always making the first move, does not dispense favours promiscuously, but seeks to build and bless a people that knows him and his ways. Ezra, therefore, resolves to demonstrate the faith of his party.

The demonstration is quite calculated. He has refused the king's proffered protection, feeling that his protestations about the character of his God would be compromised by the acceptance of such help (v. 22). The passage is structured so as to state the conflict between trust in God and trust in man most starkly:

v. 21: *seek* from God a straight way
v. 22: ashamed to *ask* the king
v. 22: the hand of God . . . upon all that *seek* him.

In setting the two kinds of trust against each other thus the author of Ezra is in line with other biblical thinking; Ps. 20:7. (Nehemiah, however, would choose differently. See on—or wait for!—Neh. 2:9.)

The act of dependence on God would prove his faithfulness both to the king and to the people themselves. The king would see that these Yahweh worshippers took their God seriously, and were no mere nationalists. The effect on the community itself, however, might prove the more important. The decision to seek God's help *to the exclusion* of any other meant that their faith could be no nominal thing. Rather it would be tested. They believed in a God who *could* deliver—therefore they would entrust themselves to him. It is well to *affirm* faith, as many Christians do regularly in the creeds. Yet it is salutary to ask whether anything that one ever does actually *requires* faith. If not, then what does it mean to say that life is lived by faith (Hab. 2:4)? Can a faith that is never drafted into service survive? Ezra's confidence was based on the fact that, in obtaining Artaxerxes' decree, he had discerned that "the hand of the Lord my God was upon me" (7:28); so now he would prove that "the hand of our God is for good upon all that seek him" (v. 22).

(ii)

Ezra's final preparation before departure is to make proper arrangements for the care and transport of the immensely valuable gifts which the king has made, a task which constitutes half of his royal commission (7:15). His charge to the twelve priests chosen to be responsible for them represents their consecration (v. 28). As the priests are already "holy", i.e. set apart to the sacred sphere of the Temple and its service, so now the vessels pass into that sphere and belong in a special way to God. As "holy things" they must be ritually "fenced off" from common use, and handled only by those who are themselves "holy". (The term is used, therefore, in a sense distinct from the ethical sense in which *all* Israelites were required to be holy; cf. Lev. 19:2.) So Sherebiah and his colleagues would have exclusive responsibility for the vessels until they handed them over to their fellow priests who were already functioning in the Temple at Jerusalem (vv. 29–30, 33–34).

This sort of concern for external beautification can strike the modern reader as at best irrelevant and at worst misplaced. It is, however, indispensable to the proper restoration of the exiles. This could never consist merely of repatriating Jews to their homeland. Rather, as in the case of the exodus from Egypt centuries before, it must be the release of a people united in their resolve *to worship God* (cf. Exod. 7:16, where "serve" = "worship"). For Israel, the Temple, with its adornments, was the place above all others in which God's praises should be sung, and its rituals were correct accompaniments to prayer and penitence. (Protests by prophets and psalmists should not be taken to be against ritual *as such*, but against the error of thinking that it was adequate in itself; so Pss. 40:6–8; 50:7–15; Isa. 1:11–17.) Proper attention to prescribed ritual, therefore, was part of obedience, scarcely separable in the Israelite mind from ethical requirements. Ezra's arrangements for these huge offerings, then, was no frustrating delay, but time well spent, perhaps even prompted by the period so recently spent in prayer (vv. 21–23. King David had learnt a harder way that such precautions were not superfluous; 1 Chr. 15:13; cf. 13:9–11.)

What makes the Jews' restoration so remarkable is not simply that they should return, but that kings should supply their needs in relation to worship (cf. 7:27). It is this that makes the "new exodus" so evidently an act of God's salvation. When Ezra's people arrived safely in Jerusalem, therefore (vv. 31–32), it was right that they should offer sacrifices (v. 35), not merely because the king had said they should (7:17), nor even as an isolated act of thanksgiving (the emphasis of sin offerings and burnt offerings is in any case on penitence and atonement; Lev. 4:22–26; 5:10), but because they were reconstituted as the people of God and therefore *must* worship.

A FLY IN THE OINTMENT

Ezra 9:1–4

[1]After these things had been done, the officials approached me and said, "The people of Israel and the priests and the Levites have not separated themselves from the peoples of the lands with their abominations, from the Canaanites, the Hittites, the Perizzites, the Jebusites, the Ammonites, the Moabites, the Egyptians, and the

Amorites. ²For they have taken some of their daughters to be wives for themselves and for their sons; so that the holy race has mixed itself with the peoples of the lands. And in this faithlessness the hand of the officials and chief men has been foremost." ³When I heard this, I rent my garments and my mantle, and pulled hair from my head and beard, and sat appalled. ⁴Then all who trembled at the words of the God of Israel, because of the faithlessness of the returned exiles, gathered round me while I sat appalled until the evening sacrifice.

(i)

If Ezra's return had been attended by euphoria it was soon cruelly dispelled. Chapters 9 and 10 tell of the sin which had crept back into the covenant community since the days of Zerubbabel, of Ezra's shock and of the people's repentance.

Chapter 9 is central to the whole book because of the sharp contrast which it draws between the people of God as it ought to be and as it actually is. The potential and true status of the people are suggested, for example, by the term "the holy race", or more literally, "holy seed", a reminiscence of the promise of Isaiah that despite all the punishments which would come upon Israel for her sin, yet her life would never be extinguished (Isa. 6:13) because she was God's holy people (cf. also Exod. 19:6). This idea is akin to that of the "remnant" (vv. 8, 15), also prominent in Isaiah (10:20–23) and connoting primarily the restoration of a people that will be once again in covenant harmony with God.

There is irony, however, in the use of these expressions here, conveying the utter incongruity of sin among the holy people. The Book of Isaiah's great proclamation of liberty had declared that satisfaction had been made for Israel's iniquity again (the same word, *awon*, is used in both Isa. 40:2 and Ezra 9:7). The "faithlessness" of verse 2 is precisely that repudiation of God and covenant which led to the condemnation and death of Saul (1 Chr. 10:13).

The issue confronting Ezra, therefore, is no mere peripheral matter, but covenant breach itself. Whether intermarriage with non-Jews was the only sin of the returned exiles we do not know. The sufficient point of it is that it represents a denial of their status as God's people. The prohibition of intermarriage was of crucial importance in their ancient charter (Exod. 34:11–16; Deut. 7:3), and was designed to secure their continued existence as a distinct people. Yet now the exiles were marrying among the successors of those very peoples who had posed a threat to them from time immemorial (cf. Deut 7:1). And Ezra is "appalled" (v. 3). In a day when marriage between people of different nationalities is a perfectly acceptable commonplace Ezra's dismay can seem like a gross overreaction. Yet in reality, the need for the purity of the race was simply a logical extension of the fact that the people of God, in those days, took the form of a nation. It was a nation, not a church, that manifested the possibilities of life with God.

The underlying issue, therefore, is purity of *religion*. The Old Testament writers knew well enough that confusion with other peoples would inevitably lead to confusion with their religions (Deut. 7:4). For Christians, therefore, the implication of this false trail of the exiles is in terms of basic commitments which run counter to the commitment to Christ. This can happen where whole churches seek to "marry" Christian belief with current philosophies, and the Gospel is reduced to a code of decent behaviour, rather than the word of life. In this, as in Ezra's Israel, the "chief men", or leaders, can often be in the van (v. 2). In a slightly different vein, some of those who are interested in establishing dialogue between Christianity and other religions have found that Christianity must remain resolutely true to what it is, for otherwise it has no integrity at all. In its relationship with Hinduism, for example, which is by its nature omni-tolerant, a Christianity which seeks a middle way, or tries to establish a *tertium quid*, has actually become Hindu and is no longer Christian. On a personal level, the pursuit of goals and interests which are in themselves neutral is reprehensible if it has taken the place of a zeal for God and for the holiness of his people.

(ii)

So Ezra rends his garments and trembles and is appalled and fasts (vv. 3–4). The spiritual scenery is strange to us here. The people of the Old Testament did not easily separate inward conviction and emotion from outward manifestation. The tearing of the clothes and the plucking of the beard, together with the fasting, testify therefore to the mighty emotional disturbance which Ezra experiences. And strange though the scenery be, the power of the reaction can neither be lost on us nor dismissed as archaic. It is the trauma of one who has made God's cause his own and who sees it scorned. There is a spirit today which passes for broad-mindedness and tolerance, but which is really indifference to the hastening of God's kingdom in the world. It has much to learn from Ezra's immoderate godliness.

IF WE SAY WE HAVE NO SIN . . .

Ezra 9:5–15

⁵And at the evening sacrifice I rose from my fasting, with my garments and my mantle rent, and fell upon my knees and spread out my hands to the Lord my God, ⁶saying: "O my God, I am ashamed and blush to lift my face to thee, my God, for our iniquities have risen higher than our heads, and our guilt has mounted up to the heavens. ⁷From the days of our fathers to this day we have been in great guilt; and for our iniquities we, our kings, and our priests have been given into the hand of the kings of the lands, to the sword, to captivity, to plundering, and to utter shame, as at this day. ⁸But now for a brief moment favour has been shown by the Lord our God, to leave us a remnant, and to give us a secure hold within his holy place, that our God may brighten our eyes and grant us a little reviving in our bondage. ⁹For we are bondmen; yet our God has not forsaken us in our bondage, but has extended to us his steadfast love before the kings of Persia, to grant us some reviving to set up the house of our God, to repair its ruins, and to give us protection in Judea and Jerusalem.

¹⁰"And now, O our God, what shall we say after this? For we have forsaken thy commandments, ¹¹which thou didst command by thy servants the prophets, saying, 'The land which you are entering, to take possession of it, is a land unclean with the pollutions of the peoples of the lands, with their abominations which have filled it from end to end with their uncleanness. ¹²Therefore give not your daughters to their sons, neither take their daughters for your sons, and never seek their peace or prosperity, that you may be strong, and eat the good of the land, and leave it for an inheritance to your children for ever.'

¹³And after all that has come upon us for our evil deeds and for our great guilt, seeing that thou, our God, hast punished us less than our iniquities deserved and hast given us such a remnant as this, ¹⁴shall we break thy commandments again and intermarry with the peoples who practise these abominations? Wouldst thou not be angry with us till thou wouldst consume us, so that there should be no remnant, nor any to escape? ¹⁵O Lord the God of Israel, thou art just, for we are left a remnant that has escaped, as at this day. Behold, we are before thee in our guilt, for none can stand before thee because of this."

Ezra's dismay drives him to prayer. It is significant that he does not run angrily into action. (Contrast Nehemiah's more direct approach; Neh. 13:15.) Rather, he brings the matter to God. His prayer exhibits four important characteristics.

(a) *Solidarity*. Ezra does not seek to dissociate himself from the condition of the people. Rather his prayer is in terms of *"our* iniquities . . . *our* guilt" (v. 6). He sees himself involved not only in the sin of the contemporary community but in the chronic rebelliousness of all the preceding generations of Israel (v. 7), a chord which had been struck by the prophets too (cf. Ezek. 20; Jer. 2). Though he utterly rejects the people's sin, his kinship with them is such that he cannot simply forsake them. He thus fulfils a kind of mediatorial role such as we meet elsewhere in the pages of the Old Testament. Moses pleaded with God not to make an end of the Israel of *his* day in the face of the offer of being made the patriarch of an entirely new covenant people (Exod. 32:9–14). In Ezekiel's day the Lord sought for one who would "stand in the breach before me for the land, that I should not destroy it" (Ezek. 22:30). The apostle Paul could wish that he were "accursed and cut off from Christ" for the sake of his natural kinsmen the Jews (Rom. 9:3). Ezra's prayer is thus not only an example of deeply sincere intercession, though it is that, but it also illustrates the powerful bond between members of the covenant community. The Bible's examples of intercession are all based on the powerful feeling of the unity of God's people, whereby the intercessor desires with all his being the good—and the righteousness—of the *whole*, because he cannot ultimately distinguish himself and his interests from it.

(b) *Confession*. Ezra draws no veil over the failures of either past or present (vv. 6–7, 10–12, 15. The quotation in vv. 11–12, incidentally, is a digest of ideas found in the prophets and Deuteronomy.) Past punishments have been well deserved (v. 7). The people can bring nothing to God but their guilt (v. 15). The element of confession thus accounts for a large part of the prayer, showing that Ezra has avoided the temptation to pass it over and concentrate on other things. This temptation was known also to the apostle John when he wrote: "If we say we have no sin, we deceive ourselves, and the truth is not in us" (1 John 1:8). The tacit argument that "God does not need to be told" is misleading, because the business of telling is not a matter of conveying information—as if one could tell anything to the omniscient God—but is rather a spiritual activity; *we* need to be reminded of our own condition, and the willingness or otherwise to go on our knees with our confessions says something about how we truly stand with God.

(c) *Readiness to change*. Recognition of past guilt is of no value unless it issues in the determination to be different in the future. Ezra thus sows the seeds of his actions in chapter 10 in the words of verses 13–14. He is saying, in a nutshell: "We have had all this in the past and look where it got us; we shall not let it happen again, for the wilful disobedience of God's people must always issue in their impoverishment or worse." In true prayer, the will is pledged to do right. And while it is true that "good intentions" are notoriously unproductive, there is help at hand for those who live by the Spirit of God (Rom. 8:1–17, especially vv. 9–11).

(d) *Faith in God's mercy*. Corresponding to the community's need for change, recognized by Ezra, is the belief that God is merciful. This mercy is reflected in the exiles' current independence from Persia, which indeed has been the main theme of the book hitherto. The circumstances of the exiles in the Books of Ezra and Nehemiah are not subject to massive fluctuations depending upon their obedience or disobedience. (Our books thus differ in this respect from Chronicles, in which the much greater span of history has lent itself to the discernment of such a pattern.) Rather, their situation changes little. The effect of God's mercy in Ezra is complex. We have noticed several times that our author is by no means given to triumphalism. And we are close here to the centre of his concept of the exiles' standing with God. Rather than finding the effects of obedience and disobedience in different phases of the exiles' experience, he finds both at the same time. The exiles have been released from Persia. Yet Ezra can still say "we are bondmen" (v. 9). Read simply as a historical statement, this might mean that, though released, they have little political power and are still in vassal status. Ezra probably means more, however, applying the idea of slavery to the effects of the exiles' sin. This is not to spiritualize Ezra's plain meaning away. For the practice of intermarriage will have the actual effect of subjugating the Jews and their God to the surrounding peoples and their religions.

Ezra feels, therefore, that the enslaving effects of sin are all round. This is the reason for his cautious statement about God's mercy in verses 8–9: "for a *brief moment* favour has been shown" (suggesting the tenuousness of the exiles' position); "a secure hold" (literally a tent-peg; RSV, therefore, overstates the idea of security, for the tent-peg too connotes impermanence); "a *little* reviving in our bondage" (v. 8; cf. "some reviving", v. 9); "protection [lit. 'a wall'] in Judea and Jerusalem" (the word for wall is that which is used in agricultural contexts, e.g. for a wall round a vineyard, cf. Isa. 5:5, and is therefore distinct from the sort of walls which Nehemiah would later build; it is thus to be taken metaphorically, and again—as Isa. 5:5 shows—could be very impermanent).

These statements about God's mercy are in no way meant to diminish his *readiness* to be merciful. That is clear enough from the very existence of a Jewish community in Judea. Rather, the prayer is meant to convey to us (and perhaps we are to suppose that Ezra's contemporaries were listening too) that God's mercy is by no means to be taken for granted. Rather let it be a spur to obedience. When the people—or the Church—that has known mercy (as the Church has in the Cross of Christ) responds to it with a pure desire to do right, then mercy will abound still more, and there will be no doubt about the will of our God to do us good.

A DESPERATE REMEDY—I

Ezra 10:1–44

[1]While Ezra prayed and made confession, weeping and casting himself down before the house of God, a very great assembly of men, women, and children, gathered to him out of Israel; for the people wept bitterly. [2]And Shecaniah the son of Jehiel, of the sons of Elam, addressed Ezra: "We have broken faith with our God and have married foreign women from the peoples of the land, but even now there is hope for Israel in spite of this. [3]Therefore let us make a covenant with our God to put away all these wives and their children, according to the counsel of my lord and of those who tremble at the commandment of our God; and let it be done according to the law. [4]Arise, for it is your task, and we are with you; be strong and do it." [5]Then Ezra arose and made the leading priests and Levites and all Israel take oath that they would do as had been said. So they took the oath.

[6]Then Ezra withdrew from before the house of God, and went to the chamber of Jehohanan the son of Eliashib, where he spent the night, neither eating bread nor drinking water; for he was mourning over the faithlessness of the exiles. [7]And a proclamation was made throughout Judah and Jerusalem to all the returned exiles that they should assemble at Jerusalem, [8]and that if any one did not come within three days, by order of the officials and the elders all his property should be forfeited, and he himself banned from the congregation of the exiles.

[9]Then all the men of Judah and Benjamin assembled at Jerusalem within the three days; it was the ninth month, on the twentieth day of the month. And all the people sat in the open square before the house of God, trembling because of this matter and because of the heavy rain. [10]And Ezra the priest stood up and said to them, "You have trespassed and married foreign women, and so increased the guilt of Israel. [11]Now then make confession to the Lord the God of your fathers, and do his will; separate yourselves from the peoples of the land and from the foreign wives." [12]Then all the assembly answered with a loud voice, "It is so; we must do as you have said. [13]But the people are many, and it is a time of heavy rain; we cannot stand in the

open. Nor is this a work for one day or for two; for we have greatly transgressed in this matter. [14]Let our officials stand for the whole assembly; let all in our cities who have taken foreign wives come at appointed times, and with them the elders of every city, till the fierce wrath of our God over this matter be averted from us." [15]Only Jonathan the son of Asahel and Jahzeiah the son of Tikvah opposed this, and Meshullam and Shabbethai the Levite supported them.

[16]Then the returned exiles did so. Ezra the priest selected men, heads of fathers' houses, according to their fathers' houses, each of them designated by name. On the first day of the tenth month they sat down to examine the matter; [17]and by the first day of the first month they had come to the end of all the men who had married foreign women.

[18]Of the sons of the priests who had married foreign women were found Ma-aseiah, Eliezer, Jarib, and Gedaliah, of the sons of Jeshua the son of Jozadak and his brethren. [19]They pledged themselves to put away their wives, and their guilt offering was a ram of the flock for their guilt. [20]Of the sons of Immer: Hanani and Zebadiah. [21]Of the sons of Harim: Ma-aseiah, Elijah, Shemaiah, Jehiel, and Uzziah. [22]Of the sons of Pashhur: Eli-o-enai, Ma-aseiah, Ishmael, Nethanel, Jozabad, and Elasah.

[23]Of the Levites: Jozabad, Shim-e-i, Kelaiah (that is, Kelita), Peth-ahiah, Judah, and Eliezer. [24]Of the singers: Eliashib. Of the gatekeepers: Shallum, Telem, and Uri.

[25]And of Israel: of the sons of Parosh: Ramiah, Izziah, Malchijah, Mijamin, Eleazar, Hashabiah, and Benaiah. [26]Of the sons of Elam: Mattaniah, Zechariah, Jehiel, Abdi, Jeremoth, and Elijah. [27]Of the sons of Zattu: Eli-o-enai, Eliashib, Mattaniah, Jeremoth, Zabad, and Aziza. [28]Of the sons of Bebai were Jehohanan, Hananiah, Zabbai, and Athlai. [29]Of the sons of Bani were Meshullam, Malluch, Adaiah, Jashub, She-al, and Jeremoth. [30]Of the sons of Pahath-moab: Adna, Chelal, Benaiah, Ma-aseiah, Mattaniah, Bezalel, Binnui, and Man-asseh. [31]Of the sons of Harim: Eliezer, Isshijah, Malchijah, Shemaiah, Shime-on, [32]Benjamin, Malluch, and Shemeriah. [33]Of the sons of Hashum: Mattenai, Mattattah, Zabad, Eliphelet, Jeremai, Manasseh, and Shime-i. [34]Of the sons of Bani: Ma-adai, Amram, Uel, [35]Ben-aiah, Bedeiah, Cheluhi, [36]Vaniah, Meremoth, Eliashib, [37]Mat-taniah, Mattenai, Jaasu. [38]Of the sons of Binnui: Shime-i, [39]Shelemiah, Nathan, Adaiah, [40]Machnadebai, Shashai, Sharai, [41]Azarel, Shelemiah, Shemariah, [42]Shallum, Amariah, and Joseph. [43]Of the sons of Nebo: Je-iel, Mattithiah, Zabad, Zebina, Jaddai,

Joel, and Benaiah. ⁴⁴All these had married foreign women, and they put them away with their children.

(i)

We are struck first of all in this chapter by the effect which Ezra's reaction to the sin of the exiles had upon his contemporaries. It appears already from 9:4 that his horror had produced a similar response from some, who joined him in his vigil. We now find (10:1) "a very great assembly of men, women, and children" coming to him weeping bitterly. It may be that some of the women and children wept because of their imminent fate. Nevertheless, Shecaniah the son of Jehiel evidently represents a consensus of the people when he accepts the need to divorce the foreign wives and urges Ezra to take the necessary action (vv. 2–4). All this has happened without any recorded word of Ezra to the people. Even after he responds to Shecaniah by putting the leaders in Israel under oath to carry through their resolve (v. 5), he delays yet again to appear in the thick of the action, withdrawing rather to a private room in the Temple (Jehohanan being presumably a priest, though not necessarily the man mentioned in Neh. 12:22) to continue his fasting and mourning over the faithlessness of the people (v. 6).

By now the process has been set in motion. A proclamation is issued (v. 8) that *all* the returned exiles who have married foreign women should come to Jerusalem on pain of confiscation of property and expulsion from the community (v. 8). The penalty invoked was harsh. Confiscation meant the giving over of property to the sacred sphere (effectively the Temple) so that it was withdrawn for ever from human use. Separation from the community would deprive the offender permanently of any interest in the salvation which God was effecting in it. Here then is all the vigour which might have been expected from Ezra himself. Yet Ezra is nowhere to be seen. He is praying in the Temple.

The whole is a striking picture of the nature of influence. Ezra was not the only Old Testament leader to exercise a quiet but powerful ministry. The prophet Ezekiel had actually been struck dumb by God, if only temporarily (Ezek. 3:26), and was obliged to portray visually Judah's coming doom through his own suffering (4:4). Both men remind us forcefully that real leadership cannot be a detached thing, but must be fully engaged. It was the godliness and commitment of Ezra, testifying more powerfully than any harangue to the reality of God, of right and wrong and of judgment, that brought others to repentance. And this is true not only for those who are prominent among the people of God; rather it means that all who practise godliness have a power far beyond what is apparent. The Church in recent decades has reawakened, rightly, to the need to speak and act on social issues, to be seen to be concerned about the countless outrages against humanity in this world. Yet it must ultimately be powerless if it comes to imagine that the unseen spiritual life, the cultivated sensitivity to the mind of God, is time and energy squandered.

A DESPERATE REMEDY—II

Ezra 10:1–44 (*cont'd*)

(ii)

Many readers of Ezra have taken offence at what they consider the harshness of enforcing mass divorce, with all the consequent misery for the rejected women and children. The measure is the more astonishing because it is impossible to plead that divorce is regarded as a natural or easily justifiable thing in the Old Testament. True, Old Testament law reckons with it (Deut. 24:1–4); yet this is not done in such a way as to approve it. And the prophet Malachi, possibly ministering close in time to Ezra, shows the Lord's real attitude to the matter, when he writes: "I hate divorce, says the Lord" (Mal. 2:16). The Old Testament is thus not significantly different from the New, where Jesus himself speaks strongly against divorce (though not without leaving a loophole for the offended party, Matt. 19:3–9), and where Paul commands that believers should remain with their unbelieving spouses, regarding the children of the marriage as "holy" and expressing the hope that the unbeliever might become "consecrated" through the believer (1 Cor. 7:10–16). This seems to place Ezra well out on a limb.

Ezra's rigour hardly becomes more palatable when we think of the modern western world in which divorce has become such a way of life that many marriages are prejudiced from the start because social expectations often make the idea of lifelong commitment seem rather quaint. Shattered men and women, bewildered children, the heavy burdens of lone responsibility for upbringing have become commonplace. It would be wrong, of course, to picture modern society as callous and indifferent to all this. There is evidence that the rate of divorce in the USA, where it is highest, is actually decreasing, possibly because a new generation is resisting the experience of its parents—the first generation to have a high degree of liberty in the matter. Modern books and films—such as 'Kramer vs Kramer'—have almost certainly contributed to this resistance by their exposure of the intractable frustrations of separation. Is the Book of Ezra, in contrast, utterly without sensitivity to human distress?

Three considerations, in ascending order of importance, may be offered in defence of Ezra here (and we must bear in mind that he has the community behind him, and that Nehemiah will later be implicated also, Neh. 13:23–37).

Firstly, it is misleading to read back into Old Testament times the sorts of social consequences which divorce today brings in its train. The one-parent family would have been unheard of. The actual effect of the measure on the divorced wives, with their children, would have been to drive them back into the extended—non-Jewish—families from which they came, and which would have been flexible enough to receive them. So the measure may not have been so harsh as it first appears.

Secondly, we cannot be quite sure just how lax the attitude to marriage had become among the exiles. Malachi, in the passage already quoted (2:15f.), hints that the practice of divorce may have been gaining ground at this period for reasons which were basically selfish and godless. Could it be that some of those whom Ezra forced to divorce had *already* divorced Jewish women in order to marry these others? The intermarriage which strikes us as so innocent may not have been so.

Thirdly, and most importantly, the *action* of Ezra is without analogies because his *situation* is without analogies, certainly in modern times. The returned exiles, that community which now represented Israel and in which God's plan of salvation was being carried forward, was marked out from all other peoples only by its adherence to faith in its Lord. It had no political power, no armies, as yet no walls. And it was subject all the time to the lure of the softer option of being swallowed up by its stronger neighbours, who offered gods enough to satisfy its unfastidious conscience.

Furthermore, the list of those families of which members had married foreigners is formidable (vv. 18–44), and shows by its extensive similarities with the lists in chapters 2 and 8 that the problem was deep and thorough-going in the community. Taken in the abstract, Ezra may have liked the idea of divorce ill enough. But a desperate situation called for a desperate remedy. And the willingness of the people (especially the men, but no doubt including not a few scorned Jewish women too!) to co-operate shows that, a spirit of repentance being upon them, the matter was really a religious one and that a new resolve to be God's people and do his will left them no choice. An evil had been done which jeopardized the very existence of the people of God and the only right course was to undo it.

(iii)

Modern applications of Ezra's stern measures are scarcely in the realm of marriage at all (though it is true that the path of discipleship is that much steeper where a partner is not equally committed to it). The issue that is raised for the Church is rather its faithfulness to its heritage and its goals. Perhaps the biggest difficulty for us in seeing Ezra as relevant to our needs (in chapter 10 as throughout) is the fact that his central concerns often seem to spell death for churches today. Features of modern church life which are reminiscent of Ezra include an attachment to buildings and traditional roles, and a rather conservative introspection with regard to those outside the Church. These are the things which, today, obscure the real character of the Church as a dynamic body of those whose Lord is Christ and who are led by the Spirit.

How necessary, therefore, in reading Ezra, to strip away the things that belong to his time. Behind the outward manifestations of his zeal, which are strange to us, there is precisely the same concern that exercises many in the Church today, namely that the people of God should be devoted to the things which really count, rather than being deflected by what passes for "adequate" religion, convenient in its demands, but scarcely open to the voice of God (cf. Col. 3:1–4). Faithfulness to the heritage of the Church can be simply restated as faithfulness to Christ—and that can never be *merely* a respect for the past, but is primarily an openness to the future which puts itself at the disposal of all mankind for the sake of bringing the lordship of Christ in the world, already a reality, to its final consummation (Phil. 2:9–11).

NEHEMIAH

TROUBLE AND SHAME

Nehemiah 1:1–11

¹The words of Nehemiah the son of Hacaliah.

Now it happened in the month of Chislev, in the twentieth year, as I was in Susa the capital, ²that Hanani, one of my brethren, came with certain men out of Judah; and I asked them concerning the Jews that survived, who had escaped exile, and concerning Jerusalem. ³And they said to me, "The survivors there in the province who escaped exile are in great trouble and shame; the wall of Jerusalem is broken down, and its gates are destroyed by fire."

⁴When I heard these words I sat down and wept, and mourned for days; and I continued fasting and praying before the God of heaven. ⁵And I said, "O Lord God of heaven, the great and terrible God who keeps covenant and steadfast love with those who love him and keep his commandments; ⁶let thy ear be attentive, and thy eyes open, to hear the prayer of thy servant which I now pray before thee day and night for the people of Israel thy servants, confessing the sins of the people of Israel, which we have sinned against thee. Yea, I and my father's house have sinned. ⁷We have acted very corruptly against thee, and have not kept the commandments, the statutes, and the ordinances which thou didst command thy servant Moses. ⁸Remember the word which thou didst command thy servant Moses, saying, 'If you are unfaithful, I will scatter you among the peoples; ⁹but if you return to me and keep my commandments and do them, though your dispersed be under the farthest skies, I will gather them thence and bring them to the place which I have chosen, to make my name dwell there.' ¹⁰They are thy servants and thy people, whom thou hast redeemed by thy great power and by thy strong hand. ¹¹O Lord, let thy ear be attentive to the prayer of thy servant, and to the prayer of thy servants who delight to fear thy name; and give success to thy servant today, and grant him mercy in the sight of this man."

Now I was cupbearer to the king.

(i)

The Book of Nehemiah introduces us straight away to Nehemiah himself, who will dominate it to a much greater extent than Ezra did in the preceding book. He is introduced to us as "cupbearer to the king" (v. 11), and therefore at Susa, where the king, presumably, was in residence at the time. (We have seen that the Persian kings resided at different seasons in Babylon, Ecbatana and Susa in a kind of "circuit".) As cupbearer he occupied a position of immense influence within the Empire because of his closeness to the king, a closeness which could actually make the cupbearer second only to the king himself. He is thus perfectly placed to lay the petitions of his Jewish brethren before the highest authority. The embassy that comes to him from Judah, including his own brother (v. 2), comes knowing that it will have a natural access to Nehemiah's sympathy, and that he in turn has access to the monarch.

The general historical background can be sketched out a little further by noting that the twentieth year of Artaxerxes I was 445 B.C. This, then, is thirteen years after Ezra's arrival (on the chronology we have adopted, see Introduction). Whether Ezra was still in Jerusalem at the time of Hanani's embassy is unclear. What is clear is that the community of those who had returned from the Babylonian exile, now almost a century earlier, was at a low ebb. This may not have been a *religious* low. It is likely that the reforms effected by Ezra (Ezra 9–10) still held, for it is only on Nehemiah's *second* visit to Jerusalem that he is obliged to take similar measures (Neh. 13:23ff.). Indeed the concern for the walls of Jerusalem, expressed here by Hanani (v. 3), is equated everywhere in the Book of Nehemiah with religious zeal, the thought being that the preservation of the community of faith necessitated a certain defence capability *vis-à-vis* those who wished it ill. The fact that the walls are broken down thus represents the possibility of the community's extinction. It is not easy to know why Nehemiah should have been unaware of Jerusalem's condition. He must have known of its destruction by the Babylonians. It may be that, never having lived there and having perhaps had little communication with those who did, he had never fully appreciated its parlous state. It is possible, of course, that the report of Hanani relates to a *more recent* deterioration of Jerusalem's defences, possibly effected by the action of the Samaritans which was sanctioned by Artaxerxes himself, and which is reported in Ezra 4:23.

We speculate, of necessity, on the exact historical circumstances. What is clear is that the people is "in great trouble and shame", and that this shame reflects upon God in the eyes of the world.

GIVE SUCCESS

Nehemiah 1:1–11 (*cont'd*)

(ii)

As important as the news itself is the manner of Nehemiah's reaction to it. Despite having the ear of the *king*, and the fact that—as events will show—he himself is by disposition a man of *action*, he turns first to *God* and to *prayer* (vv. 4ff.). This is not to say that resort to human power and action is *incompatible* with resort to divine power and prayer. (Indeed their compatibility is a fundamental tenet of the book.) Nevertheless it is significant that he prays *first*.

Two features of the prayer are important. First, it is *committed*. The picture in verse 4 is of an intense emotion, expressed in weeping, fasting and prayer, and continuing for days (probably in the midst of his serving duties, to judge by 2:2). We need hardly elaborate upon such intensity, since we have discussed it in relation to Ezra (Ezra 9:3ff.). It is important, however, that both men regarded this sort of engagement with God as a prerequisite of action.

The second feature of the prayer is the way in which Nehemiah places the present need in the *context* of God's long history of dealing with his people. That history, as perceived by Ezra as well as Nehemiah (cf. Ezra 9:7), was one of persistent rebellion against God (v. 7). And Nehemiah, again like Ezra, confesses that sinfulness in a way which acknowledges his own complicity in it (v. 6*b*). There is no blame-shifting here. When Nehemiah muses on the imperfection of the people of God, he is driven to reflect upon his own. His own sinfulness is part of that broad canvas of wrong which accounts for all the displeasure of God which his people has known.

(iii)

The idea of Nehemiah's appeal to the wider context of the Jews' current situation can be elaborated by the observation that his prayer is entirely in terms of the *covenant* between God and Israel. The theology of the prayer is stated centrally in verse 5 where we find (a) something about the character of God, viz. that he *keeps covenant and steadfast love*, i.e. he is fundamentally disposed to be faithful to his promises to Israel, which begin with the promise to Abraham (Gen. 12:1–3); and (b) something about what he expects of those who are in covenant with him, viz. that they should "love him and keep his commandments". These two elements are in a significant order, reflected in the line of a well-known hymn, where the believer's response to God is characterized as: "Loving him who *first* loved me". The same order is found *universally* in the Bible, without any distinction between the Old Testament and the New (cf. John 14:15).

Nevertheless, the expectation that Israel would respond to God's love by keeping his commandments was absolute and attended by sanctions. The Book of Deuteronomy had insisted that, ultimately, disobedience would result in loss of the land (Deut. 28:63ff.). This was what had actually occurred when the people was carried into exile in Babylon (as far as that part of the people was concerned which was subsequently restored), and it is to this that Nehemiah refers in verse 8. Beyond the "curse", Deuteronomy had also foreseen a restoration (30:1–10) following the people's repentance. Nehemiah's prayer goes on, then, to lay claim to this aspect of the covenant promise (v. 9—a free representation of the thought of Deut. 30), relating it not only to the initial restoration from Babylon but to God's present and future dealings with his people (v. 10). This is similar to the prayer of Solomon at the dedication of the first Temple, when he prays that the "eyes [of God] be open and thy ears attentive" to the prayers of repentant Israel (2 Chr. 6:40; cf. vv. 6, 11 for identical phraseology).

The prayer, then, is essentially an appeal to God's mercy, based on a knowledge of his character expressed in his covenant with Israel. Though Israel has sinned, though indeed she has done so repeatedly, the Lord is always willing to restore her to a rich, living relationship with himself when she repents and recognizes that it depends—on Israel's part—upon a loving, and therefore obedient, response to her Redeemer. Nehemiah's prayer, therefore, which he believes is shared by other faithful Jews, can strike a note of confidence, mixed with commitment (v. 11). The same combination (confidence and commitment) can characterize the prayer of any Christian today, however much his or her practice of faith has lapsed.

(iv)

Only in the last line of the chapter are we told of Nehemiah's exalted position in the Persian Court. The information serves to introduce the theme of the relationship between the divine and human powers which was prominent in Ezra and will be no less so here. Nehemiah's confidence, to which his prayer wins through, is achieved in the face of potentially huge obstacles.

WISE AS SERPENTS

Nehemiah 2:1-8

¹In the month of Nisan, in the twentieth year of King Artaxerxes, when wine was before him, I took up the wine and gave it to the king. Now I had not been sad in his presence. ²And the king said to me, "Why is your face sad, seeing you are not sick? This is nothing else but sadness of the heart." Then I was very much afraid. ³I said to the king, "Let the king live for ever! Why should not my face be sad, when the city, the place of my fathers' sepulchres, lies waste, and its gates have been destroyed by fire?" ⁴Then the king said to me, "For what do you make request?" So I prayed to the God of heaven. ⁵And I said to the king, "If it pleases the king, and if your servant has found favour in

your sight, that you send me to Judah, to the city of my fathers'
sepulchres, that I may rebuild it." ⁶And the king said to me (the queen
sitting beside him), "How long will you be gone, and when will you
return?" So it pleased the king to send me; and I set him a time. ⁷And I
said to the king, "If it pleases the king, let letters be given me to the
governors of the province Beyond the River, that they may let me pass
through until I come to Judah; ⁸and a letter to Asaph, the keeper of the
king's forest, that he may give me timber to make beams for the gates
of the fortress of the temple, and for the wall of the city, and for the
house which I shall occupy." And the king granted me what I asked,
for the good hand of my God was upon me.

The scene shifts to the king's banqueting hall. Nehemiah is now
carrying out his official duties. It is not clear whether the occasion
is public or private. If it were a banquet this might explain the
king's concern about his cupbearer's long face (vv. 1–2). On the
other hand it could equally probably arise from his attachment to
a trusted servant. The mention of the queen's presence (v. 6) may
be incidental, or may reflect her interest in Nehemiah's affairs.
Queens, like Esther, could be highly influential.

(i)

Three aspects of Nehemiah's bearing here deserve mention.
First, he shows *courage*. It was a bold beginning simply to appear
disgruntled around the king. Court mores dictated cheerfulness,
if only to dispel notions of disloyalty. Nehemiah's remark that he
had not been sad in the king's presence before (v. 1) testifies to
the seriousness of the matter. This is not to say that he is exhibit-
ing deliberate sullenness. His condition probably owes more to
his grief at the vulnerability of Jerusalem together, perhaps, with
debility from lack of sleep and food (cf. 1:4—this could by now
have been going on for several months).

A more positive display of his courage comes when he decides
to respond to the king by making his request about Jerusalem,
doubtless following long, anxious waiting for the right opportunity. He will have known well enough that the possible consequences were dire; (cf. again Esther's reluctance to risk her life
by making a request to Ahasuerus, Esth. 4:11.) Quite apart from

the possibility of stepping out of line in terms of court etiquette, a request for the fortification of any city in the realm was potentially suspicious. And the king had already been prejudiced against Jerusalem in particular by the cunning of Rehum and his friends in Samaria, to the extent that he had, at an unspecified earlier stage in his reign, put a stop to the very business of fortification which Nehemiah now wished to resume (cf. Ezra 4:7–23—which is, at that point, a "flash-forward" to the present king's reign). No wonder, then, that Nehemiah feared greatly when he saw that the moment of decision had come (v. 2). Yet it did not weaken his resolve, and his fear becomes the measure of his courage.

(ii)

Second, the *godliness* of the man appears again in his reaction to stress. Here, tailored to the need of the moment and in contrast to the extended mourning of chapter 1, it takes the form of a rapid heavenward plea. At the root of his courage was a clear knowledge of the relative greatness of powers, which was not dimmed even in the splendid presence of the lesser. And the moment of danger past, he kept this perception before him, recognizing that the king's favour had been obtained *because* "the good hand of my God was upon me" (v. 8).

(iii)

The third feature of Nehemiah's handling of his request is its *wisdom*, or, as we might say, cunning. It is widely noted by commentators that nowhere in the exchange between the king and his servant is the name of Jerusalem mentioned. It is, of course, highly unlikely that Artaxerxes did not know which city Nehemiah came from, or indeed that he would have authorized the strengthening of any city without taking a moment to ascertain which one! Nehemiah's cleverness lies in the way in which he explains his request in terms of personal grief about *his* city. It was a matter of shame for Nehemiah—and Artaxerxes could understand this—that "the place of [his] fathers' sepulchres" (vv.

3, 5) lay undefended. The purpose of rebuilding the walls of Jerusalem is thus presented to the king as a matter of Nehemiah's, and by extension the Jews', self-esteem, rather than as a bid for political power, and this we must put down to Nehemiah's fine judgment.

It may be, indeed, that Nehemiah was even more skilful than we know. The timing of his request may have been informed in part by observation of the king's thinking about his Empire. In the decade and a half prior to the conversation before us there had been serious rebellions in Egypt and the province Beyond the River. The desire for a stable and friendly Judah (adjoining Egypt and a part of Beyond the River, yet not—as far as we know—*involved* hitherto in any rebellion) is thus perfectly understandable on the king's part, and his authorization of Nehemiah entirely plausible. Yet Nehemiah will have had to discern the change in the king's mood from the suspicions kindled by Rehum. When the request came, furthermore, it was clear-headed, fully reckoning with the opposition he was likely to meet, and determined to secure the full authority of the king to enable the work to be done well (vv. 7–8). There was no question of making the request more palatable to the king by being half-hearted and half-equipped. Partly-built walls would be a waste of time. So Nehemiah's wisdom had to gel with his courage and require all that was necessary to do the thing properly.

We have referred now to the cunning of Rehum on the one hand (Ezra 4) and that of Nehemiah on the other. The one (Rehum's) met with a success so temporary that it must be judged a failure; the success of the other knows no such qualification. The walls of Jerusalem would not be destroyed in the time of Nehemiah nor for generations to come. The difference between the two is not that they are different *kinds* of intellectual activity. Words for cleverness in the Old Testament are often capable of both good and bad connotations, just as in English (e.g. "a *scheming* rogue", but "an impressive *scheme*"). The difference is entirely in motivation. The mind cannot be divorced from what a person *is*. Every potentiality of the human mind can be applied well or ill. Human wisdom is by no means scorned by God. But he would *sanctify* it. In Jesus' words, "Be wise as serpents and innocent as doves" (Matt. 10:16).

THE FIGHT

Nehemiah 2:9–20

⁹Then I came to the governors of the province Beyond the River, and gave them the king's letters. Now the king had sent with me officers of the army and horsemen. ¹⁰But when Sanballat the Horonite and Tobiah the servant, the Ammonite, heard this, it displeased them greatly that some one had come to seek the welfare of the children of Israel.

¹¹So I came to Jerusalem and was there three days. ¹²Then I arose in the night, I and a few men with me; and I told no one what my God had put into my heart to do for Jerusalem. There was no beast with me but the beast on which I rode. ¹³I went out by night by the Valley Gate to the Jackal's Well and to the Dung Gate, and I inspected the walls of Jerusalem which were broken down and its gates which had been destroyed by fire. ¹⁴Then I went on to the Fountain Gate and to the King's Pool; but there was no place for the beast that was under me to pass. ¹⁵Then I went up in the night by the valley and inspected the wall; and I turned back and entered by the Valley Gate, and so returned. ¹⁶And the officials did not know where I had gone or what I was doing; and I had not yet told the Jews, the priests, the nobles, the officials, and the rest that were to do the work.

¹⁷Then I said to them, "You see the trouble we are in, how Jerusalem lies in ruins with its gates burned. Come, let us build the wall of Jerusalem, that we may no longer suffer disgrace." ¹⁸And I told them of the hand of my God which had been upon me for good, and also of the words which the king had spoken to me. And they said, "Let us rise up and build." So they strengthened their hands for the good work. ¹⁹But when Sanballat the Horonite and Tobiah the servant, the Ammonite, and Geshem the Arab heard of it, they derided us and despised us and said, "What is this thing that you are doing? Are you rebelling against the king?" ²⁰Then I replied to them, "The God of heaven will make us prosper, and we his servants will arise and build; but you have no portion or right or memorial in Jerusalem."

(i)

This passage constitutes the centre of the present chapter, not
only in terms of a verse count, but as an indicator of its real
theme, namely that the welfare of the "children of Israel" dis-
pleases their enemies. (Sanballat and Tobiah were governors
respectively in Samaria and Ammon, v. 10. Together with
Geshem the Arab, who was influential on Judah's southern flank,
they are known from non-biblical documents and must have been
a powerful and determined trio.)

The contrast between good (*tob*) and evil (*ra'*) pervades the
chapter in a way that is not immediately obvious from the English
translation. When Nehemiah's face is said to be "sad" (vv. 1–3)
the word is actually "evil". The "trouble" of Jerusalem (v. 17, as
in 1:3) is "evil". On the other hand, the expression "it pleased the
king" (v. 6, cf. v. 7) is literally "it was *good* to the king". Similarly, the *good* hand of God is upon Nehemiah (vv. 8, 18). And
"the good work" (v. 18) is simply "the good", or perhaps "the
good thing". This contrast is most pointed in verse 10, where "it
displeased them" is literally "it was evil to them", and the "welfare" of the Israelites is simply their "good".

Underlying the action in this chapter, therefore, is a conflict
between good and evil. Everything that serves the interests of the
returned exiles—the king's decision, the rebuilding of the walls—
is good; all that tends towards, or is the product of, their loss—the
broken walls, Nehemiah's grief, the aspirations of Sanballat,
Tobiah and Geshem—is evil. The clear implication of verse 10 is
that the opposition to Judah from these powerful leaders is a
spiritual thing. As with the "adversaries of Judah and Benjamin"
in Zerubbabel's day (Ezra 4:1), there is an implicit claim to faith
in Yahweh in the form of Tobiah's name. (The ending -iah
represents the name Yahweh. There is evidence that Sanballat's
sons' names were similarly formed.) We know too that Tobiah
had friends in high places at Jerusalem (13:4–9). Yet this purely
superficial suggestion of sympathy is belied by the bitterness of
their antagonism, which is not simply a legitimate concern for
their own security, but an actual hostility to the well-being of
Judah. The opposition of Sanballat and his allies may well have

appeared to the returned exiles to be a struggle against human might only. The letter to the Ephesians, however, points us beyond such appearances and articulates the true nature of the battle, when it unequivocally locates it in "the heavenly places", and names the real antagonists of God's people as "the spiritual hosts of wickedness" (Eph. 6:12). The outward forms of such opposition vary from age to age. Yet it is *war*. And the only recourse for the people of God is to "take the whole armour of God" (Eph. 6:13–20).

(ii)

Nehemiah's journey to Jerusalem, unlike Ezra's (Ezra 8), occupies no narrative space beyond the notice that Nehemiah delivered the king's letters of authority to the governors of Beyond the River, and that he was accompanied *en route* by a military escort (v. 9). This latter circumstance is in direct contrast to Ezra who refused such help (Ezra 8:22). It may be that the king insisted on this measure, regarding Nehemiah's mission as affecting the interests of the Empire more closely than that of Ezra.

It is clear that, on his arrival, the purpose of his mission was not widely known (v. 16). Clearly, too, he was careful to guard its secrecy for a time. And so we find him making his preliminary reconnaissance of the walls at night, with only a few companions and a single mount (v. 12). Presumably Nehemiah was anxious not to let information about his purpose get into the wrong hands. The people of Judah were not necessarily unified in their will to undertake such an operation as he had in mind. There was always the danger of a fifth column within. His secrecy, therefore, is related to our point about spiritual warfare (above), and indeed to Nehemiah's down-to-earth, but sanctified, cunning.

(iii)

The description of Nehemiah's night-ride (vv. 13–15) affords incidental information, more than anywhere else in the Old Testament, about the layout of ancient Jerusalem. The lines of the city have always been governed by the contours of the two hills on which it is built. These run side by side from north to south with a valley between, and their slopes are most precipitous to the east, west and south. The eastern hill is that which David originally conquered, and the city only gradually spread to the western hill in the time of the monarchy. Nehemiah's problem was probably not simply that of rebuilding walls, but also of deciding which lines they should follow, as there would have been remains both of David's original walls and later expansions.

The decision would be most difficult on the east, west and south of the city because, as we have seen, the terrain was exceptionally rough there. The actual features mentioned in Nehemiah's description are all on these sides. (See Diagram of Jerusalem in Nehemiah's Day, p. xii.) The Valley Gate was on the western side of the city (named because it led into the valley between the two hills). What is unclear is whether it was located on the eastern or western hill—i.e. how *far* west was the west of the city?—and what Nehemiah decided to do on this side. On the eastern side of the city, scholars agree that Nehemiah's walls were built from scratch on the crest of the ridge rather than lower on the eastern slope as previously. Some have deduced from this that Nehemiah built along a line that would require as little fortification as possible and that the city was therefore much smaller than that which had been destroyed. This may not be so, however. On the east, where Nehemiah at one point could not pass (v. 14), the decision to move uphill may have been determined by the extent of the damage to the walls here, which was considerable. The only reason for the earlier lower line was the need for water, which was now supplied in any case by Hezekiah's famous tunnel (2 Kings 20:20). So on the east Nehemiah was free to build higher.

The western wall still puzzles us. Nehemiah, however, evidently formulated a plan quickly, before coming to the business of persuasion. He was about to make an appeal for a major commitment from the people of Judah. It was imperative to know clearly what it was that he was calling them to.

(iv)

Having surveyed the extent of the damage, Nehemiah reveals his intention publicly in the form of an exhortation. There is no discussion of the matter. Once again we need to realize that the issue is one of spiritual contention. A democratic spirit is not what the moment requires. Nehemiah proceeds rather from his conviction that the project is of God and persuades the people that the current state of Jerusalem is incompatible with their status as God's people (v. 17). He also brings to bear his own experience of God's provision for the project, discerned in the acquiescence of the king (v. 18). The people respond with a readiness that is perhaps surprising (v. 18), given that Nehemiah was a stranger in those parts. Their eagerness is a measure of the truth of what Nehemiah said. And when, as here, truth is *moral* truth, it is irresistible. The people are instantly convinced that it is right to build and that, under God, the moment has come to do it. And so it is first blood to God's battalions.

The blow is, not surprisingly, met with a riposte from Sanballat *et al.* It takes the form of the old accusation of disloyalty to the king (v. 19). But how ironically hollow it sounds when we know what we know, namely that the work was sanctioned by the king himself, and the real rebels are those who would oppose it. We have not heard the last of Sanballat in the Book of Nehemiah. But in a sense these first chapters guarantee from the start that his machinations *cannot* frustrate God's good intentions for his people. Nehemiah in reply (v. 20) does not even bother to refute the disloyalty charge. Instead he goes to the heart of the matter. Those who maintain the cause of God will prosper. There can be no nominal allegiance to the Lord, mixed with a self-seeking contempt for genuine religion.

BUILDING TOGETHER

Nehemiah 3:1–32

¹Then Eliashib the high priest rose up with his brethren the priests and they built the Sheep Gate. They consecrated it and set its doors; they consecrated it as far as the Tower of the Hundred, as far as the Tower of Hananel. ²And next to him the men of Jericho built. And next to them Zaccur the son of Imri built.

³And the sons of Hassenaah built the Fish Gate; they laid its beams and sets its doors, its bolts, and its bars. ⁴And next to them Meremoth the son of Uriah, son of Hakkoz repaired. And next to them Meshullam the son of Berechiah, son of Meshezabel repaired. And next to them Zadok the son of Baana repaired. ⁵And next to them the Tekoites repaired; but their nobles did not put their necks to the work of their Lord.

⁶And Joiada the son of Paseah and Meshullam the son of Besodeiah repaired the Old Gate; they laid its beams and set its doors, its bolts, and its bars. ⁷And next to them repaired Melatiah the Gibeonite and Jadon the Meronothite, the men of Gibeon and of Mizpah, who were under the jurisdiction of the governor of the province Beyond the River. ⁸Next to them Uzziel the son of Harhaiah, goldsmiths, repaired. Next to him Hananiah, one of the perfumers, repaired; and they restored Jerusalem as far as the Broad Wall. ⁹Next to them Rephaiah the son of Hur, ruler of half the district of Jerusalem, repaired. ¹⁰Next to them Jedaiah the son of Harumaph repaired opposite his house; and next to him Hattush the son of Hashabneiah repaired. ¹¹Malchijah the son of Harim and Hasshub the son of Pahath-moab repaired another section and the Tower of the Ovens. ¹²Next to him Shallum the son of Hallohesh, ruler of half the district of Jerusalem, repaired, he and his daughters.

¹³Hanun and the inhabitants of Zanoah repaired the Valley Gate; they rebuilt it and set its doors, its bolts, and its bars, and repaired a thousand cubits of the wall, as far as the Dung Gate.

¹⁴Malchijah the son of Rechab, ruler of the district of Beth-haccherem, repaired the Dung Gate; he rebuilt it and set its doors, its bolts, and its bars.

¹⁵And Shallum the son of Colhozeh, ruler of the district of Mizpah, repaired the Fountain Gate; he rebuilt it and covered it and set its doors, its bolts, and its bars; and he built the wall of the Pool of Shelah of the king's garden, as far as the stairs that go down from the City of David. ¹⁶After him Nehemiah the son of Azbuk, ruler of half the district of Beth-zur, repaired to a point opposite the sepulchres of David, to the artificial pool, and to the house of the mighty men. ¹⁷After him the Levites repaired: Rehum the son of Bani; next to him Hashabiah, ruler of half the district of Keilah, repaired for his district. ¹⁸After him their brethren repaired: Bavvai the son of Henadad, ruler of half the district of Keilah; ¹⁹next to him Ezer the son of Jeshua, ruler of Mizpah, repaired another section opposite the ascent to the armoury at the Angle. ²⁰After him Baruch the son of Zabbai

repaired another section from the Angle to the door of the house of Eliashib the high priest. [21] After him Meremoth the son of Uriah, son of Hakkoz repaired another section from the door of the house of Eliashib to the end of the house of Eliashib. [22] After him the priests, the men of the Plain, repaired. [23] After them Benjamin and Hasshub repaired opposite their house. After them Azariah the son of Ma-aseiah, son of Ananiah repaired beside his own house. [24] After him Binnui the son of Henadad repaired another section, from the house of Azariah to the Angle [25] and to the corner. Palal the son of Uzai repaired opposite the Angle and the tower projecting from the upper house of the king at the court of the guard. After him Pedaiah the son of Parosh [26] and the temple servants living on Ophel repaired to a point opposite the Water Gate on the east and the projecting tower. [27] After him the Tekoites repaired another section opposite the great projecting tower as far as the wall of Ophel.

[28] Above the Horse Gate the priests repaired, each one opposite his own house. [29] After them Zadok the son of Immer repaired opposite his own house. After him Shemaiah the son of Shecaniah, the keeper of the East Gate, repaired. [30] After him Hananiah the son of Shelemiah and Hanun the sixth son of Zalaph repaired another section. After him Meshullam the son of Berechiah repaired opposite his chamber. [31] After him Malchijah, one of the goldsmiths, repaired as far as the house of the temple servants and of the merchants, opposite the Muster Gate, and to the upper chamber of the corner. [32] And between the upper chamber of the corner and the Sheep Gate the goldsmiths and the merchants repaired.

We have here a picture of concerted industry on a grand scale. The chapter is tantalizing on one level, because the topographical features, which the author could presume to be familiar to his readers, are largely lost on us. However, the Sheep Gate (v. 1) is usually located in the north wall of the city (closest to the Temple and therefore built, and consecrated, by the priests). The description follows the walls in an anti-clockwise direction, as did Nehemiah's night-ride.

Despite the obscurity of the topographical details, the purpose of the chapter is clear enough. Two points may be made.

(i)

There was obviously little doubt in the community (with some exceptions, v. 5) about the virtue of building walls. And the author agrees with the builders. This is not unremarkable in view of the many things that are said in the Old Testament about the essential weakness of human might and the folly of trusting in it (cf. the walls of Jericho, Josh. 6:20, and the apparent impregnability of a later and grander Jerusalem than Nehemiah's, Mark 13:1–2). We have noticed on another occasion, however, that the temptations facing the returned exiles were chiefly those of assimilation rather than of pride in their own might. The building of these walls would be a testimony to God's power rather than to their own, and to their determination to be a holy people, separated from others by their faithfulness to him.

It is important to bear in mind the potency of walls as *symbols*, quite apart from their physical strength. For Nehemiah, as we have noticed, news of the sad condition of Jerusalem's fortifications had been a matter of personal humiliation. (See 2:3 and comment.) Walls have a significance which outlasts their actual usefulness. Anyone who has witnessed the annual rituals focusing on the walls of the old city of Derry in Northern Ireland, at which the resistance to and relief of a siege of centuries ago is commemorated, knows of this kind of power. Walls, like a flag, can provide identity and solidarity. It is in these terms that we should view the present activity. The Lord was giving his people a badge, a further token—alongside the Temple—that they *were* his people.

(ii)

The second point to note is that the solidarity or *esprit de corps* which walls can produce was actually experienced by the people. Everyone, apparently, was involved, from the High Priest down (v. 1). We need not suppose that the list is exhaustive. (It is often pointed out that there are a number of references to "second sections", e.g. vv. 11, 19, 20—where RSV has "*another* section"—without information about their corresponding *first* sections.) The point is that all *kinds* of people participated, named—besides the priests—according to family (e.g. v. 3), town (v. 5) or even profession (v. 8). Some of those named were evidently influential (e.g. Shallum, v. 12, ruler of half of Jerusalem). Many did not actually belong to Jerusalem. Their co-operation on the walls is one of the Old Testament's finest pictures of its ideal of Israelite brotherhood. Each worked, literally "by the side of" the next, apparently without rivalry or envy. If there were differences of wealth and standing—and there are some hints that there were, in that some men are called "rulers", and there is evidence of a burgeoning merchant class, v. 8—they do not appear here. The only distinction recognized is that of belonging to the people of God and being engaged in his business.

This is not to say that there was no organization or authority. The whole enterprise is highly organized, and the authority of Nehemiah himself seems implicit. But these things do not obtrude. The dominant impression is of each individual cheerfully accepting his role, and seeing how his work contributed to the whole. The pressure of adverse circumstances undoubtedly contributed to this—just as the experience of wartime in living memory teaches us that it does. A mood like this ought to characterize the Church at *all* times, however. The most challenging instance of it is recorded in Acts 2:43–47.

THE PRESSURE ON

Nehemiah 4:1–23

¹Now when Sanballat heard that we were building the wall, he was angry and greatly enraged, and he ridiculed the Jews. ²And he said in the presence of his brethren and of the army of Samaria, "What are these feeble Jews doing? Will they restore things? Will they sacrifice? Will they finish up in a day? Will they revive the stones out of the heaps of rubbish, and burned ones at that?" ³Tobiah the Ammonite was by him, and he said, "Yes, what they are building—if a fox goes up on it he will break down their stone wall!" ⁴Hear, O our God, for we are despised; turn back their taunt upon their own heads, and give them up to be plundered in a land where they are captives. ⁵Do not cover their guilt, and let not their sin be blotted out from thy sight; for they have provoked thee to anger before the builders.

⁶So we built the wall; and all the wall was joined together to half its height. For the people had a mind to work.

⁷But when Sanballat and Tobiah and the Arabs and the Ammonites and the Ashdodites heard that the repairing of the walls of Jerusalem was going forward and that the breaches were beginning to be closed, they were very angry; ⁸and they all plotted together to come and fight against Jerusalem and to cause confusion in it. ⁹And we prayed to our God, and set a guard as a protection against them day and night.

¹⁰But Judah said, "The strength of the burden-bearers is failing, and there is much rubbish; we are not able to work on the wall." ¹¹And our enemies said, "They will not know or see till we come into the midst of them and kill them and stop the work." ¹²When the Jews who lived by them came they said to us ten times, "From all the places where they live they will come up against us." ¹³So in the lowest parts of the space behind the wall, in open places, I stationed the people according to their families, with their swords, their spears, and their bows. ¹⁴And I looked, and arose, and said to the nobles and to the officials and to the rest of the people, "Do not be afraid of them. Remember the Lord, who is great and terrible, and fight for your brethren, your sons, your daughters, your wives, and your homes."

¹⁵When our enemies heard that it was known to us and that God had frustrated their plan, we all returned to the wall, each to his work. ¹⁶From that day on, half of my servants worked on construction, and half held the spears, shields, bows, and coats of mail; and the leaders stood behind all the house of Judah, ¹⁷who were building on the wall. Those who carried burdens were laden in such a way that each with one hand laboured on the work and with the other held his weapon. ¹⁸And each of the builders had his sword girded at his side while he built. The man who sounded the trumpet was beside me. ¹⁹And I said to the nobles and to the officials and to the rest of the people, "The work is great and widely spread, and we are separated on the wall, far from one another. ²⁰In the place where you hear the sound of the trumpet, rally to us there. Our God will fight for us."

²¹So we laboured at the work, and half of them held the spears from the break of dawn till the stars came out. ²²I also said to the people at that time, "Let every man and his servant pass the night within Jerusalem, that they may be a guard for us by night and may labour by day." ²³So neither I nor my brethren nor my servants nor the men of the guard who followed me, none of us took off our clothes; each kept his weapon in his hand.

(i)

The concerted effort reported in chapter 3 seemed to Sanballat and the other enemies of Judah all too likely to have a successful outcome. Consequently we now find a build-up of bitter and determined resentment. Sanballat himself is desperately angry (v. 1). What is more, the circle of enemies is expanding. The Ashdodites, occupying former Philistine territory on Judah's western flank, have now joined the unholy alliance (v. 7). And it seems that the Ammonites (on the east) are no longer represented by Tobiah alone. With the Samaritans holding the north and the Arabs threatening from the south, the conspiracy looks powerful indeed, and Judah's situation precarious. It seems too that the enemies are ready to go beyond mere ridicule (vv. 8, 11–12), risking the opprobrium of Persia itself, so opposed were they to the re-emergence of an old and hated foe. Their frustration will have been the deeper because it had so recently appeared that the threat from Judah was gone forever (Ezra 4:23).

Nor were the builders insensitive to a danger which they may well have felt was the greater for the measures they were taking. As the work progressed the unremitting demands which it made brought on a dispiriting weariness. The cry in verse 10, "there is much rubbish", conjures up for us something of the arduousness of their heavy task. This rubbish was not the beer can variety, but heavy rubble. On the eastern slopes in particular—but no doubt more widely too—there had been serious collapse of houses and walls as a result of Nebuchadnezzar's activities. (This was where Nehemiah had been unable to pass during his night-time reconnaissance; 2:14.) The terrain itself, on all but the northern side, is often very steep. The business of stumbling over uncertain and precipitous ground, and fumbling through the rubble for the best building material—and this all day long (v. 21)—will soon have become exceedingly wearisome.

The cry of the builders in verse 10 is to be understood against this background. It is not, as it may appear, a single declaration of intent. Rather, being in poetic meter (which the English can hardly reproduce), it appears to be a kind of chorus chanted during the work. Despite its rather negative tone it may actually have had the function of keeping the men going—not unlike the "spirituals" which encouraged enslaved labourers of more recent times. Taken in this way it is more readily intelligible in the light of verse 6, where the people had "a mind to work". Nevertheless, the mood of the builders by verse 12, when they are brought disheartening news by some who perhaps meant well but probably did more for the cause of the enemies (cf. the faithless spies of old, Num. 13:22ff.) is evidently low. The temptation to unbelief must have been immense. Those especially who did not even live in Jerusalem, and may have worried about the security of their own towns, may have wondered whether their present task was just the fanaticism of a misguided idealist.

DRY POWDER

Nehemiah 4:1–23 (*cont'd*)

(ii)

Despite the bleak appearances, however, the aspirations of the enemies were doomed to frustration from the outset. This frustration is already implicit in the scornful words of Sanballat and Tobiah (vv. 2–3). Outwardly, their words seem all too true, in Tobiah's case even picturesque. The Jews *were* feeble; their success *did* look implausible; the walls they built—as we know from archaeological excavations—were not of the quality of those which their forefathers had built, and Tobiah's fox might indeed have sent the odd stone tumbling into the Kidron valley. Yet Sanballat's anger already shows his fear that the very things he derides as impossible may come to pass. And we the readers, knowing that God is with his people, can answer all his hollowly confident questions with a "Yes", for God has ordained it.

Nehemiah now shows himself a leader in more than mere organizational terms or by virtue of the trappings of Persian authority. He shows that he is also a *spiritual* leader in Judah, by his perception, before any other, of how things really lie. His words in verses 4–5 constitute a curse, reminiscent of some

Psalms (e.g. Pss. 68:1–3; 139:19–24). It is tempting to read words like these as the personal bitterness of the one who prays, and to condemn them for vindictiveness. Clearly, in seeking to derive edification from such sentiments, we must in no way diminish the force of Christ's command to "love your enemies" (Matt. 5:44); for if there *can* be a godly hatred, there is no doubt whatever that *un*godly hatred is a powerful temptation in stressful situations.

Having said that, it is possible to attribute to Nehemiah a motivation that is other than personal bitterness. His words are in effect a prayer that God will be just. In the covenant that existed between God and Israel it was axiomatic that the blessing of the people followed upon their obedience. Nehemiah invokes that blessing. And because Sanballat *et al.* perceive their interests as diametrically opposed to those of Judah, they must suffer by Judah's blessing. Nehemiah is thus declaring the consequences for them of their antipathy to *God* (for that is the real issue), which will be a turning upon themselves of the things they wish upon Judah. (The exactness of the justice that will be done is contained in the words: "we are *despised*; turn back their taunt ... and give them up to be *plundered* in a land where they are captives." It is neatly captured in the italicized words, which sound very similar in Hebrew.)

Nehemiah's curse is thus a declaration of God's opposition to those who wilfully oppose Judah. The sentence is not irreversible. Sanballat and his allies *could* repent; others had done so and joined the exiles (Ezra 6:21). Nehemiah shows that he sees God's way. It is his perception and confidence which fit him to lead the people out of despair and into possession of their promised reward.

(iii)

The threat from the enemy evidently reached a head with the report from the Jews who lived in the hostile territories (v. 12). Nehemiah therefore puts the people on battle-alert (v. 13), thus temporarily suspending the work. How exactly he mustered them (v. 13) is difficult to visualize because we cannot picture the layout of the city in any detail. The "lowest parts" he might have deemed the safest. The gathering of the families along with the men (rather than hiding the women and children in houses) may have been designed to heighten their appreciation of just what was at stake. (In the battle for Jerusalem in 1948 the Jewish military leaders refused to evacuate women and children for just this sort of reason.) In any case, the measure was never intended as a heroic last stand, nor was the attitude a stoical "wait and see". Rather, the muster will have had the effect of demonstrating to the people their own strength. In the "open spaces" they may well have been able to get a clear impression of just how much progress was being made (v. 6). And Nehemiah uses the occasion to exhort the people to trust in God (v. 14), of whose readiness to help in battle Israel's history afforded ample evidence (e.g. Judg. 7:19–23).

It is not clear just in what way the battle-alert influenced the enemy. It has been suggested that an army was actually at the walls, though there is no evidence for this. Clearly, however, they heard that their desired advantage of secrecy (4:11) was illusory, the prospect of an attack receded, and the people were able to resume work on the walls (v. 15). In all this Nehemiah's practical and powerful piety dominates. His ability to bring a word from the Lord influences the people in a remarkable way—just as when he first exhorted them to build (2:17ff.)—and they are able to go back to the onerous and dangerous task with renewed courage.

(iv)

Part of the people's renewed vigour lay in an appreciation of the *human* resources God had given them. They had taken stock and seen that they were on the way to being a relatively formidable garrison. And this combination of initiative and piety, so characteristic of Nehemiah himself, now dominated the remainder of the building activity. Even as the work progressed the instruments of battle were held in readiness (vv. 16, 21). As far as possible work was done weapon in hand (vv. 17–18). There was watchfulness by night (v. 22), and Nehemiah led the way by remaining constantly—whether he slept or not—more or less in battle-dress (v. 23). The trumpeter (v. 18) stood by Nehemiah (could we say like the man who stands in constant attendance on the US President and whose sole purpose is to convey the message that the "button" is to be pushed) ready to summon the dispersed labourers to close ranks. None of this can have eased the sheer physical arduousness of the labour.

Yet there is now a purposefulness about their activity which has evidently shed the fears which threatened to be so destructive. The formula that has produced this is very close to that expressed in Oliver Cromwell's immortal dictum: "Trust in God and keep your powder dry". The whole enterprise is conceived as a work of God which he superintends and guarantees (v. 20*b*). Yet the faithful see clearly that the means which God will use is themselves, their faculties well trained, and fully exploiting all their resources. Translated into the arena of the making of modern disciples (though the point pertains to all areas of Christian endeavour), we might recall the 19th-century preacher Spurgeon's advice to his students that they should "pray as if everything depended on God, then preach as if everything depended on you."

STRIFE WITHIN

Nehemiah 5:1–13

¹Now there arose a great outcry of the people and of their wives against their Jewish brethren. ²For there were those who said, "With our sons and our daughters, we are many; let us get grain, that we may eat and keep alive." ³There were also those who said, "We are mortgaging our fields, our vineyards, and our houses to get grain because of the famine." ⁴And there were those who said, "We have borrowed money for the king's tax upon our fields and our vineyards. ⁵Now our flesh is as the flesh of our brethren, our children are as their children; yet we are forcing our sons and our daughters to be slaves, and some of our daughters have already been enslaved; but it is not in our power to help it, for other men have our fields and our vineyards."

⁶I was very angry when I heard their outcry and these words. ⁷I took counsel with myself, and I brought charges against the nobles and the officials. I said to them, "You are exacting interest, each from his

brother." And I held a great assembly against them, [8]and said to them, "We, as far as we are able, have bought back our Jewish brethren who have been sold to the nations; but you even sell your brethren that they may be sold to us!" They were silent, and could not find a word to say. [9]So I said, "The thing that you are doing is not good. Ought you not to walk in the fear of our God to prevent the taunts of the nations our enemies? [10]Moreover I and my brethren and my servants are lending them money and grain. Let us leave off this interest. [11]Return to them this very day their fields, their vineyards, their olive orchards, and their houses, and the hundredth of money, grain, wine, and oil which you have been exacting of them." [12]Then they said, "We will restore these and require nothing from them. We will do as you say." And I called the priests, and took an oath of them to do as they had promised. [13]I also shook out my lap and said, "So may God shake out every man from his house and from his labour who does not perform this promise. So may he be shaken out and emptied." And all the assembly said "Amen" and praised the Lord. And the people did as they had promised.

(i)

Ever since the days of Zerubbabel, we have been accustomed to reading of the difficulties put in the way of the returned exiles by those outside the community. We now discover a new threat from *within*, potentially more dangerous than the others because it strikes at the exiles' most precious asset, their unity.

The events of chapter 5 surprise the reader because the account of them follows directly upon the picture of co-operation presented in chapter 4. Yet we should not be too surprised. It is often the way of Hebrew narrative to use stark contrasts in order to qualify statements. Our author wishes to avoid giving the impression that, in the concerted effort on the walls, everything in the community was sweetness and light. On the contrary, there were deep problems. In determining their character, we need to bear in mind at the outset the factor of time-scale. Nehemiah is here reflecting on his twelve years as governor in Judah (v. 14). It is not quite clear whether the events described here took place during the time of the building, which was, after all, relatively brief (cf. 6:15). Verse 16 does not necessarily suggest that they did. Problems like these could, therefore, have been more or less acute at different times during Nehemiah's tenure of office. Matters may have come to a head in Nehemiah's great assembly (v. 7), either during the building, or at some later stage. Nevertheless they were almost certainly present in some degree during the time of the building, and that is the author's justification for placing the account here. A similar use of time-scale occurs in Ezra 4.

That the grievances were in any case no light matter is already hinted at in verse 1. The term "great outcry" suggests a cry from the heart in deep distress. Furthermore, the fact that the *women* are expressly mentioned only here in Ezra–Nehemiah suggests that they are to the forefront in issuing a protest about conditions. This in itself indicates the life-and-death urgency of the matter. It was the women who had, ultimately, to provide the basic needs of their, perhaps large, families. Their husbands—especially during the time of the wall-building—may have been shielded from the realities at home by their prolonged absence. (We cannot help thinking of the role that men's wives often play today in lengthy industrial disputes.) Yet it is not the women alone who protest. The real division here is between rich and poor.

(ii)

What has gone wrong, then, in the community so devoted to the ideal of brotherhood? For many in Judah there was no safety margin built into the family budget. Nor was there the security of a welfare state. If the crops were poor in any year then some would be hungry. In a desperate situation there were measures that could be taken. Property could be mortgaged until better times came along. This could apply to houses and fields, and even to children, whom the rich were always ready to acquire as slaves. The system was not directly opposed by Israelite law. At its best it could help the unfortunate over a bad patch. The laws sought rather to prevent *abuse* of the system, for which, obviously, there was considerable scope. Thus interest-taking on loans was forbidden (Deut. 23:19–20). After a certain period both loans and slaves were to be remitted (Deut. 15:1ff.), and generosity was enjoined (Deut. 15:10, 13–14).

On matters like this, therefore, Israelite law appealed to the heart. Dry regulations are made to point to their underlying principles: e.g. "there will be no poor among you" (Deut. 15:4). Rights were not to be insisted on to the extent of exploitation or the causing of intolerable poverty (Deut. 24:10–13). In short, all actions in the area of economic relations were to be governed by *love* (cf. Lev. 19:18). The ideal of brotherhood, therefore, was no mere pipe-dream. Rather, it was backed up by a system of laws which, if taken seriously, could create a very different kind of society from any other. All this is hardly less radical than the teaching of Jesus himself on love. Has any other society been based on a system which ran on love? Are our own dealings in business etc.—where our actions largely affect people we have never met—so motivated?

(iii)

Sadly, the appeal to the human heart often does little more than show up its reluctance to love beyond the natural family ties. Nehemiah was not the first to be disappointed at this discovery. The prophet Isaiah, three centuries before, had put his finger on the same problem (Isa. 5:8). When the year of release was ignored, when creditors had no regard for the consequences of their exactions upon the poor, then the poor quickly lost all prospect of a way back. (With their land in pledge they had no resources available for economic recovery.) Creditors did not even need to exact interest. They could crush the poor without it, thus remaining within the law while pursuing their murderous greed. It is probable that there is in fact no question of interest-taking in this chapter. Nehemiah's words in verse 7 can as well be taken to mean "You are imposing too heavy a burden . . . " (The same is true of v. 10.)

The time of Nehemiah for all its idealism and new opportunity was not exempt from such abuses. The emergence of a relatively wealthy class is probably connected with that other great abuse already treated in Ezra chapters 9–10. That is to say, some Israelites had not only intermarried, but had done so advantageously. On the principle that "money makes money", even the dissolution of such marriages will not necessarily have deprived them of their initial gains.

Nehemiah is enraged at this new revelation (v. 6) and holds a popular assembly designed to expose and terminate the abuses (v. 7). This is a measure of the man's natural—or rather God-given—authority. The assembly would have consisted of the powerful alongside the disadvantaged. Its very gathering was a triumph for the brotherhood ideal, and was therefore far more effective than the use of the normal legal process, which would in any case have been biased towards the rich. In his appeal to the wealthy he refers to the redemption of Jewish people who had been "sold to the nations" (v. 8). The allusion is obscure, but presumably means that at some stage since the first return of exiles from Babylon members of the community had succumbed to slavery to neighbouring non-Jewish peoples, and that the community had subsequently been able to free them. Nehemiah points out the ironic contrast between this triumph for Jewish idealism and the current situation in which the Jews are themselves exploiting their own brothers. The repetition of "selling" in verse 8 hammers home the point. The last phrase in Nehemiah's accusation suggests that some of those who were being brought back from the "nations" had actually been sold off in the first place by Jews. The exposure of the offensiveness of these practices, when all present knew well what loyalty to Yahweh implied, leaves the guilty without defence.

TRUE LOVE

Nehemiah 5:14–19

14Moreover from the time that I was appointed to be their governor in the land of Judah, from the twentieth year to the thirty-second year of Artaxerxes the king, twelve years, neither I nor my brethren ate the food allowance of the governor. 15The former governors who were before me laid heavy burdens upon the people, and took from them food and wine, besides forty shekels of silver. Even their servants lorded it over the people. But I did not do so, because of the fear of God. 16I also held to the work on this wall, and acquired no land; and all my servants were gathered there for the work. [17]Moreover there were at my table a hundred and fifty men, Jews and officials, besides those who came to us from the nations which were about us. [18]Now that which was prepared for one day was one ox and six sheep; fowls likewise were prepared for me, and every ten days skins of wine in abundance; yet with all this I did not demand the food allowance of the governor, because the servitude was heavy upon this people. [19]Remember for my good, O my God, all that I have done for this people.

(i)

Having exposed the abuses and induced a proper sense of shame in the guilty, Nehemiah proceeds to his appeal (vv. 9–11). He begins by showing that any lapse into injustice on the part of the people of God reflects upon God himself in the eyes of the nations. It was no mere fancy to suppose that outsiders would look at Judah and draw conclusions about her God. This was part of the ancient mentality. A powerful nation must have a powerful god, and a weak nation a weak god. Through Ezekiel, God had said that he had spared Israel again and again "for the sake of my name . . . in the sight of the nations" (Ezek. 20:9, 22). For the community of returned exiles the idea should have been especially meaningful because Cyrus' restoration was essentially a restoration of their God to his Temple (Ezra 1:2–4).

Nehemiah's allusion to the reputation of God may be taken in one of two ways. The thought may be that, if the exiles do not obey God, God will punish them, and that therefore he will be thought weak because of the reduced state of his people. (This is the thought underlying Ezek. 20.) Alternatively—and more probably—Nehemiah makes the point that the character of the community reflects that of God. The brotherhood within Israel is meant to be a showpiece, a model of the potential human society. The nations should look at Israel and see a people harmonious, prosperous and content, and organized so as to be so rather than for the aggrandizement of the few. Israel was to be a radical challenge to the nations, a specimen of love.

Love in action is extraordinarily powerful. Those whose whole experience of life has been moulded by other principles are shocked by love. The Church exists in order to exhibit this love, and shock the world into belief in the God of love. Too often it merely confirms the world's view that all actions illustrate the principle of "every man for himself". (How sections of the press love to get their hands on stories of lapses on the part of church people! Their celebration of such things is spiritual—part of that battle we spoke of in chapter 4.) The call to the Church to love, therefore (John 15:12), is not simply for our own good, or because it is "nice", but because it shows the world what God is like.

Nehemiah's words produce repentance and an oath to restore all that had been lent (v. 12). Nehemiah himself, incidentally, does not hide the fact that he too has been lending (v. 10). Since everything here depends on motive, however, we need attribute nothing unworthy to him. His preaching is therefore backed up by practice and it is costly. (The "hundredth", v. 11, suggests interest-taking. Here too, however, it is possible to adopt a slightly different text, and read "burden".) The assembly closes with a "curse" (v. 13). When Nehemiah "shakes out his lap" it is the equivalent of emptying his pockets, thereby symbolizing the loss of all that one has. If the people break their oath—and therefore proceed along the path of self-interest—Nehemiah invokes the Lord's judgment so that they shall, after all, possess nothing. (cf. Hag. 1:9–11 for a similar thought.) The people's acceptance of these terms—always implicit in the covenant relationship with God (cf. Exod. 24:7–8, signifying the people's acceptance that death is the due reward for covenant-breach)— shows their seriousness about a new commitment to God.

(ii)

The closing verses of the chapter form a sort of appendix to the main action which has preceded them. They show other ways in which Nehemiah remained faithful to the idea of Israel which he has been preaching. He tells how, during his term of office, he renounced the governor's food allowance, which was a tax upon the people (v. 14); how he refused to exploit the people (v. 15), in contrast to his predecessors (referring to governors since Zerubbabel, of whom, individually, our account tells us nothing); how he acquired no land, probably highly unusual among officials of the time, choosing rather to channel all his energies and all the advantages of his position into achieving the people's good (v. 16).

It is clear that the honest policy cost Nehemiah dear. Verses 17–18 give a glimpse of the daily demands upon his hospitality, partly occasioned by his diplomatic responsibilities as governor, and partly, it seems, acceded to simply from his generosity. Nehemiah's motives in acting thus were (a) his fear of God (v. 15), which means simply that he acted out of awareness of what was appropriate for one who *worshipped* God, and (b) compassion for the people's suffering (v. 18). His motives in *telling* us about it may be similar to those of the apostle Paul, who, while insisting strongly on his *right* to share in the material welfare of those among whom he worked (1 Cor. 9:8ff.), *renounced* that right lest his motivation come in question (1 Cor. 9:15).

The closing words in this section (v. 19) reflect this same spirit. As a prayer, it is a claim to innocence now made, not to the reader, but to God himself. It is thus testimony to his utter sincerity. It is possible to maintain a façade of righteousness before men, but not before God. The invocation of God's favour is not so much a plea for a reward as an emphatic way of claiming that he has acted in good faith and from right motives. It is a statement of confidence that God is judge, and judges favourably those who sincerely seek to do his will. The same judgment will be invoked in similar terms but to different effect in 6:14.

DEATH THROES?

Nehemiah 6:1–19

[1]Now when it was reported to Sanballat and Tobiah and to Geshem the Arab and to the rest of our enemies that I had built the wall and that there was no breach left in it (although up to that time I had not set up the doors in the gates), [2]Sanballat and Geshem sent to me, saying, "Come and let us meet together in one of the villages in the plain of Ono." But they intended to do me harm. [3]And I sent messengers to them, saying, "I am doing a great work and I cannot come down. Why should the work stop while I leave it and come down to you?" [4]And

they sent to me four times in this way and I answered them in the same manner. ⁵In the same way Sanballat for the fifth time sent his servant to me with an open letter in his hand. ⁶In it was written, "It is reported among the nations, and Geshem also says it, that you and the Jews intend to rebel; that is why you are building the wall; and you wish to become their king, according to this report. ⁷And you have also set up prophets to proclaim concerning you in Jerusalem, 'There is a king in Judah.' And now it will be reported to the king according to these words. So now come, and let us take counsel together." ⁸Then I sent to him, saying, "No such things as you say have been done, for you are inventing them out of your own mind." ⁹For they all wanted to frighten us, thinking, "Their hands will drop from the work, and it will not be done." But now, O God, strengthen thou my hands.

¹⁰Now when I went into the house of Shemaiah the son of Delaiah, son of Mehetabel, who was shut up, he said, "Let us meet together in the house of God, within the temple, and let us close the doors of the temple; for they are coming to kill you, at night they are coming to kill you." ¹¹But I said, "Should such a man as I flee? And what man such as I could go into the temple and live? I will not go in." ¹²And I understood, and saw that God had not sent him, but he had pronounced the prophecy against me because Tobiah and Sanballat had hired him. ¹³For this purpose he was hired, that I should be afraid and act in this way and sin, and so they could give me an evil name, in order to taunt me. ¹⁴Remember Tobiah and Sanballat, O my God, according to these things that they did, and also the prophetess No-adiah and the rest of the prophets who wanted to make me afraid.

¹⁵So the wall was finished on the twenty-fifth day of the month Elul, in fifty-two days. ¹⁶And when all our enemies heard of it, all the nations round about us were afraid and fell greatly in their own esteem; for they perceived that this work had been accomplished with the help of our God. ¹⁷Moreover in those days the nobles of Judah sent many letters to Tobiah, and Tobiah's letters came to them. ¹⁸For many in Judah were bound by oath to him, because he was the son-in-law of Shecaniah the son of Arah: and his son Jehohanan had taken the daughter of Meshullam the son of Berechiah as his wife. ¹⁹Also they spoke of his good deeds in my presence, and reported my words to him. And Tobiah sent letters to make me afraid.

The story of opposition to the work of re-establishing the exiles in Jerusalem and Judah, which began in Ezra 4, now reaches its climax, with Sanballat, Tobiah and Geshem playing their last great scene. Their actions exhibit the desperation of those who see the growing inevitability of something which is anathema to them. In verse 1 the walls are up—there is not much time left. They will, therefore, try anything to subvert Nehemiah, and the chapter records numerous attempts to do so. There are clearly distinguishable stages. At first (v. 2) the approach has all the plausible chumminess of the opponent who wishes to minimize real differences. "At the end of the day, we are not far apart. Let's bury the hatchet. We're all reasonable people and we shall find a way of preserving the interests of all concerned": so it might go, if we use our imagination a little. The adversaries evidently have high hopes of this tactic, for they try it four times (v. 4). A previous generation of opponents of Judah had tried it also (Ezra 4:2). The attempt had good reason behind it, because the appeal of such an approach is powerful. The Church *can* be embarrassed by its radical differentness from the world and by the unremitting need to throw down a gauntlet to its ways. Only the clear-headed resoluteness of Nehemiah weathers this challenge.

On the fifth approach the tactic has altered to one of thinly-disguised menace (vv. 5–7). The tenor of Sanballat's letter on this occasion is that a great rumour of Judah' intended rebellion is going up in the Empire. The allusion to a plan to make Nehemiah king, with a religious sanction furnished by the prophets (vv. 6–7), is designed to raise the spectre of the former strength of the kingdoms of Judah and Israel in a way which had been so effective on an earlier occasion (Ezra 4:11–16, 20). (The allegation was almost certainly without foundation, even if messianic hopes had been attached decades earlier to Zerubbabel.) The prognosis which looks so sympathetic—"Come; I am telling you this for your own good"—is a falsehood, calculated to be self-fulfilling. The *open* letter is precisely designed to *foment* the rumours, not to allay them.

The final ploy is subtle and thoroughly unscrupulous. The leading figure here is probably Tobiah, because of his known influence with certain inhabitants of Jerusalem (cf. vv. 18–19, 13:4–9). Shemaiah is in his pay (v. 13), but apparently pretending to be in danger from the same quarter as Nehemiah. The phrase "who was shut up" (v. 10) has puzzled commentators by its ambiguity, but probably means that Shemaiah was making a point of being confined to his house because of fear. This would provide a plausible "cover" for his purpose of coaxing Nehemiah into the Temple, driven by the threat of death and lured, perhaps, by vague thoughts of asylum (Exod. 21:13–14; 1 Kings 1:50–53). In fact the law of asylum was not intended for a case like this, and would not in any case have involved going into the Temple. To do that, for a layman like Nehemiah, would have been a serious infringement of the laws of holiness. Yet Shemaiah makes it quite clear that this is what he is suggesting. The terms of verse 10 leave no doubt that he wants Nehemiah right inside. He wants to make very sure that Nehemiah well and truly sins, with no possibility of evading the issue afterwards. Shemaiah is clearly compromised himself, and has no qualms about dragging another down. In addition to the gravity of the sin itself, to have violated the Temple, without which Judah would have neither identity nor hope, would have utterly compromised Nehemiah in the eyes of those very people whom he needed to carry with him. This was Tobiah's hope. Whereas the enemies' early ploys, had they deflected Nehemiah at all, might actually have steeled the purpose of Judah in the end, this would more probably have destroyed it for ever.

The enemies' last stand, therefore, exhibits both cunning and determination, even obsession. History shows that this is no accident or aberration. Wherever the people of God goes about its business of extending the knowledge of God in the world with clear-headed vigour, there will be those, perhaps with power and influence, who will take strong exception. The most sinister aspect of the story is the success of Tobiah in obtaining a foothold within Jerusalem to the extent of dividing the allegiance of "many" of its people (v. 18). Shemaiah's approach to Nehemiah must initially have carried conviction because to some extent it must have been difficult to know who one's friends were, or how *far* they were friends. It was not only a question of some being "bound by oath" to Tobiah (v. 18), in the sense of an unwelcome commitment; rather he had many willing friends, mainly perhaps because of a marriage relationship. (For Shecaniah and Meshullam cf. 3:4, 29.) It was a link which many were reluctant to break, and it made undivided allegiance to God's word extraordinarily difficult.

Although this is almost the last appearance of Sanballat, Tobiah and Geshem, it is just a little disquieting that the chapter ends with a reference to Tobiah's continued badgering of Nehemiah (v. 19). In the Christian life no victory over the temptation to do wrong can ever be final, because the temptation is always sure to return.

TRIUMPH

Nehemiah 6:1–19 (*cont'd*)

The concern of the enemies of Judah was to weaken their resolve and stop the work on the walls (v. 9). The story of the chapter, nevertheless, is one of strength, and indeed of the project completed (v. 15). (This verse presumably refers to the setting of gates in the wall, since apart from these the wall was already standing by v. 1; without them, however, it was impossible to speak of the walls being complete.) What are the ingredients in the triumphant conclusion of this, Nehemiah's main task?

(i)

The first is his *perception* of what was really going on. The invitation to meet Sanballat and Geshem "in one of the villages in the plain of Ono" (v. 2) may have seemed innocent enough. Ono was neutral territory, not far from modern Israel's airport just east of Tel-Aviv. It looked a good place for a "summit conference". But Nehemiah knows their mind. They want to do him harm (v. 2).

At each stage of the attack upon his integrity he shows similar insight. He knows that the rumour-mongering about his ambition is an attempt to stop the work (v. 9). He also sees through Shemaiah, though verse 12 is phrased in such a way as to suggest

that he did not see this immediately but rather that the truth
dawned in the midst of his dealings with him. Literally it reads:
"Then I recognized, and behold, it was not God who had sent
him". The problem of false prophecy was already an old one in
Nehemiah's time, and always knotty (cf. Deut. 18:20). Jeremiah
was plagued all his ministry by the widespread belief that *he* was a
false prophet, and had confrontations with some who really were
(e.g. Jer. 28). If a man *said* he was a prophet and *sounded* like one
(Shemaiah speaks in v. 10 in the sort of couplets which characterized prophetic speech), how could anyone tell whether he was
genuine or not? Nehemiah could scarcely wait around to apply
the fulfilment-test of Deut. 18:21–22! So his perception of
Shemaiah's hypocrisy is purely and simply God-given insight.
How did he get it? We can only answer in the terms of Prov. 1:7:
"The fear of the Lord [cf. Neh. 5:15!] is the beginning of knowledge." The knowledge of which Proverbs speaks embraces all
kinds of understanding. It was because Nehemiah walked closely
with his God that he had such a sure eye for the true nature of
things.

(ii)

The second secret of Nehemiah's success is his *prayerfulness*
(which we have noted before). It is characteristic of his memoir
that the narrative of what happened is peppered not only with
explanations of *why* things happen, but also with prayers. They
are often one-liners (v. 9), sometimes longer (v. 14). But they all
show how finely intermeshed were Nehemiah's life of action and
his life of prayer. He brought problems to God even as he was in
the thick of them (2:4). And he thought fit—presumably in
tranquil recollection—to record them afterwards in his memoir.

The prayer of verse 9 shows us just where to look for the deep
cause of the frustration of Sanballat's cohorts and the triumph of
Judah. The human might of the enemy aims to *weaken* the
builders (the picture is one of limp exhaustion, the kind close at
hand in 4:10 and all too readily comprehensible); a higher might
can give a thoroughly *un*natural strength—and Nehemiah claims
it. The verse is structured (hands ... drop/strengthen ... hands;

the word-order is slightly different in the Hebrew, but to the same effect) so as to bring out the conflict between two kinds of power, the utter futility of anyone measuring himself against God, and the need for God's servants to draw on the power he would give. Even the attempt to induce fear in those who are so armed is doomed to failure.

The prayer of verse 14 is an exact counterpart of that of 5:19. It is once again a claim upon God's covenant faithfulness. We cannot recover the "tone of voice" with which Nehemiah prayed. It is tempting to regard the sentiment as vindictive, and indeed we need not suppose that Nehemiah was "perfect in every way". Yet if we are content to characterize the prayer as vindictive we shall miss its real significance. Nehemiah is dedicated to the rebuilding of Jerusalem, and that not as an end in itself but as the context for the *continuing* life of the community. He will have had no reason to think that the likes of Tobiah would throw in the towel, in pliant resignation, once the walls were up: the letters that kept dropping on the mat (v. 19) were a sufficient reminder not to indulge in foolish optimism of that sort. Nor can he suppose that "the enemy within"—here represented by Noadiah and other prophets—will simply go away. So the sentiment of verse 14 cannot be explained apart from Nehemiah's devotion to the people and the work of God. Like 5:19 it is based on the belief that God will do right. Fashionable pooh-poohing of such thoughts is belied by the fact that the need for justice and the rage against perceived wrong is very deep-seated in the human heart. The modern world can scarcely cope with the Jewish holocaust of the Second World War without some doctrine—spoken or not— of right vengeance. Where it is absent, a sense of right may be missing altogether.

(iii)

There is, thirdly, an element of that *cunning* which we have noticed before. Nehemiah plays the enemy along a bit. He answers them in their own terms. He declines the invitation to Ono on the grounds that he is too busy, while the real reason is reserved for the memoir (v. 2). There is a similar discrepancy between word and thought in verses 8–9, and again in verse 11, where there is no open accusation of Shemaiah. Rather he waxes indignant about the implications of cowardice. (His two rhetorical questions make essentially the same point. The reading in RSV margin is probably to be preferred: i.e. What man such as I could go into the Temple "to save his life"?) The effect of this policy is probably to defer further open confrontation. In adopting it, he never lies. All his words are true, and indeed would be described as "frank" in the jargon of modern negotiation. Once again, however, he has used all his skills in the cause of furthering God's purpose.

(iv)

The completion of the walls (v. 15) comes as an early promise of God's continuing faithfulness. The credit is given to God. Nehemiah has not only sought his help while the crisis remained (v. 9) but remembered it when it was past (v. 16). Furthermore the name of God—prejudiced by the abuses recorded in chapter 5 (5:9)—has been vindicated because the nations perceived that something very remarkable had happened under Nehemiah (v. 16). They were also *afraid*, falling victim therefore to the very thing they had wished upon the builders of Jerusalem (v. 9), i.e. a sense of their *own* vulnerability in the world (cf. 4:2).

The real nature of judgment is very clear here. Human pretensions are put in perspective. God is exalted. What appears to be strong proves to be weak; and what seems weak is shown to be strong, by virtue of the strength of God. (The theme is very important in the Old Testament. See further Isa. 2:12–19; 11:3–4.)

PRIORITIES

Nehemiah 7:1–73*a*

¹Now when the wall had been built and I had set up the doors, and the gatekeepers, the singers, and the Levites had been appointed, ²I gave my brother Hanani and Hananiah the governor of the castle charge over Jerusalem, for he was a more faithful and God-fearing man than

many. ³And I said to them, "Let not the gates of Jerusalem be opened until the sun is hot; and while they are still standing guard let them shut and bar the doors. Appoint guards from among the inhabitants of Jerusalem, each to his station and each opposite his own house." ⁴The city was wide and large, but the people within it were few and no houses had been built.

⁵Then God put it into my mind to assemble the nobles and the officials and the people to be enrolled by genealogy. And I found the book of the genealogy of those who came up at the first, and I found written in it:

. . . .

⁷³So the priests, the Levites, the gatekeepers, the singers, some of the people, the temple servants, and all Israel, lived in their towns.

(i)

The bulk of this chapter (vv. 6–73*a*) has been met already, being to all intents and purposes identical with Ezra 2:1–70. Our interest in it at this point, therefore, can be limited to asking why the list of the first returnees from Babylon is produced at this juncture as well as at the more obvious position at the beginning of Ezra–Nehemiah.

The answer to this question lies in verses 1–5. To all appearances Nehemiah's work is now complete. The walls have been rebuilt. The inhabitants of Judah and Jerusalem stand at the end of the long process, covering almost a century, which has led from Cyrus' decree, via the rebuilding of the Temple and false starts upon the city itself, to their present security. Nehemiah, for his part, appears to contemplate a return to the centre of Empire, whether to resume his cup-bearing duties or merely to bring a report to the king. (We deduce this from the commission to Hanani in v. 2. The trip would be a separate one from that recorded in 13:6. It may be that he made several journeys during his twelve-year tenure of the office of governor, 5:14.)

The job is not quite done, however. The walls may be up, but the city has as yet an inadequate population. In all the information we have had about the resettlement to this point, little has been said about the relative population of Jerusalem and the other towns of Judah. The city is not expressly mentioned in the list of Ezra, repeated in this chapter. When there has been talk of a return "to Jerusalem and Judah" (as in v. 6 here) the significance of the former has been primarily *religious*, referring to the re-establishment of the Temple and its worship. During the re-building the population was no doubt artificially inflated by the influx of workers—some, perhaps, with their families (cf. 4:14)—from the province. But with that work complete, Nehemiah can now lament that his fine new city is hardly worth the name because of the few people who live there (v. 4). Walls would afford poor protection for the Temple without people behind them. If they survived at all in a hostile environment they would stand, at best, as silent accusers of a people which, when all was said and done, cared little for the name of its God.

Nehemiah's concern, therefore, says two things. The *first* is that the short-term commitment which was required of the people for the building project itself was meaningless unless it was actually a token of a commitment that was *enduring*. They could not simply rest on the laurels of their achievements and a once-for-all sacrifice. Rather they must be ready for self-sacrifice to become a hallmark of their whole lives. (Clearly—and as 11:1–2 will bear out—to live in Jerusalem must have been *perceived* as a sacrifice by the many who had chosen not to live there.) So it is with Christian faith. In the depths of our consciousness we are tempted to regard duties done in the line of Christian service as a pay-off against God's mercies. Of course, we would never admit it, and it needs no demonstration that such a thought is scandalous. The Christian is in the position of the servant in Luke 17:7–10 who, having served his master all the day, must yet serve. How fortunate that the Master, unlike the run of masters, is compassion itself!

The *second* point to be observed from Nehemiah's concern is that the walls are nothing in themselves. The call to obedience in the Old Testament takes many forms. In this book, it involves the fortification of a city. Yet no activity to which the people of God is called is *identical* with obedience. Many times the Old Testament writers call their people to repent *because they have equated what obedience should produce (e.g. sacrifice) with obedience itself* (cf.

Mic. 6:6–8). Here, as everywhere in the Bible, the Lord looks upon the heart.

(ii)

Our passage gives us a further glimpse of Nehemiah's painstaking ability as a leader. Having won many victories he was anxious to ensure that all was not squandered through carelessness. The gatekeepers of verse 1 refer here to keepers of the *city* gates. (The grouping of gatekeepers, singers and Levites usually relates to the Temple. It is hard to see what the appointment of singers and Levites has to do with the completion of the walls. However, 13:22 shows that Nehemiah apparently thought it appropriate that Levites should guard the gates on the sabbath. This may account for the association of ideas in v. 1.) Verse 3 provides for a closing of the gates at siesta time, and for a vigilante-style guard upon the city. All this is simply what we might have expected by way of final measures from one who had so single-mindedly given himself to a God-given task which he would see through to its end.

More striking, perhaps, is what these verses have to say about *priorities*. Nehemiah appoints Hanani his brother as his deputy in Jerusalem, the same, presumably, who had first alerted him to Jerusalem's straits, 1:2. (Hananiah, incidentally, is probably a mistaken scribal repetition of Hanani—in Hebrew it looks very similar to "my brother Hanani".) That mission had suggested what Nehemiah now tells us, that he was "a more faithful and God-fearing man than many." Here are the qualities that are important to Nehemiah in a leader. Astuteness, forcefulness, yes; these he himself had shown. But it is godliness that he picks out as being indispensable.

Similarly, verse 4 records the significant fact that, though the walls stood complete, "no houses had been built." This can hardly mean that Jerusalem was *devoid* of houses. Houses have been mentioned in verse 3, and it is clear that *some* people lived in Jerusalem. What is meant is that no houses had been built in the course of the building which Nehemiah had guided. In more leisurely circumstances the walls might have been built so as to *incorporate* houses, thus stretching resources and fully utilizing limited space (cf. Rahab's house in Jericho, Josh. 2:15). But the urgency of the task meant that the walls had had to go up without either embellishment or thought for the people's future lifestyle.

We have thus two cameo-glimpses of the kind of thinking which had led to the accomplishment of the goal of building the walls. A leader who knows that all true success is the product of godliness—a people that comes to terms, in a clear-headed way, with the demands of a call from God and subjects all other considerations to meeting them: these are the things which have established Jerusalem and frustrated the malevolence of her antagonists.

It hardly needs to be added that the reason for the inclusion of the census list at this point is to show how Nehemiah took stock of the whole population pattern in Judah before conceiving a plan for the peopling of Jerusalem. That, when it happened, would both ensure that the gains made so far were not forfeited, and require the people to continue to maintain right priorities, to the point of subordinating their own interests to the common good and to the will of God.

THE NEED TO KNOW

Nehemiah 7:73*b*–8:8

And when the seventh month had come, the children of Israel were in their towns. [1]And all the people gathered as one man into the square before the Water Gate; and they told Ezra the scribe to bring the book of the law of Moses which the Lord had given to Israel. [2]And Ezra the priest brought the law before the assembly, both men and women and all who could hear with understanding, on the first day of the seventh month. [3]And he read from it facing the square before the Water Gate from early morning until midday, in the presence of the men and the women and those who could understand; and the ears of all the people were attentive to the book of the law. [4]And Ezra the scribe stood on a wooden pulpit which they had made for the purpose; and beside him stood Mattithiah, Shema, Anaiah, Uriah, Hilkiah, and Maaseiah on his right hand; and Pedaiah, Misha-el, Malchijah, Hashum,

Hashbaddanah, Zechariah, and Meshullam on his left hand. ⁵And Ezra opened the book in the sight of all the people, for he was above all the people; and when he opened it all the people stood. ⁶And Ezra blessed the Lord, the great God; and all the people answered, "Amen, Amen," lifting up their hands; and they bowed their heads and worshipped the Lord with their faces to the ground. ⁷Also Jeshua, Bani, Sherebiah, Jamin, Akkub, Shabbethai, Hodiah, Ma-aseiah, Kelita, Azariah, Jozabad, Hanan, Pelaiah, the Levites, helped the people to understand the law, while the people remained in their places. ⁸And they read from the book, from the law of God, clearly; and they gave the sense, so that the people understood the reading.

(i)

The census list of chapter 7 not only prepares for the measures which Nehemiah will take to populate the city of Jerusalem, but also leads directly into the present account of a huge public assembly which brought the people from their towns into the capital. The occasion is the seventh month of the year (in the autumn, according to the calendar of Old Israel) in which were kept both the Day of Atonement, on the tenth of the month (Lev. 23:27ff.) and the Feast of Booths (or Harvest), beginning on the fifteenth and lasting for a week (Lev. 23:34–36). The Day of Atonement does not feature in the celebration recorded here; it may be that it was not kept, its spirit having been poured into the sombre event beginning on the twenty-fourth of the month and recorded in chapters 9 and 10. Here the Feast of Booths dominates, with its tone of rejoicing (cf. Lev. 23:40), an appropriate first response to the completion of the walls. On this occasion, the more contemplative ceremony can take second place.

The omission of the Day of Atonement is not the only oddity in the chapter. It comes as a surprise suddenly to find Ezra in the midst of things once again (v. 1), with Nehemiah taking a back seat. Ezra's abrupt re-emergence, together with the atmosphere of new discovery in relation both to the law and the Feast of Booths—even though these featured already in Ezra 3 (vv. 2, 4)—has led some scholars to suppose that the present chapter is displaced and must have belonged originally in the Book of Ezra. However, the narrative does picture both Ezra and Nehemiah working together at this point (v. 9). And it is possible to account for the surprising features of the narrative. Ezra has naturally remained on the sidelines during a work which was rightly under- taken by a *political* leader. (He may even, as already suggested, have returned to Babylon following his own reform, and have come back again to lend his authority to Nehemiah's further exhortations of the people, just as the work of the latter reaches its climax.) In a ceremony which is now essentially *religious*, however, Ezra would naturally play a leading role.

As for the Feast of Booths, it seems impossible, on the face of it, to reconcile verse 17*b* with Ezra 3:4. There is an interesting parallel, however, between the Passover celebrations of Hezekiah (2 Chr. 30:5ff.) and Josiah (2 Chr. 35), where the latter is described in very similar terms to the Feast of Booths here (2 Chr. 35:18) even though Hezekiah's was no paltry affair (2 Chr. 30:23ff.). The explanation may simply lie in a tendency to exaggeration which seems to accompany the description of such feasts.

(ii)

The chapter is most important, however, for its picture of Israel at worship. The buzz of excitement at finishing the walls has hardly had time to settle by the first day of the seventh month (since the twenty-fifth of Elul—the sixth month—was only four or five days earlier, cf. 6:15). We might expect a *natural* readiness to praise God on this occasion, therefore. It is interesting to find, then, that behind the thanksgiving lies, not the mere fact of the new walls, but a reading of the law (vv. 1ff.). Israel rejoices in response to the word of God. The building of the walls is set in its context. The enemies of Israel have been thwarted not because of an isolated, once-for-all action of God—that could always be interpreted as a fluke—but because the God of Israel is the same, yesterday, today and forever.

A number of points can be made here. We confine ourselves initially to observing what this relationship between the word and thanksgiving says about *worship*. We have in these verses one of the most graphic portrayals of Israel at worship in the Old Testament. There is in the first place a tremendous solemnity about it. Ezra stands on a wooden *pulpit.* (The word actually means "tower". It looks as if there was no ready-made word for pulpit.) We are close here to the beginnings of the Jewish synagogue, which may have originated in the Babylonian exile, where the law was regularly read from a raised platform, and where places were reserved for the most eminent synagogue members close to the spot where the law was read (cf. v. 4*b*). The effect was to show that those who wielded authority in the community were themselves under the authority of God, and that therefore it was the word of God that regulated the whole life of the community. We can almost hear the hush as Ezra opens the book and the people stand (v. 5). Something of this has been preserved in those church traditions where the Bible is carried solemnly to the pulpit before the minister arrives, so that the whole congregation places itself symbolically under the authority of the word.

Ezra's congregation showed no reluctance, it seems, to listen to the long sermon (v. 3)! Rather, there is great concern that as many as possible should hear and understand. "All who could hear with understanding" (v. 2) probably refers to children who are old enough to "stay with the grown-ups for the sermon", as we might put it. But even among those who were mature enough to understand, Ezra did not take understanding for granted. The activity of the Levites in verses 7–8 could either be translation— on the supposition that the people's language had been influenced by the Aramaic of Babylon and perhaps other dialects—or simply, and most probably, elucidation of things which may have been difficult to grasp. The law-reading thus entirely corresponds to what is laid down in Deut. 31:9–13, where provision is made for reading the law every seven years at the Feast of Booths. There, as here, we find a concern that those who hear may really understand and not just pay lip-service. For on their understanding depends the reality of their experience of God, and the likelihood of its being transmitted to the next generation. Ezra may have been stepping into the seven-year cycle. The tone of the chapter makes it more likely, however, that he is re-initiating something that had lapsed.

This need for understanding the word of God, and the fact that it cannot be taken for granted, has been recognized by the Church in its most active periods. Creeds and hymns, passion plays and the lowly jingle have all played their part. In the 20th century a whole world of communications aids lies at our feet. We may not know how the Levites "gave the sense" (v. 8—they may have done it in an *ad hoc* way as questions arose); but if it is our real concern to pass on a *knowledge* of the Christian faith that goes beyond a meagre minimum, we will refuse to make a "sacred cow" of any inherited method and tap all the expertise of the day in order that we might know more of our God.

(iii)

The setting was solemn, but it was evidently not inhibiting. The people cried "Amen", raised their hands in prayer and prostrated themselves in adoration. Certain modern church movements have sought to recapture something of this self-expression. For others it seems to be, well, overdoing it a bit! Of course, the preferences of ancient Israel cannot be made the measure of acceptable style in modern worship. Our spiritual forefathers were informed by their culture, as we are. For the Hebrew, emotion inevitably expressed itself in physical attitude. This was because the self was conceived as a unity to a far greater extent than in most modern western culture, where there has been, in many reaches of the Church, a reaction against externalism in religion and a concentration upon inwardness. This is well and good apart from the constant danger that, when outward expression of emotion has been abolished, the vaunted inner passion can be well gone before anyone—including the person concerned—has noticed! The point that is enduring here is that the reading of the word produced a response which was *heartfelt* and which was *evident to and shared by the congregation.* Whatever our cultural or temperamental prejudices, we must find ways, as congregations of God's people, not only of hearing, but of knowing that we have heard *together.* For the experience of togetherness is *part* of hearing, and that way lies increased faith.

A TIME TO DANCE

Nehemiah 8:9–18

⁹And Nehemiah, who was the governor, and Ezra the priest and scribe, and the Levites who taught the people said to all the people, "This day is holy to the Lord your God; do not mourn or weep." For all the people wept when they heard the words of the law. ¹⁰Then he said to them, "Go your way, eat the fat and drink sweet wine and send portions to him for whom nothing is prepared; for this day is holy to our Lord; and do not be grieved, for the joy of the Lord is your strength." ¹¹So the Levites stilled all the people, saying, "Be quiet, for this day is holy; do not be grieved." ¹²And all the people went their way to eat and drink and to send portions and to make great rejoicing, because they had understood the words that were declared to them.

¹³On the second day the heads of fathers' houses of all the people, with the priests and the Levites, came together to Ezra the scribe in order to study the words of the law. ¹⁴And they found it written in the law that the Lord had commanded by Moses that the people of Israel should dwell in booths during the feast of the seventh month, ¹⁵and that they should publish and proclaim in all their towns and in Jerusalem, "Go out to the hills and bring branches of olive, wild olive, myrtle, palm, and other leafy trees to make booths, as it is written." ¹⁶So the people went out and brought them and made booths for themselves, each on his roof, and in their courts and in the courts of the house of God, and in the square at the Water Gate and in the square at the Gate of Ephraim. ¹⁷And all the assembly of those who had returned from the captivity made booths and dwelt in the booths; for from the days of Jeshua the son of Nun to that day the people of Israel had not done so. And there was very great rejoicing. ¹⁸And day by day, from the first day to the last day, he read from the book of the law of God. They kept the feast seven days; and on the eighth day there was a solemn assembly, according to the ordinance.

(i)

The reading of the law, as we have seen (vv. 1–8), produced a profound emotional response. There was clearly a strong element of penitence in this, for we are told that "the people wept" (v. 9). Ezra and Nehemiah, however, believe that the appropriate first response to the rebuilding of the walls is joy. They therefore send the people off to feast and make merry, drawing the under-privileged into their festivities (vv. 10–12). If there is to be a time of rigorous self-examination (chs. 9, 10) let it first be remembered that God is good, and means it well with Israel.

The people's initial tearful response, followed by the command to rejoice and to share with the poor, raises the question of what was read to the people that produced such reactions. The words of Ezra and Nehemiah, backed up by the Levites, in verses 9–12, suggest that there were two elements which made an impression. (This is apart from the law's many commands, which had evidently produced a sense of sin and therefore weeping. Since Ezra and Nehemiah postpone consideration of these we shall do likewise!)

The first element in the law-reading was evidently God's desire to bless Israel. This might have stemmed from Gen. 1, with its declaration of God's intent to bless the world he has made (vv. 28–31). With respect to Israel in particular, it will have emerged most strongly from Deuteronomy, with its descriptions of the wealth of the promised land (8:7–10). Perhaps it was because they had squandered all this that the people first wept. Now, however, they are directed to go and eat the fat of the land (v. 10). (There is some confirmation here that the famine of 5:3, as we noted there, did not occur at the time of the construction of the walls.) This is in close conformity to the pattern in Deuteronomy where worship is conceived as a joyful participation in the plenty which God has provided (Deut. 12:7; 14:24–26).

This note of joy is sustained for a considerable period. The study to which the people give themselves on the second day (v. 13) issues in the Feast of Booths, which begins some weeks later and which is also characterized by rejoicing (v. 17*b*). The dwelling in booths was symbolic on more than one level. We have noticed already that it could be a sobering reminder of imperma-nence against a *false* trust in the walls. Yet it is also appropriate as a celebration of the wall-building because the success of this has marked a final stage of the "new exodus" similar to that first exodus which gave the feast its original meaning (Lev. 23:42–43). Rejoicing like this in response to God's goodness shows that the people of the Old Testament did not fall into the trap, which has not been universally avoided, of making all worship uniformly sombre. Such would be an insult to the God who desires above all joy in his creatures. The joy of Israel in her feast will have had more of that uninhibitedness we have noticed already (cf. David's abandon after bringing the ark to Jerusalem; 2 Sam. 6:12*b*–15). And it cannot be overstressed that this is *not* self-indulgence. Rather, like the more solemn response of verse 6, it has a function for faith, expressed in the assurance that "the joy of the Lord is your strength" (v. 10). It is vital for Israel to experience and affirm *together* the goodness of God. Thanksgiving to God for what he has done for a *people* cannot be dissipated into a thousand separate and unrelated responses. It is when the voice of thanksgiving is unanimous that it takes on an authentic ring and becomes *strength*, the strength of a sure faith.

Let it be stressed, however, that it is *joy in God*. What we witness here is not the tacking on of vacuous festivity to an act of worship which is itself kept drab. The rejoicing *is* worship. What must be cultivated is a rejoicing together *in the goodness of God*.

(ii)

The second element in the law-reading which has conditioned the worship of the people is the call to neighbour-love. The good things of the land belong *as of right* to the poor, and their interest in it is guarded by the command to those who have to share with those who have not. It is no coincidence that the call to rejoice is accompanied by such a command. Exactly the same association of ideas occurs in those passages in Deuteronomy which we have already found to have exerted an influence on the present chapter (Deut. 12:12; 14:29). The right of the poor is an implication of the brotherhood of Israel, an idea which we saw to underlie chapter 5. Indeed there *should* be no poor at all (Deut. 15:4). The point is plain. There can be no conscientious exultation in the plenty of God's world while brothers and sisters go needy. It is hard to put limits to the radicalness of this principle for a western world that is shielded from want but knows all too well that much of the world is dying from it. "Let every one be fully convinced in his own mind" (Rom. 14:5).

A TIME TO MOURN

Nehemiah 9:1–38

¹Now on the twenty-fourth day of this month the people of Israel were assembled with fasting and in sackcloth, and with earth upon their heads. ²And the Israelites separated themselves from all foreigners, and stood and confessed their sins and the iniquities of their fathers. ³And they stood up in their place and read from the book of the law of the Lord their God for a fourth of the day; for another fourth of it they made confession and worshipped the Lord their God. ⁴Upon the stairs of the Levites stood Jeshua, Bani, Kadmi-el, Shebaniah, Bunni, Sherebiah, Bani, and Chenani; and they cried with a loud voice to the Lord their God. ⁵Then the Levites, Jeshua, Kadmi-el, Bani, Hashabneiah, Sherebiah, Hodiah, Shebaniah, and Pethahiah, said, "Stand up and bless the Lord your God from everlasting to everlasting. Blessed be thy glorious name which is exalted above all blessing and praise."

⁶And Ezra said: "Thou art the Lord, thou alone; thou hast made heaven, the heaven of heavens, with all their host, the earth and all that is on it, the seas and all that is in them; and thou preservest all of them; and the host of heaven worships thee. ⁷Thou art the Lord, the God who didst choose Abram and bring him forth out of Ur of the Chaldeans and give him the name Abraham; ⁸and thou didst find his heart faithful before thee, and didst make with him the covenant to give to his descendants the land of the Canaanite, the Hittite, the Amorite, the Perizzite, the Jebusite, and the Girgashite; and thou hast fulfilled thy promise, for thou art righteous.

⁹"And thou didst see the affliction of our fathers in Egypt and hear their cry at the Red Sea, ¹⁰and didst perform signs and wonders against Pharaoh and all his servants and all the people of his land, for thou knewest that they acted insolently against our fathers; and thou didst get thee a name, as it is to this day. ¹¹And thou didst divide the sea before them, so that they went through the midst of the sea on dry land; and thou didst cast their pursuers into the depths, as a stone into mighty waters. ¹²By a pillar of cloud thou didst lead them in the day, and by a pillar of fire in the night to light for them the way in which they should go. ¹³Thou didst come down upon Mount Sinai, and speak with them from heaven and give them right ordinances and true laws, good statutes and commandments, ¹⁴and thou didst make known to them

thy holy sabbath and command them commandments and statutes and a law by Moses thy servant. [15]Thou didst give them bread from heaven for their hunger and bring forth water for them from the rock for their thirst, and thou didst tell them to go in to possess the land which thou hadst sworn to give them.

[16]"But they and our fathers acted presumptuously and stiffened their neck and did not obey thy commandments; [17]they refused to obey, and were not mindful of the wonders which thou didst perform among them; but they stiffened their neck and appointed a leader to return to their bondage in Egypt. But thou art a God ready to forgive, gracious and merciful, slow to anger and abounding in steadfast love, and didst not forsake them. [18]Even when they had made for themselves a molten calf and said, 'This is your God who brought you up out of Egypt,' and had committed great blasphemies, [19]thou in thy great mercies didst not forsake them in the wilderness; the pillar of cloud which led them in the way did not depart from them by day, nor the pillar of fire by night which lighted for them the way by which they should go. [20]Thou gavest thy good Spirit to instruct them, and didst not withhold thy manna from their mouth, and gavest them water for their thirst. [21]Forty years didst thou sustain them in the wilderness, and they lacked nothing; their clothes did not wear out and their feet did not swell. [22]And thou didst give them kingdoms and peoples, and didst allot to them every corner; so they took possession of the land of Sihon king of Heshbon and the land of Og king of Bashan. [23]Thou didst multiply their descendants as the stars of heaven, and thou didst bring them into the land which thou hadst told their fathers to enter and possess. [24]So the descendants went in and possessed the land, and thou didst subdue before them the inhabitants of the land, the Canaanites, and didst give them into their hands, with their kings and the peoples of the land, that they might do with them as they would. [25]And they captured fortified cities and a rich land, and took possession of houses full of all good things, cisterns hewn out, vineyards, olive orchards and fruit trees in abundance; so they ate, and were filled and became fat, and delighted themselves in thy great goodness.

[26]"Nevertheless they were disobedient and rebelled against thee and cast thy law behind their back and killed thy prophets, who had warned them in order to turn them back to thee, and they committed great blasphemies. [27]Therefore thou didst give them into the hand of their enemies, who made them suffer; and in the time of their suffering they cried to thee and thou didst hear them from heaven; and according to thy great mercies thou didst give them saviours who saved them

from the hand of their enemies. ²⁸But after they had rest they did evil again before thee, and thou didst abandon them to the hand of their enemies, so that they had dominion over them; yet when they turned and cried to thee thou didst hear from heaven, and many times thou didst deliver them according to thy mercies. ²⁹And thou didst warn them in order to turn them back to thy law. Yet they acted presumptuously and did not obey thy commandments, but sinned against thy ordinances, by the observance of which a man shall live, and turned a stubborn shoulder and stiffened their neck and would not obey. ³⁰Many years thou didst bear with them, and didst warn them by thy Spirit through thy prophets; yet they would not give ear. Therefore thou didst give them into the hand of the peoples of the lands. ³¹Nevertheless in thy great mercies thou didst not make an end of them or forsake them; for thou art a gracious and merciful God.

³²"Now therefore, our God, the great and mighty and terrible God, who keepest covenant and steadfast love, let not all the hardship seem little to thee that has come upon us, upon our kings, our princes, our priests, our prophets, our fathers, and all thy people, since the time of the kings of Assyria until this day. ³³Yet thou hast been just in all that has come upon us, for thou hast dealt faithfully and we have acted wickedly; ³⁴our kings, our princes, our priests, and our fathers have not kept thy law or heeded thy commandments and thy warnings which thou didst give them. ³⁵They did not serve thee in their kingdom, and in thy great goodness which thou gavest them, and in the large and rich land which thou didst set before them; and they did not turn from their wicked works. ³⁶Behold, we are slaves this day; in the land that thou gavest to our fathers to enjoy its fruit and its good gifts, behold, we are slaves. ³⁷And its rich yield goes to the kings whom thou hast set over us because of our sins; they have power also over our bodies and over our cattle at their pleasure, and we are in great distress."

³⁸Because of all this we make a firm covenant and write it, and our princes, our Levites, and our priests set their seal to it.

(i)

It was right to celebrate God's goodness to the returned exiles in enabling Jerusalem to be built. Their leaders however—and Ezra is still in the forefront (v. 6)—know that the story is not over. The remainder of the Book of Nehemiah, consequently, is taken up with the need for the people to extricate themselves from their mediocrity—a mediocrity in devotion to God, which is reflected in their status as a vassal-people (v. 36). Chapter 9 must be seen in this wider context. It belongs particularly closely with chapter 10. It was common in the ancient world to cement relationships (normally political ones) by agreements (or treaties) between the parties, which were characterized (a) by a rehearsal of *past* relations between them and (b) by formal commitments about the *future*. The Old Testament often adopts this practice, somewhat loosely, for the relationship between God and Israel. Neh. 9 and 10 together are a case in point. Neh. 9 rehearses the past in the form of a prayer of confession (vv. 6–37), and prepares for the new commitment to God in 9:38–10:39. The form in its entirety is one which commends itself for Christian prayer in general, and solemn acts of renewal in particular. We look first, however, at the great confession.

(ii)

The atmosphere is sharply different from that which prevailed during the Feast of Booths. Once again outward manifestations betoken the condition of the worshippers' hearts (v. 1). The sackcloth and the earth on the worshippers' heads are signs of humility and mortality. The note of praise which prefaces the confession (v. 5) heralds what will in fact be the tone of the prayers, namely that, despite the sin of Israel, the relationship with Israel's God is a continuing one, and that praise and confession belong intimately together, both appropriate because of the greatness of God. It is important to notice that the confession—like the earlier joy—has been engendered by the reading of God's word (v. 3). The Levites have a prominent place again, showing that Ezra's prayer speaks for the community in the totality of its religious authority structure.

THE SURE MERCIES

Nehemiah 9:1–38 (*cont'd*)

(iii)

The confession itself encompasses the whole history of the people of Israel, from creation (v. 6) through the election of Abraham and promises to him (vv. 7–8), to the fulfilment of those promises in the miraculous exodus of the earlier Israelites from Egypt by the division of the Red Sea (v. 11), their guidance and sustenance in the wilderness (vv. 12, 15), the giving of commandments at Sinai (v. 13), and the ultimate possession of the rich land of Canaan as a numerous and victorious people (vv. 22–25). (The reader who wishes to follow the story in detail will need to read large parts of the Pentateuch and beyond. The events that are expressly alluded to here occur in Gen. 1; 12; 17:5; Exod. 2:23–25; 7–12; 13:21; 14; 16; 19–24; 32; Num. 21:21–35; Josh. 1–12.)

Ezra thus claims a solidarity between the people of his day and their ancestors in the faith. This is two-edged. On the one hand it is to claim the mercies of God all down the ages for the contemporary community. On the other hand, it means that the people of the present have a share in the *guilt* of the past. The "sins of the fathers" are in no way minimized in Ezra's prayer. Indeed, the prayer oscillates between statements of God's goodness (vv. 9–15, 17b, 19–25, 27, 28b, 31) and statements of the people's sinfulness (vv. 16–17a, 18, 26, 28a, 29–30) in such a way as to throw their ingratitude into sharp relief. The high point of their sin was the manufacture of a golden calf (v. 18; cf. Exod. 32), an act of idolatry at the very moment when Yahweh was setting his seal to the election of Israel as his own at Sinai. Yet this was merely typical of what was to come. Every act of love on God's part was met and matched by one of disloyalty on the part of his people (e.g. v. 26). Ezra is in no sense exonerating his own generation by this catalogue. Rather, he is allowing the character of former generations to reflect upon it.

There is an obvious point here for the faithful of today as we reflect upon our own failures. Our confessions can be very individualistic. In relation to the Church in other times and places we even tend to distance ourselves from its inadequacies and lean towards self-congratulation. How much better to try to see with God's eye the failures of the Church in all the ages, to admit that we are made of similar stuff, and to admire far more his gracious-

ness! This is not blame-shifting. It is entirely to accept that the
sins of the past are our own heritage, and is a sure defence against
self-justification or the feeling that one has nothing to confess.

(iv)

Yet at the heart of Ezra's prayer is the mercy of God. It is
instructive to notice how often the word "but" occurs in it. Whole
sermons have been preached on the words "But now..." in
Rom. 3:21, representing the great turning-point of the gospel.
Men are chronically sinful, *but* God has shown in Jesus Christ that
he *justifies* the sinful, not because of any price *they* pay, but as a
free gift (Rom. 3:22–26). The same principle is present here, even
if its final exhibition (in Christ) was yet withheld. "*But* thou art a
God ready to forgive" (v. 17); "*Even when* they had made [a
calf]...thou in thy great mercies..." (vv. 18–19); "*yet* when
they turned...thou didst hear" (v. 28). There is, of course, a
corresponding succession of "buts" and "neverthelesses", showing the people's ingratitude. This only serves, however, to bring
out more forcefully the Lord's determination to be gracious.

Notice the terms that describe his character, especially in v.
17*b*. He is a God, literally, "of forgiveness"; more than simply
being "ready to forgive" (RSV), he has forgiven and goes on
doing so times without number. He is *gracious*, i.e. he is fundamentally disposed to be kind, giving, favourable to his people. He
is *merciful*. The word has overtones of the warm, passionate
feeling a mother has for her child. He is *slow to anger and
abounding in steadfast love*. That is, he is slow to apply the terms
of the covenant strictly to Israel (by punishing them), but is more
than ready to fulfil all the obligations which it imposes upon
himself. It is thus that he has *not forsaken* them. By all natural
justice he should have done. It is only because his love goes far
deeper than any duty could demand that he has borne with his
people still.

The extent of his favour to them emerges from a comparison
of verses 10 and 29. The Egyptians' "insolence" becomes a
ground for their judgment. Israel is no better—she too is "pre-

sumptuous". (The word is the same in v. 29 as in v. 10 and
connotes high-handed defiance.) Yet because it is through Israel
that God desires ultimately to manifest his salvation to the whole
world, he did not "make an end of them or forsake them" (v. 31).
If we seek evidence that it is purely by God's goodwill that *any*
experience his salvation, the history of his dealings with Israel
furnishes it (cf. also Eph. 2:8.) And a prayer like Ezra's teaches
us to make a sober evaluation of our own need of God's mercy.

(v)

The prayer of Ezra is one of a number of places in the Old
Testament where we are given a potted version of Israel's in-
glorious history. Others are Deut. 1; Jer. 2; Ezek. 20; Pss. 78,
105, 106, 135, 136. These all have different emphases according
to the situations they address. Thus Jer. 2 speaks to the nation
while it still persists in the worst excesses of its idolatry, before the
axe that is Nebuchadnezzar has fallen, and stresses the justness of
God's anger. Ezra's prayer stands close to Ps. 106. In it, as in the
Psalm, a balance is kept between the rightness of God's periodic
chastisement of the people (vv. 17*a*, 30*b*) and the ultimately
merciful intentions which we have seen to be the real keynote of
the prayer.

Ezra is careful, therefore, to avoid giving wrong impressions.
In his praying he is aware that the assembled people are listening,
and that this lends to the activity—inevitably—a didactic dimension. (It is in this respect similar in character to the prayers in
certain Christian liturgies which precede the sacrament of Holy
Communion.) The grace of God which is so inexhaustible is not
therefore indifferent to Israel's faithfulness or lack of it. The
urgency of this point for Ezra's generation is that, while they have
so signally experienced God's goodness, there is a clear sense in
which they nevertheless continue to suffer. Ezra refers to "hardship" that has been the lot of Israel for generations (v. 32), and
more particularly a "slavery" in which they labour here and now
(vv. 36–37; note the bitter irony here). All this is attributable to
sin (vv. 33–34, 35*b*). Resistance to grace is *still* the problem of

Israel, and explains their rather ambiguous situation, in which they remain a subject people despite the new fortifications of their city.

The balance of the prayer is intended, therefore, both to point to the open-ended possibilities of future blessing from God, and to call the people to set their house in order, so that it might be realized. This call is not to compromise what we have said already about God's grace, nor to lead into ideas of merited salvation. Rather it calls God's people to take seriously their status as such, and the fact that God's purposes for them are that they should be holy (cf. Lev. 20:26, echoed in v. 2 of our chapter). The right goal of Israel is faithfulness. Her history has furnished at least one example of the quality, in a sea of disobedience, namely Abraham (vv. 7–8). This she should emulate, so that there might be a grander fulfilment than there has yet been of the promises to him. In this way the prayer leads into the affirmations of chapter 10. The word for "covenant" in 9:38 is not the usual word (*berith*) but *amana*, meaning an act of faithfulness. It is closely related, therefore, to the quality shown by Abraham (v. 8). Israel is thus exhorted to become, by their faithfulness, Abraham's children. Gal. 3:6–14 guards against any wrong interpretation of what that implies.

AN OATH—I

Nehemiah 10:1–39

[1]Those who set their seal are Nehemiah the governor, the son of Hacaliah, Zedekiah, [2]Seraiah, Azariah, Jeremiah, [3]Pashhur, Amariah, Malchijah, [4]Hattush, Shebaniah, Malluch, [5]Harim, Meremoth, Obadiah, [6]Daniel, Ginnethon, Baruch, [7]Meshullam, Abijah, Mijamin, [8]Ma-aziah, Bilgai, Shemaiah; these are the priests. [9]And the Levites: Jeshua the son of Azaniah, Binnui of the sons of Henadad, Kadmi-el; [10]and their brethren, Shebaniah, Hodiah, Kelita, Pelaiah, Hanan, [11]Mica, Rehob, Hashabiah, [12]Zaccur, Sherebiah, Shebaniah, [13]Hodiah, Bani, Beninu. [14]The chiefs of the people: Parosh, Pahath-moab, Elam, Zattu, Bani, [15]Bunni, Azgad, Bebai, [16]Adonijah, Bigvai, Adin, [17]Ater, Hezekiah, Azzur, [18]Hodiah, Hashum, Bezai,

¹⁹Hariph, Anathoth, Nebai, ²⁰Magpiash, Meshullam, Hezir, ²¹Mesh-ezabel, Zadok, Jaddua, ²²Pelatiah, Hanan, Anaiah, ²³Hoshea, Hana-niah, Hasshub, ²⁴Hallohesh, Pilha, Shobek, ²⁵Rehum, Hashabnah, Ma-aseiah, ²⁶Ahiah, Hanan, Anan, ²⁷Malluch, Harim, Baanah.

²⁸The rest of the people, the priests, the Levites, the gatekeepers, the singers, the temple servants, and all who have separated them-selves from the peoples of the lands to the law of God, their wives, their sons, their daughters, all who have knowledge and understand-ing, ²⁹join with their brethren, their nobles, and enter into a curse and an oath to walk in God's law which was given by Moses the servant of God, and to observe and do all the commandments of the Lord our Lord and his ordinances and his statutes. ³⁰We will not give our daughters to the peoples of the land or take their daughters for our sons; ³¹and if the peoples of the land bring in wares or any grain on the sabbath day to sell, we will not buy from them on the sabbath or on a holy day; and we will forgo the crops of the seventh year and the exaction of every debt.

³²We also lay upon ourselves the obligation to charge ourselves yearly with the third part of a shekel for the service of the house of our God: ³³for the showbread, the continual cereal offering, the continual burnt offering, the sabbaths, the new moons, the appointed feasts, the holy things, and the sin offerings to make atonement for Israel, and for all the work of the house of our God. ³⁴We have likewise cast lots, the priests, the Levites, and the people, for the wood offering, to bring it into the house of our God, according to our fathers' houses, at times appointed, year by year, to burn upon the altar of the Lord our God, as it is written in the law. ³⁵We obligate ourselves to bring the first fruits of our ground and the first fruits of all fruit of every tree, year by year, to the house of the Lord; ³⁶also to bring to the house of our God, to the priests who minister in the house of our God, the first-born of our sons and of our cattle, as it is written in the law, and the firstlings of our herds and of our flocks; ³⁷and to bring the first of our coarse meal, and our contributions, the fruit of every tree, the wine and the oil, to the priests, to the chambers of the house of our God; and to bring to the Levites the tithes from our ground, for it is the Levites who collect the tithes in all our rural towns. ³⁸And the priest, the son of Aaron, shall be with the Levites when the Levites receive the tithes; and the Levites shall bring up the tithe of the tithes to the house of our God, to the chambers, to the storehouse. ³⁹For the people of Israel and the sons of Levi shall bring the contribution of grain, wine, and oil to the

chambers, where are the vessels of the sanctuary, and the priests that minister, and the gatekeepers and the singers. We will not neglect the house of our God.

(i)

We saw that it was common in the ancient world when formalizing relationships to recall the course they had taken in the past, then to assume obligations for the future. We come now to the exiles' "firm covenant", or resolution to be faithful (9:38). Its formal and binding character is indicated by the fact that it is *written*, and that the leaders of the community, with governor Nehemiah at their head, set their seal to the document (9:38–10:26)—just as witnesses were called to observe and validate political treaties—following which it was read publicly for the general consent of the community. The solemnity of the pledge is expressed in strong terms in 10:29, where the people "enter into a *curse and an oath* to walk in God's law". The meaning is that they recognize the justice of incurring the wrath of heaven should they depart from the commitment they now give (cf. the curses—and alternative blessings—of Deut. 28, the classic Old Testament model for this idea).

We have thus a further instance of the importance for Old Testament piety of the outward sign and the communal act. Two thousand years of church history teach us that this is never adequate in itself as an offering to God. Yet it has a value which we may too readily despise. Solemn and public undertakings can make us forcefully come to terms with the obligations that rest upon us as God's people. The correct insistence on inwardness in religion can degenerate into indiscipline. And once again it is of value to know that pious intentions are shared.

(ii)

The pledge itself falls into general and particular affirmations (vv. 28–29, 30–39). The general affirmation, explicitly involving the whole community, recalls the measures of Ezra 9, 10. The people will hold themselves separate from "the peoples of the lands". We have noted before that this is, in practice, a *religious* separation. All who wished to affirm loyalty to Yahweh were welcome to do so (Ezra 6:21). By the same token, the "peoples of the lands" are those who worship other gods, and who will tend to seduce the exiles into idolatry. (The principle of separation, on these grounds, was first articulated in Exod. 34:10–16.) The need to be separate is simply a logical inference from the first commandment: "You shall have no other gods before me" (Exod. 20:3); cf. also Exod. 34:17 for a restatement of the same fundamental principle, following immediately upon the prohibition of intermarriage to which we have just referred. That prohibition, therefore, was of paramount importance to Israel's faith.

The point is further stressed by the expression "all who have separated themselves ... *to the law of God*". This is to say that obedience to the law is a whole way of life which marks out *God's* people as a people apart from others by the very way in which they function as a community. (We have elaborated this in our comments on Neh. 5.) Adherence to the law was never meant to be what it later became in some quarters, a pedantic and nitpicking attention to detail that knew and cared little about real rights and wrongs (cf. Matt. 23:23). Rather it was the mark of those whose governing desire was to be like God and to show in a community what a people of God could be like. If we are tempted to think of the Books of Ezra and Nehemiah as unattractively exclusivist, we may reflect that the separation of Judah *from* the peoples was part of a plan of God which was ultimately *for* the peoples. The religious element is present here in the qualification "all who have knowledge and understanding". This, and the fact that the separation from the "peoples of the lands" clearly involves an act of the will, shows that mere pedigree is not the same as faithfulness to God.

AN OATH—II

Nehemiah 10:1–39 (*cont'd*)

(iii)

The people's pledge continues (vv. 30–39) with particular obligations which they lay upon themselves. These relate to intermar-

riage (again) (v. 30), to the sabbath (v. 31) and to provision for
the upkeep of the Temple and clergy (vv. 32–39). There is clearly
no attempt to assent to all the extant laws (of the Pentateuch) one
by one. In a sense those which are reflected here are representative of the whole law. All the elements of the people's affirmation
can be traced to one requirement or another, implicit or explicit,
in the Pentateuch. Yet they are not simply a random selection.
Nor do they constitute mere enumeration of laws. Rather they
correspond to issues which faced the community at the time. And
they often show signs of modification and conscious reapplication
of the laws in question.

The former point hardly needs demonstration. The commitment to the Temple occupies most space here and is a dominant
concern of Ezra–Nehemiah (in the latter book as well as the
former, since the impulse to rebuild the city is closely bound up
with the fact that it is the place where, above all, Israel's God is
worshipped). The need to furnish and maintain it may have been
felt with increasing acuteness following the initial generosity of
both Cyrus (Ezra 1:4) and Artaxerxes (Ezra 7:15–16). There is
an analogy, therefore, between the people's readiness to meet
the *ongoing* needs in the area of worship and the need, already
identified (Neh. 7:4), to populate Jerusalem. The business of
being faithful to God would require a commitment that was
open-ended and which made its mark upon every day of the life
of the community, and of every member of it. The Temple,
then, is a burning issue. So too, as we know well by now, is intermarriage. And sabbath-breach is also singled out as a problem
in 13:19ff.

(iv)

More interesting than the mere identification of these problems is
the way in which they are faced, i.e. by reapplication of known
laws. The reader who wishes to follow up all the elements of
Judah's pledge should consult one of the more technical commentaries. We shall note some general observations and notice how
laws are reapplied.

The underlying point is that the law is respected *in its spirit*. There is no attempt to evade the implications of the law by adhering to the letter, and therefore to the loophole. The resolution not to *buy* on the sabbath is not, strictly speaking, required by the sabbath laws (Exod. 20:9–11; 34:21). The determined legalist might have justified his shopping expedition on the grounds that the work was really being done by the foreign traders (v. 31). The people see that this is a dishonest subterfuge and set their faces against it. Similarly regarding intermarriage: it *could* have been argued that this was only prohibited with Canaanites, Hittites, Hivites, Perizzites and Jebusites (Exod. 34:11, 16). As these terms were by now anachronistic and could not describe in any accurate way the populations of Palestine in the fifth century B.C., why not marry Ashdodites? This thinking too is scorned (cf. 13:23), and for "Canaanites" *et al.* Nehemiah's community reads "the peoples of the land", thus rightly sensing the *intention* of the law.

The same principle is at work in the regulations for the temple provision. The half-shekel levy for the Temple (Exod. 30:11–16) (here re-calculated as a third because of a different system of evaluating the shekel), becomes for the first time a regular, annual tax on the whole population. Clearly, the need to supply the Temple created such urgent demands that new ways were sought of doing it, and they were not shirked. Similarly, there is nowhere in the law an actual levy on *wood*. Yet it was clear that wood was needed for the sacrificial fire (Lev. 1:17), and so wood there would be (v. 34). Furthermore, the list of offerings in verses 35–37 appears to take a maximal view of what the law requires. There are basically five kinds: first fruits (v. 35; cf. Exod. 23:19), firstlings (v. 36; cf. Exod. 13:11–13), choice produce, or the "first" (v. 37; cf. Deut. 26:2), contributions (v. 37—offerings that were essentially voluntary, on occasions of thanksgiving etc.; cf. Lev. 7:32, where the same word is translated "offering"), and tithes (v. 37; cf. Num. 18:21–26). The various laws on offerings in the Pentateuch leave a considerable degree of unclarity— especially to generations removed from the original practices— about how they all related to each other. Leaving nothing to chance, Nehemiah's community adds them all together. The gathering of the tithe has become systematic, with the Levite—the chief beneficiary—permitted to take the initiative (v. 37) rather than leaving it to the donor.

The people's pledge, then, was not the rigmarole of lip-service. It was the acceptance of a heavy burden. When they declared: "We will not neglect the house of our God" (v. 39), they were embarking on a path, to use a term more characteristic of the New Testament, of discipleship. For modern Christians—for whom the service of God is not chiefly expressed in furnishing the rituals of a temple—there is also a cost in discipleship. Do we regard the best of all we have, in terms of material wealth and natural endowment, as belonging first of all to God? Do we seek to apply God's standards with rigour, and a sense of how they apply to the situation in which we are now? The idea that much of the Bible is "out of date" is little better than an excuse for not listening to it. Those who would do God's will have met the first and most important condition for being able to apply this ancient book today.

SETTLEMENT

Nehemiah 11:1–36

¹Now the leaders of the people lived in Jerusalem; and the rest of the people cast lots to bring one out of ten to live in Jerusalem in the holy city, while nine tenths remained in the other towns. ²And the people blessed all the men who willingly offered to live in Jerusalem.

³These are the chiefs of the province who lived in Jerusalem; but in the towns of Judah every one lived on his property in their towns: Israel, the priests, the Levites, the temple servants, and the descendants of Solomon's servants. ⁴And in Jerusalem lived certain of the sons of Judah and of the sons of Benjamin. Of the sons of Judah: Athaiah the son of Uzziah, son of Zechariah, son of Amariah, son of Shephatiah, son of Ma-halalel, of the sons of Perez; ⁵and Ma-aseiah the son of Baruch, son of Col-hozeh, son of Hazaiah, son of Adaiah, son of Joiarib, son of Zechariah, son of the Shilonite. ⁶All the sons of Perez who lived in Jerusalem were four hundred and sixty-eight valiant men.

⁷And these are the sons of Benjamin: Sallu the son of Meshullam,

son of Joed, son of Pedaiah, son of Kolaiah, son of Ma-aseiah, son of Ithi-el, son of Jeshaiah. ⁸And after him Gabbai, Sallai, nine hundred and twenty-eight. ⁹Joel the son of Zichri was their overseer; and Judah the son of Hassenuah was second over the city.

¹⁰Of the priests: Jedaiah the son of Joiarib, Jachin, ¹¹Seraiah the son of Hilkiah, son of Meshullam, son of Zadok, son of Meraioth, son of Ahitub, ruler of the house of God, ¹²and their brethren who did the work of the house, eight hundred and twenty-two; and Adaiah the son of Jeroham, son of Pelaliah, son of Amzi, son of Zechariah, son of Pashhur, son of Malchijah, ¹³and his brethren, heads of fathers' houses, two hundred and forty-two; and Amashsai, the son of Azarel, son of Ahzai, son of Meshillemoth, son of Immer, ¹⁴and their brethren, mighty men of valour, a hundred and twenty-eight; their overseer was Zabdi-el the son of Haggedolim.

¹⁵And of the Levites: Shemaiah the son of Hasshub, son of Azrikam, son of Hashabiah, son of Bunni; ¹⁶and Shabbethai and Jozabad, of the chiefs of the Levites, who were over the outside work of the house of God; ¹⁷and Mattaniah the son of Mica, son of Zabdi, son of Asaph, who was the leader to begin the thanksgiving in prayer, and Bakbukiah, the second among his brethren; and Abda the son of Shammu-a, son of Galal, son of Jeduthun. ¹⁸All the Levites in the holy city were two hundred and eighty-four.

¹⁹The gatekeepers, Akkub, Talmon and their brethren, who kept watch at the gates, were a hundred and seventy-two. ²⁰And the rest of Israel, and of the priests and the Levites, were in all the towns of Judah, every one in his inheritance. ²¹But the temple servants lived on Ophel; and Ziha and Gishpa were over the temple servants.

²²The overseer of the Levites in Jerusalem was Uzzi the son of Bani. son of Hashabiah, son of Mattaniah, son of Mica, of the sons of Asaph, the singers, over the work of the house of God. ²³For there was a command from the king concerning them, and a settled provision for the singers, as every day required. ²⁴And Pethahiah the son of Meshezabel, of the sons of Zerah the son of Judah, was at the king's hand in all matters concerning the people.

²⁵And as for the villages, with their fields, some of the people of Judah lived in Kiriath-arba and its villages, and in Dibon and its villages, and in Jekabzeel and its villages, ²⁶and in Jeshua and in Moladah and Beth-pelet, ²⁷in Hazarshual, in Beer-sheba and its villages, ²⁸in Ziklag, in Meconah and its villages, ²⁹in En-rimmon, in Zorah, in Jarmuth, ³⁰Zanoah, Adullam, and their villages, Lachish

and its fields, and Azekah and its villages. So they encamped from Beer-sheba to the valley of Hinnom. [31]The people of Benjamin also lived from Geba onward, at Michmash, Aija, Bethel and its villages, [32]Anathoth, Nob, Ananiah, [33]Hazor, Ramah, Gittaim, [34]Hadid, Zeboim, Neballat, [35]Lod, and Ono, the valley of craftsmen. [36]And certain divisions of the Levites in Judah were joined to Benjamin.

There follows a long section consisting largely of lists of people who occupied the land at various times from Zerubbabel (12:1) down to Ezra and Nehemiah (12:26). This is occasioned by the issue which was first introduced in 7:4 and is now taken up again in 11:1–2. Following the completion of the walls there were not enough people to populate Jerusalem. A right balance had to be achieved in order to make the holy city viable. The list in chapter 7, of those who had returned at first from Babylon, had laid out the raw material, as it were, for the solution of the problem. The list which now appears (specifically that of chapter 11) pictures the spread of population after Nehemiah's measure to bring people to Jerusalem. Verses 4–6 name numbers of the tribe of Judah who went to live there, followed by Benjaminites (vv. 7–9), then priests, Levites, gatekeepers and the officials (as far as v. 24). The remainder of the chapter relates to the population of outlying parts of Judah. It is often noted that Jewish population is surprisingly far-flung, as far even as Beersheba (11:30), which, though belonging within the classical borders of the land, might have been presumed to be at this time in the sphere of influence of Geshem the Arab. The picture of a reoccupied Jerusalem, surrounding by outlying villages and towns which are traditional border-posts of Judah, subtly suggests a re-emergence of the old kingdom: just what Sanballat, Tobiah and Geshem had feared.

The picture is strengthened by the first two verses, which describe the means by which the city was populated. The aim was to achieve a ratio of one person in Jerusalem for every nine in the outlying areas (v. 1). It seems that some *volunteered* to live in Jerusalem (v. 2). The decision about how the numbers should be made up was then taken by lot (a way of discovering the will of God in the matter and ensuring that there were no grounds for envy or complaint). Whether the lot had to be cast to make up the numbers by coercion or to keep them down because of a surfeit of volunteers, or whether verse 2 simply means that those who were selected were also willing, is unclear.

In any case, some or all of those who went to live in Jerusalem "willingly offered", and were blessed by the people. We have noticed in connection with chapter 7 that many clearly regarded it as a matter of sacrifice to live in the city—whether from attachment to ancestral homesteads, or from the fact that the terrain around Jerusalem is less hospitable than in many other more fertile parts of Judah. There were, as far as we know, no "re-settlement grants" or other inducements of the sort that have been on offer in Britain in connection with the development of new towns. Those who went simply subordinated personal interest to the good of the people as a whole. The fine balance between individual assent and prompting from the community is analogous to what happens, rightly, in the Church, when individuals feel their suitability for a particular role, and at the same time have their talent "spotted" by others. The Church has, to an extent, a directive role in such matters. Yet it should harmonize with the individual's own perceptions.

The terms of verse 2 suggest a further point. They resemble strongly those of Judg. 5:2, 9, in the ancient song of Deborah. There too the people "offered themselves willingly", and there is a call to "bless the Lord'. It is quite likely that the author of Nehemiah had these verse in Judges in mind when he wrote. If so, he may have been hinting at the theme of the Lord as warrior and as victor over all his enemies which characterizes the song. The peopling of Jerusalem was another step—by the willing obedience of the people—towards a greater fulfilment of God's promises of redemption than had yet been experienced by the returned exiles.

DEDICATION

Nehemiah 12:1–13:3

[1]These are the priests and the Levites who came up with Zerubbabel

the son of She-alti-el, and Jeshua: Seraiah, Jeremiah, Ezra, ²Amariah, Malluch, Hattush, ³Shecaniah, Rehum, Meremoth, ⁴Iddo, Ginnethoi, Abijah, ⁵Mijamin, Ma-adiah, Bilgah, ⁶Shemaiah, Joiarib, Jedaiah, ⁷Sallu, Amok, Hilkiah, Jedaiah. These were the chiefs of the priests and of their brethren in the days of Jeshua.

⁸And the Levites: Jeshua, Binnui, Kadmi-el, Sherebiah, Judah, and Mattaniah, who with his brethren was in charge of the songs of thanksgiving. ⁹And Bakbukiah and Unno their brethren stood opposite them in the service. ¹⁰And Jeshua was the father of Joiakim, Joiakim the father of Eliashib, Eliashib the father of Joiada, ¹¹Joiada the father of Jonathan, and Jonathan the father of Jaddu-a.

¹²And in the days of Joiakim were priests, heads of fathers' houses: of Seraiah, Meraiah; of Jeremiah, Hananiah; ¹³of Ezra, Meshullam; of Amariah, Jehohanan; ¹⁴of Malluchi, Jonathan; of Shebaniah, Joseph; ¹⁵of Harim, Adna; of Meraioth, Helkai; ¹⁶of Iddo, Zechariah; of Ginnethon, Meshullam; ¹⁷of Abijah, Zichri; of Miniamin, of Moadiah, Piltai; ¹⁸of Bilgah, Shammu-a; of Shemaiah, Jehonathan; ¹⁹of Joiarib, Mattenai; of Jedaiah, Uzzi; ²⁰of Sallai, Kallai; of Amok, Eber; ²¹of Hilkiah, Hashabiah; of Jedaiah, Nethanel.

²²As for the Levites, in the days of Eliashib, Joiada, Johanan, and Jaddu-a, there were recorded the heads of fathers' houses; also the priests until the reign of Darius the Persian. ²³The sons of Levi, heads of fathers' houses, were written in the Book of the Chronicles until the days of Johanan the son of Eliashib. ²⁴And the chiefs of the Levites: Hashabiah, Sherebiah, and Jeshua the son of Kadmi-el, with their brethren over against them, to praise and to give thanks, according to the commandment of David the man of God, watch corresponding to watch. ²⁵Mattaniah, Bakbukiah, Obadiah, Meshullam, Talmon, and Akkub were gatekeepers standing guard at the storehouses of the gates. ²⁶These were in the days of Joiakim the son of Jeshua son of Jozadak, and in the days of Nehemiah the governor and of Ezra the priest the scribe.

²⁷And at the dedication of the wall of Jerusalem they sought the Levites in all their places, to bring them to Jerusalem to celebrate the dedication with gladness, with thanksgiving and with singing, with cymbals, harps and lyres. ²⁸And the sons of the singers gathered together from the circuit round Jerusalem and from the villages of the Netophathites; ²⁹also from Beth-gilgal and from the region of Geba and Azmaveth; for the singers had built for themselves villages around

Jerusalem. [30]And the priests and the Levites purified themselves; and they purified the people and the gates and the wall.

[31]Then I brought up the princes of Judah upon the wall, and appointed two great companies which gave thanks and went in procession. One went to the right upon the wall to the Dung Gate; [32]and after them went Hoshaiah and half of the princes of Judah, [33]and Azariah, Ezra, Meshullam, [34]Judah, Benjamin, Shemaiah, and Jeremiah, [35]and certain of the priests' sons with trumpets: Zechariah the son of Jonathan, son of Shemaiah, son of Mattaniah, son of Micaiah, son of Zaccur, son of Asaph; [36]and his kinsmen, Shemaiah, Azarel, Milalai, Gilalai, Maai, Nethanel, Judah, and Hanani, with the musical instruments of David the man of God; and Ezra the scribe went before them. [37]At the Fountain Gate they went up straight before them by the stairs of the city of David, at the ascent of the wall, above the house of David, to the Water Gate on the east.

[38]The other company of those who gave thanks went to the left, and I followed them with half of the people, upon the wall, above the Tower of the Ovens, to the Broad Wall, [39]and above the Gate of Ephraim, and by the Old Gate, and by the Fish Gate and the Tower of Hananel and the Tower of the Hundred, to the Sheep Gate; and they came to a halt at the Gate of the Guard. [40]So both companies of those who gave thanks stood still in the house of God, and I and half of the officials with me; [41]and the priests Eliakim, Ma-aseiah, Miniamin, Micaiah, Eli-o-enai, Zechariah, and Hananiah, with trumpets; [42]and Ma-aseiah, Shemaiah, Eleazar, Uzzi, Jehohanan, Malchijah, Elam, and Ezer. And the singers sang with Jezrahiah as their leader. [43]And they offered great sacrifices that day and rejoiced, for God had made them rejoice with great joy; the women and children also rejoiced. And the joy of Jerusalem was heard afar off.

[44]On that day men were appointed over the chambers for the stores, the contributions, the first fruits, and the tithes, to gather into them the portions required by the law for the priests and for the Levites according to the fields of the towns; for Judah rejoiced over the priests and the Levites who ministered. [45]And they performed the service of their God and the service of purification, as did the singers and the gatekeepers, according to the command of David and his son Solomon. [46]For in the days of David and Asaph of old there was a chief of the singers, and there were songs of praise and thanksgiving to God. [47]And all Israel in the days of Zerubbabel and in the days of Nehemiah gave the daily portions for the singers and the gatekeepers; and they

set apart that which was for the Levites; and the Levites set apart that which was for the sons of Aaron.

[1]On that day they read from the book of Moses in the hearing of the people; and in it was found written that no Ammonite or Moabite should ever enter the assembly of God; [2]for they did not meet the children of Israel with bread and water, but hired Balaam against them to curse them—yet our God turned the curse into a blessing. [3]When the people heard the law, they separated from Israel all those of foreign descent.

(i)

The first twenty-six verses consist of two separate lists of priests and Levites, one from the time of Zerubbabel (vv. 1–11), and one (vv. 12–26) dating from a generation later (since the Joiakim of v. 12 is presumably the son of Jeshua mentioned in v. 10, who was himself Zerubbabel's contemporary). The whole chapter seems concerned to show that the provision for the work of the Temple continued properly from the time of Zerubbabel down to that of Ezra and Nehemiah (vv. 26, 47). The link is also established with David (vv. 24, 45–46), who had appointed the Levites to their various roles, including those of gate-keeping and singing, but with the common and over-arching duty of giving the lead in praise and thanksgiving (v. 24, cf. 1 Chr. 23:30).

(ii)

The Levites' responsibility for thanksgiving leads neatly into the ceremony described in verses 27–43, in which thanksgiving is the dominant note (v. 31). The Levites who dwell in the countryside, therefore, are brought in, equipped with all the musical apparatus of praise, to prepare themselves and the people for the great occasion (v. 30). Their "purification" will have taken particular ritual form, involving perhaps fasting, abstention from sexual intercourse and the washing of garments; cf. Exod. 19:10, 14–15. The gates and walls were purified too, in some appropriate way which is not specified.

The ceremony itself consisted of a procession in two companies round the top of the walls, beginning together probably at the Valley Gate (on the south-west side) and converging at a point on the north-east near the Temple, which they then entered. (See again the plan of Nehemiah's city.) The group that went to the right, i.e. anti-clockwise (vv. 31–37), was led by Ezra (v. 36), and Nehemiah went with that which went to the left (v. 38). Along with them went "the princes of Judah" (v. 31). Here, as in the great ceremony of confession and renewal, the whole community is present (at least representatively) from the top down. All classes—those who give thanks, leaders of the community, priests, music-makers—appear to be represented in each group.

How much the purpose of the ceremony is to give thanks appears from the fact that each company is led by a group which is simply called a "thanksgiving" (RSV has to paraphrase to "company of those who gave thanks", for the sake of clarity). The procession is thus reminiscent of those which are mentioned in certain Psalms (e.g. Ps. 68:24—notice "the princes of Judah" in that context also, v. 27), where a note of praise is also struck. (This does not mean that *all* such processions were identical to that of Nehemiah, which was particularly related to the wall-building. Yet the event here may give some idea of the *kind* of background against which many of the Psalms were sung.)

THE JOY OF JERUSALEM

Nehemiah 12:1–13:3 (*cont'd*)

(iii)

When the two groups converge in the Temple the two motifs which have dominated the Books of Ezra and Nehemiah—viz. Temple and walls—are brought together. Many commentators have found it curious that the dedication of the walls should be so far removed from their completion (6:15), and have wondered whether the two events did not originally stand much closer together. There is an excellent logic in the order of the material as it stands, however. It is clear from the Books of Ezra and Nehemiah together that the walls are not an end in themselves. Yet had their official dedication come immediately upon their completion, precisely this impression might have been given.

The imminence of the seventh month, with its own cultic demands, had suggested a solution to the problem, for it produced a golden opportunity to set the walls in their proper perspective. A preliminary time of rejoicing—in the people's homes but not in the Temple (8:12)—would suffice as an interim measure, thus allowing the great act of confession and self-dedication (chapters 9, 10) to precede the climactic ceremony. When the people march on the walls to the Temple they do so *after* having placed the *Temple* once again at the centre of their thoughts (10:32–39). The walls thus appear for what they are: not a monument to the strength of Judah—heaven forbid!—but God's gift for the protection and perpetuation of his name in the world. The organization of events following the completion of the walls, therefore, was calculated to guard against one of the perennial threats to the people of God, namely the confusion of those gifts which he has given for its general good and for its path to holiness (cf. Eph. 4:11–14) with personal accomplishment.

(iv)

When the people come together in the Temple their mood is one of joy. Lest we should overlook the fact, Nehemiah uses the word (joy/rejoice) five times in verse 43. He thus identifies and marks out what was the chief characteristic of Old Testament religion. Joy was and is the only right response to the perception that God is good. It is no accident that the joy of Jerusalem is experienced in an act of worship, in which the exiles' true situation as a people that owes its life and allegiance to God is fully recognized and accepted. So it was in chapter 8, when the rejoicing followed the reading of God's word. Similarly, the apostle Paul would say: "Rejoice *in the Lord* always; again I will say, Rejoice" (Phil. 4:4): and this out of imprisonment and into a situation of persecution! If the joy of Nehemiah's Jerusalem seems alien and Paul's unnatural, it is simply a measure of the difficulty experienced by a rich western world in finding well-being in godliness itself. What Nehemiah and Paul knew—in direct contrast to the modern doctrine that he who acquires most and succeeds best is happiest—is that joy, like love, peace, self-control etc. (cf. Gal.

5:22), is *spiritual*. The people rejoiced "for God had made them rejoice" (v. 43).

(v)

Verses 44–13:3 correspond to the undertaking in 10:30–39 to maintain religious purity. The offerings in verse 44 are first enumerated there (10:37). We now find that they were in fact given, something which could not be taken for granted at many periods in Israel's history. (A very different picture is painted in Mal. 1.) The proper provision for the priesthood depended upon a readiness to give. When they were well provided for it was a sign of religious conscientiousness in Judah (v. 44).

The faithfulness of the clergy too (v. 45) is a matter for note. Driven, perhaps, to make a priority of personal interest by their countrymen's inclination to negligence, they themselves often applied mediocre standards in their sacred work. (The complaints of Malachi are in fact addressed predominantly to *them*.) Here, however, they match the vision of David and Solomon (contained in 1 Chr. 23–26; for Asaph, v. 46, see in particular 1 Chr. 25, and various Psalms, viz. 50, 73–83), and fulfil the requirements of the law (with v. 47*b*, cf. Num. 18: 21–26).

The opening verses of chapter 13 really belong with chapter 12. They are in the same vein, recalling the commitment made in 10:30, and closely following Deut. 23:3–5. Ammonites and Moabites are here lumped together, though it was strictly speaking the Moabites only who had hired Balaam (Num. 22–24). The ancient law, here as elsewhere, is in fact applied to *all* who were not of Israelite descent. The terms of the law of Deuteronomy that is invoked here suggest that the measure taken was exclusion from the cultic assembly. That is, it was a different measure from the mass divorce organized by Ezra thirteen years earlier. The fact that the problem still existed may mean that that plan had encountered difficulties because of mixed marriages generations back. This may have been a compromise, produced by the same concern but stopping short of the huge social disruption that rigorous exclusion would have required.

Finally, it needs to be said again that, presumably, neither the measure of Ezra nor this of Nehemiah was intended to foreclose the possibility of becoming "Israelite" by conversion. cf. again Ezra 6:21, and the conversion and acceptance of Ruth the Moabitess (Ruth 1:16–17).

The picture of Judah in 12:44–13:3, therefore, is one of devoted service and worship. *One* of the twin climaxes of the Books of Ezra and Nehemiah has been reached. The Temple is up. The walls surround it. The enemy is at bay. The community epitomizes the relationship between self-giving and joy. Here is one of the ever-present possibilities for the people of God.

EPILOGUE—I

Nehemiah 13:4–31

⁴Now before this, Eliashib the priest, who was appointed over the chambers of the house of our God, and who was connected with Tobiah, ⁵prepared for Tobiah a large chamber where they had previously put the cereal offering, the frankincense, the vessels, and the tithes of grain, wine, and oil, which were given by commandment to the Levites, singers, and gatekeepers, and the contributions for the priests. ⁶While this was taking place I was not in Jerusalem, for in the thirty-second year of Artaxerxes king of Babylon I went to the king. And after some time I asked leave of the king ⁷and came to Jerusalem, and I then discovered the evil that Eliashib had done for Tobiah, preparing for him a chamber in the courts of the house of God. ⁸And I was very angry, and I threw all the household furniture of Tobiah out of the chamber. ⁹Then I gave orders and they cleansed the chambers; and I brought back thither the vessels of the house of God, with the cereal offering and the frankincense.

¹⁰I also found out that the portions of the Levites had not been given to them; so that the Levites and the singers, who did the work, had fled each to his field. ¹¹So I remonstrated with the officials and said, "Why is the house of God forsaken?" And I gathered them together and set them in their stations. ¹²Then all Judah brought the tithe of the grain, wine, and oil into the storehouses. ¹³And I appointed as treasurers over the storehouses Shelemiah the priest, Zadok the scribe, and Pedaiah of the Levites, and as their assistant Hanan the son of Zaccur,

son of Mattaniah, for they were counted faithful; and their duty was to distribute to their brethren. ¹⁴Remember me, O my God, concerning this, and wipe not out my good deeds that I have done for the house of my God and for his service.

¹⁵In those days I saw in Judah men treading wine presses on the sabbath, and bringing in heaps of grain and loading them on asses; and also wine, grapes, figs, and all kinds of burdens, which they brought into Jerusalem on the sabbath day; and I warned them on the day when they sold food. ¹⁶Men of Tyre also, who lived in the city, brought in fish and all kinds of wares and sold them on the sabbath to the people of Judah, and in Jerusalem. ¹⁷Then I remonstrated with the nobles of Judah and said to them, "What is this evil thing which you are doing, profaning the sabbath day? ¹⁸Did not your fathers act in this way, and did not our God bring all this evil on us and on this city? Yet you bring more wrath upon Israel by profaning the sabbath."

¹⁹When it began to be dark at the gates of Jerusalem before the sabbath, I commanded that the doors should be shut and gave orders that they should not be opened until after the sabbath. And I set some of my servants over the gates, that no burden might be brought in on the sabbath day. ²⁰Then the merchants and sellers of all kinds of wares lodged outside Jerusalem once or twice. ²¹But I warned them and said to them, "Why do you lodge before the wall? If you do so again I will lay hands on you." From that time on they did not come on the sabbath. ²²And I commanded the Levites that they should purify themselves and come and guard the gates, to keep the sabbath day holy. Remember this also in my favour, O my God, and spare me according to the greatness of thy steadfast love.

²³In those days also I saw the Jews who had married women of Ashdod, Ammon, and Moab; ²⁴and half of their children spoke the language of Ashdod, and they could not speak the language of Judah, but the language of each people. ²⁵And I contended with them and cursed them and beat some of them and pulled out their hair; and I made them take oath in the name of God, saying, "You shall not give your daughters to their sons, or take their daughters for your sons or for yourselves. ²⁶Did not Solomon king of Israel sin on account of such women? Among the many nations there was no king like him, and he was beloved by his God, and God made him king over all Israel; nevertheless foreign women made even him to sin. ²⁷Shall we then listen to you and do all this great evil and act treacherously against our God by marrying foreign women?"

[28] And one of the sons of Jehoiada, the son of Eliashib the high priest, was the son-in-law of Sanballat the Horonite; therefore I chased him from me. [29] Remember them, O my God, because they have defiled the priesthood and the covenant of the priesthood and the Levites.

[30] Thus I cleansed them from everything foreign, and I established the duties of the priests and Levites, each in his work; [31] and I provided for the wood offering, at appointed times, and for the first fruits. Remember me, O my God, for good.

(i)

We have had a first climax to the Book of Nehemiah in the dedication of the walls through the great ceremony in the Temple (chapter 12). We now come to another, which is altogether more sombre, and all too reminiscent of the low note on which the Book of Ezra also ended (chapters 9, 10). This warning about defection from the ideal thus becomes one of the key points of the combined work.

Following the dedication of the walls, Nehemiah's movements are unclear. It is possible to interpret verse 6 to mean that he had spent twelve years continuously in Jerusalem, and only now returned to the king for the first time. Some think that 5:14 also implies this. Yet it is questionable whether he would have been given so long a leave of absence initially (2:6), and we have already suggested that his appointment of Hanani as chargé-d'affaires in Jerusalem (7:2) implied an imminent departure in the first year of his governorship. The likeliest scenario is that Nehemiah commuted a number of times between Jerusalem and the seat of Empire, and that during one of his absences—beginning in 433 B.C. (= the thirty-second year of Artaxerxes, v. 6)—the various abuses recorded in chapter 13 sprang up.

(ii)

The practices which Nehemiah discovered to his horror on his return were those, by and large, to which the community had succumbed in the past. (The exiles were what in the parlance of modern crime detection are called recidivists.) They fell into three categories: (a) failure to maintain the purity of religion and the sanctity of the Temple (vv. 4–14); (b) desecration of the sabbath (vv. 15–22); (c) intermarriage with foreign women (vv. 23ff.). These are all interconnected, because foreign influence is present in each.

The first and most serious offence is drawn to Nehemiah's attention by the circumstance that the old enemy Tobiah, with the connivance of a priest named Eliashib (vv. 4–5—probably a different person from the *high* priest of v. 28), has literally "occupied" the Temple. The closing verses of chapter 6 had led the reader to suspect that some such thing might happen. Where direct attempts to undermine the re-establishment of the people, including the threat of military action, had failed (chapters 4, 6), insidious infiltration had won a major victory. Tobiah has in fact taken over "a large chamber" (v. 5) principally used for storing temple supplies. This meant that the temple was inadequately equipped to maintain the regular activities of the cult, including the daily provision for the Levites (v. 10). How far the accommodation of Tobiah constituted an offence against the religion of Yahweh emerges from the fact that it had involved the removal of "the vessels of the house of God" from their place (vv. 5, 9). It was in large measure the return of these by Cyrus (Ezra 1:7), together with other facilities for rebuilding the Temple, that had betokened the re-establishment of the worship of Yahweh and the vindication of his people. The presence of Tobiah in the Temple belied all this and threatened to undo it. What was probably passed off as a friendly gesture to a "neighbour" was in fact the death-knell of the worship of God.

The next casualty was the sabbath (vv. 15–22). The sabbath day was not only for rest. Its other functions were (a) to allow time in busy lives for Israel to ponder God's goodness to her in the past (Exod. 20:10–11; Deut. 5:15); (b) to demonstrate that God could go on supplying her needs *despite* her temporary lapse from labour (cf. Exod. 16:4–5); and (c) to mark her out (by virtue of the *faith* required to relinquish the work of provision) from other nations. The last aspect had probably taken on particular significance in Babylon where there was little *else* to distinguish the

Jews from their neighbours. In the returned exiles' failure in this
respect—a direct abandonment of their commitment in 10:30–
31—non-Jews (men of Tyre, v. 16) were almost inevitably involved. Once again, the offence was not simply something on the
outskirts of the life of faith but at its heart. It was a denial of faith
in God and a decision to be like the nations.

The religious laxity implicit in the first two offences made it
inevitable that the old sin of intermarriage would recur (vv.
23–29): the practice which, more obviously than any other, must
lead to the gradual dissolution and disappearance of the Jews as a
people. With the involvement of a grandson of Eliashib, the high
priest, in an alliance with the family of Sanballat (v. 28) it becomes grimly evident how the offences paraded here are in reality
one and the same. Intermarriage strikes at the religious heart of
the people (symbolized in the high priest's family) and plays into
the hands of their enemies (Sanballat).

EPILOGUE—II

Nehemiah 13:4–31 (*cont'd*)

(iii)

Nehemiah, not surprisingly, is emphatic in his condemnation of
this repudiation of all he has striven for. At each stage he takes
measures to eradicate the ill. Tobiah's paraphernalia is bundled
angrily out (v. 8) (in a gesture which foreshadows Jesus' later
temple clearance, John 2:13ff.), and the Temple is cleansed of
everything unholy (v. 9). The Levites, who had fled to their
"fields" (referring to the small pieces of land surrounding their
cities in the country, on which they were permitted to raise some
animals, Num. 35:2) are restored to their position, and arrangements are made for them to receive once again their dues in
return for cultic service (vv. 11–13). Guards are set on the gates
to prevent sabbath abuse by traffic in merchandise (vv. 19, 22)
and a threat is issued which, by its effect (v. 21), says something
about the fearsomeness of the men. Most picturesque of all is
Nehemiah's treatment of those who have married foreign women

(v. 25)! Finally he banishes the errant grandson of Eliashib (v. 28).

His language is hardly less extreme. The people have forsaken the house of God (v. 11); they threaten to bring his wrath upon Israel (v. 18); they have acted treacherously against God (v. 27 —the word is *ma'al*, meaning a thorough-going renunciation of the ways of God, deserving of the direst punishment; cf. 1 Chr. 10:13–14, where "unfaithfulness" is *ma'al*). The clear implication of such strong language is that the covenant community, despite the near-incredible turns of events which reinstated them in their land a century earlier, despite a recommitment to the Lord which was now more than a decade past, could not presume upon God's goodness. It is a message which recalls that of the prophets. The Lord had been merciful indeed; but his salvation of Israel was a salvation *into* service and obedience. A covenant between God and a people that was god-less was a nonsense and could hold no future. For these reasons Nehemiah attempts to re-establish the conditions of chapters 10 and 12. He puts the people under oath once more (v. 25; cf. 10:29), and makes provision for the regular service of the Temple (vv. 30–31; cf. 10:32ff., 12:44ff.).

(iv)

The final note in Ezra–Nehemiah is thus one of ambiguity. We may wonder how the people who had so exuberantly celebrated the completion of the defences against the enemy came so readily to accept the enemy's presence within the Temple and the high priest's family. How, indeed, could those who had committed themselves so solemnly to religious purity (chapter 10) so rapidly return to practices which were essentially irreligious? If we sense a certain desperation about Nehemiah's last efforts to put the house of Israel in order, a tiredness about the need yet again to bring back the wandering sheep to the right path, a feeling that there is no reason to think that this reform will be more successful than any other, a sense that after all he himself has done his best (vv. 14, 22*b*, 31*b*), then we may be catching the right meaning here.

Had our author wished to suggest that all was now well in Judah he could have stopped at 13:3. But he chose to finish on a bleak note. In reality this has been suggested since Ezra 1 when, as we saw, the return from Babylon was carefully *not* treated as the final glorious fulfilment of the prophet's hopes. Indeed at every moment of triumph in the book there has been a "but". Most notable was the ominous conclusion to Neh. 6, when the infamous Tobiah was down but clearly not out. The present chapter shows that he got to his feet to fight on. And even though his furniture lies on the street he will still have his friends in Jerusalem. The history of Judah from Nehemiah to Christ—so far as we know it—shows that Judaism would never for long be free of threat from the enemy within. (The Sadducees of Jesus' day were, by and large, influential priests who had imbibed freely at the springs of Graeco-Roman religion and mores for the sake of prestige with the overlords of *their* day.)

(v)

This leads us to make two final points about the message of Ezra–Nehemiah.

(a) *No complacency*

Our books cannot be dismissed as pessimistic. The release from Babylon is a sign of God's saving purposes for Israel, and the beginning at least of prophecy fulfilment. The building of the Temple and then the walls are further triumphs. There is, furthermore, much to learn, not only from the sprirituality of Ezra and Nehemiah themselves, but from the whole community in its moments of devotion, about the life of worship and service. *Yet* it is clear that the community's hold upon obedience was always tenuous. The moments of joy in the Lord were, apparently, moments indeed. The tendency to go into decline was always imminent. If Neh. 12 represents one of the ever-present possibilities for the people of God, so too does chapter 13. The Church can take nothing for granted. It is never reformed once-for-all, but rather—as the Reformers in the 16th century knew well—*semper reformanda* ("always needing to be reformed"), simply because of the perversity and inconstancy within human beings.

(b) *Pointers to New Covenant*

The second point is related to the first. It is the very inconstancy of human beings which makes us realize that no mere restoration of Jerusalem *could ever* be a final fulfilment of the Old Testament's prophecies. Something totally new would be required. And that new thing was the birth, life, death and resurrection of Jesus Christ: a man, at last, who could stand in the place of all Israel, and, because he was God, render perfect obedience. Only with him could the prophecies which the Books of Ezra and Nehemiah do *not* claim to have fulfilled (e.g. Isa. 60:1–3; 61:1–4) come to have meaning. The *in*ability of the chosen people of the Old Testament to meet the terms of the covenant in any definitive way, which our books so clearly illustrate, leads naturally into these statements of the New Testament which show the need for a new way of salvation apart from the law, which was, according to Paul, but "our custodian until Christ came, that we might be justified by faith" (Gal. 3:23–26; cf. Rom. 3:21). In that time there would be "neither Jew nor Greek" in the sight of God (Gal. 3:28); since salvation was no longer tied to a law of Israel, then God's "Israel" need no longer be a political nation, and it certainly need no longer be defined by a Temple or enclosed by walls.

Yet the things that happened to the Jews in the days of Cyrus and until the days of Artaxerxes are no mere irrelevancy in the history of salvation. Had the Jews not occupied their land and provided, at least, a focus for Judaism, how could their Messiah have come first of all to "the lost sheep of the house of Israel" (Matt. 10:6) in any recognizable way? There is joy in the Books of Ezra and Nehemiah which brings us close to the heart of God and shows us some of the possibilities of real piety. And there is sadness too—but the sadness points us to Christ.

ESTHER

INTRODUCTION

BACKGROUND

The Book of Esther has in common with Ezra–Nehemiah its
setting in the Persian period of Israel's history. The king in the
story, called Ahasuerus in most English translations, is better
known to most readers as Xerxes (486–465 B.C.), the head of a
mighty Empire which nevertheless met its match in Greece. With
the role played by a Persian king, however, the similarities with
Ezra–Nehemiah end. The action is set not in Jerusalem, but in
Susa, one of the three great royal seats (along with Babylon and
Ecbatana). Indeed there is no special concern for the Jerusalem
community at all, as distinct from Jews throughout the Empire in
general, even though the action occurs at a time when that community was in a parlous state, and despite the fact that in Ezra–
Nehemiah the whole future of the Jewish people seems to depend
on the outcome of their particular struggle. Rather, the Book of
Esther shows us that the Jews of the Diaspora—i.e. those Jews
who did *not* return to Jerusalem following Cyrus' decree—were
still counted as God's people and had a role to play in the future of
the whole.

THEOLOGY

The story—of a Jewish girl who, through favourable circumstances and her native wit, saves her people from destruction at
the hands of her enemies—is too well told in the narrative itself to
be repeated in an Introduction. A word is necessary, rather, on its
reception down the ages within Judaism and by the Christian
Church. In short, both have been embarrassed by it—though

many Jews, for whom the pogrom has become an all-too-dreadful and regular reality, have come to hold it dear. The reasons for its dubiousness—which almost led to its non-acceptance as canonical scripture—were its non-mention of God, and accompanying high evaluation of human resources, and its supposed vengefulness.

These considerations do not mean, however, that the Book of Esther has no value for us. The latter charge is probably more apparent than real (as will emerge from the exposition of chapters 8 and 9). As for the fact that the name of God does not appear in the book, this does not mean that it is not "theological", or does not *teach* about God. The silence about God is quite deliberate, *not* to make the point that he is inactive in human situations, but on the contrary, that he is hidden behind *all* events. This is the implication of the numerous coincidental occurrences in the book. The story can become, therefore, a powerful statement about the reality of God in a world from which he *appears* to be absent.

HISTORICITY

Beyond the fact that Xerxes is a well-documented historical figure, there is little else in the Book of Esther that has been verified by secular historical research. Esther herself was unknown to the Greek historian Herodotus, who mentions only one Amestris as Xerxes' wife. It may be that Amestris was none other than Vashti, though we cannot be certain about this. (There have been attempts to show that Amestris and Vashti are two forms of the same name.) More promising is Mordecai, who may be identical with a high official known as Marduka, mentioned in Persian records. The other characters, like Esther, are known only from the story itself. Historical research, therefore, has to be content largely with noticing that the author was evidently very familiar with royal Susa and Persian customs. Some features have been held to argue *against* the historicity of the story. (If 2:6 means that Mordecai himself was deported from Jerusalem in 597 B.C., he would be well over 100 years old by the time of Xerxes' reign and his cousin Esther hardly in a position to win a beauty contest! On the other hand it is grammatically possible to suppose that 2:6 refers to Mordecai's grandfather Kish, which alleviates the problem and makes sense of the story.) Historical problems of this sort may not in the end be problems at all, and in fact, as with many historical narratives, it can be as difficult to show their *non-*historicity as their historicity. In our exposition we have supposed that the things narrated actually happened.

LITERARY NOTE

It remains to say that the Book of Esther is by any standards a brilliantly written story, to be savoured—even chuckled over (see e.g. on chapter 6). The reader who wishes to learn may mix business and pleasure here.

KING'S OPENING

Esther 1:1–11

[1]In the days of Ahasuerus, the Ahasuerus who reigned from India to Ethiopia over one hundred and twenty-seven provinces, [2]in those days when King Ahasuerus sat on his royal throne in Susa the capital, [3]in the third year of his reign he gave a banquet for all his princes and servants, the army chiefs of Persia and Media and the nobles and governors of the provinces being before him, [4]while he showed the riches of his royal glory and the splendour and pomp of his majesty for many days, a hundred and eighty days. [5]And when these days were completed, the king gave for all the people present in Susa the capital, both great and small, a banquet lasting for seven days, in the court of the garden of the king's palace. [6]There were white cotton curtains and blue hangings caught up with cords of fine linen and purple to silver rings and marble pillars, and also couches of gold and silver on a mosaic pavement of porphyry, marble, mother-of-pearl and precious stones. [7]Drinks were served in golden goblets, goblets of different kinds, and the royal wine was lavished according to the bounty of the king. [8]And drinking was according to the law, no one was compelled; for the king had given orders to all the officials of his palace to do as

every man desired. [9]Queen Vashti also gave a banquet for the women in the palace which belonged to King Ahasuerus.

[10]On the seventh day, when the heart of the king was merry with wine, he commanded Mehuman, Biztha, Harbona, Bigtha and Abagtha, Zethar and Carkas, the seven eunuchs who served King Ahasuerus as chamberlains, [11]to bring Queen Vashti before the king with her royal crown, in order to show the peoples and the princes her beauty; for she was fair to behold.

In the Books of Ezra and Nehemiah we became acquainted with kings only from afar, apart from a brief glimpse of Artaxerxes I in Neh. 2. Now, however, we meet King Xerxes (= Ahasuerus) "at home" and in party mood. The first impact made upon the reader is the sheer grandeur which surrounds the king's person. For the ruler over a vast territory—extending from Asia Minor down into Africa and across to the northern parts of India (v. 1)—nothing can be too magnificent. A 180-day banquet is larger than life. (It may have permitted successive waves of high-ranking Persians to come in from the provinces.) The richness of the palace—symbolizing that of the Empire—is colourfully described in verses 6–7. Hints of its lavishness have been provided by archaeologists, who have unearthed, among other things, golden goblets reminiscent of those in verse 7. The wealth of Persia has been revealed most strikingly in the spacious display of Persepolis, the *religious* capital built by Darius and Xerxes, and rather better preserved than Susa. Susa itself must have been impressive nonetheless. Verse 2 (RSV) refers to Susa "the capital". What is more particularly in view, however, is that part of the city which was given over to the palace complex, comprising residential areas for the king and his harem, large and delightful gardens, and the offices of the machinery of government. With assets like these, Xerxes could count on making the desired impression.

Display of royal grandeur, furthermore, is what the present chapter is chiefly about. It was precisely *on show* (v. 4). Nor was it only the princes in the provinces (real kinglets with minor courts of their own) who were to be impressed; the whole population of Susa was invited, as a finale to the six-month festivity (v. 5), to goggle in the king's private palace, a colonnaded pavilion with its own gardens, thus enjoying an access to things royal which must have been rare indeed; (cf. Esther's statement about the king's *in*accessibility, 4:11.) *Why* it was on show our author leaves us to speculate. It has been suggested that the purpose was to inspire Persians with confidence in preparation for the massive—and ultimately disastrous—military campaign against Greece (the only significant part of the world known to Xerxes that was not under his control) which began in the same year as the banquet (483 B.C.). Our author's purpose in preparing the high-budget set, however, is to provide the context for the story of Vashti, which in turn introduces that of Esther.

Vashti is very much part of the display. At an unspecified point in the royal stag-party (for since Vashti was staging her own women's event, v. 9, that is what it was) the king, intoxicated with wine (v. 10) and perhaps with thoughts of his own greatness, commands that his queen, in all her beauty and regalia, be added to the exhibits (v. 11).

In verses 1–11, then, we have what might be called the unacceptable face of human power. The Book of Esther is not *primarily* concerned to criticize that kind of power (in the way that certain other Old Testament books, notably Exodus, do). Yet it should not escape our notice that Ahasuerus—characterized by the ancient Greek historian Herodotus as impatient, hot-tempered and lecherous—furnishes one of the most colourful pictures in the Old Testament of power that has become self-serving and grotesque.

QUEEN'S DEFENCE

Esther 1:12–22

¹²But Queen Vashti refused to come at the king's command conveyed by the eunuchs. At this the king was enraged, and his anger burned within him.

¹³Then the king said to the wise men who knew the times—for this was the king's procedure toward all who were versed in law and judgment, ¹⁴the men next to him being Carshena, Shethar, Admatha, Tarshish, Meres, Marsena, and Memucan, the seven princes of Persia

and Media, who saw the king's face, and sat first in the kingdom—: ¹⁵"According to the law, what is to be done to Queen Vashti, because she has not performed the command of King Ahasuerus conveyed by the eunuchs?" ¹⁶Then Memucan said in presence of the king and the princes, "Not only to the king has Queen Vashti done wrong, but also to all the princes and all the peoples who are in all the provinces of King Ahasuerus. ¹⁷For this deed of the queen will be made known to all women, causing them to look with contempt upon their husbands, since they will say, 'King Ahasuerus commanded Queen Vashti to be brought before him, and she did not come.' ¹⁸This very day the ladies of Persia and Media who have heard of the queen's behaviour will be telling it to all the king's princes, and there will be contempt and wrath in plenty. ¹⁹If it please the king, let a royal order go forth from him, and let it be written among the laws of the Persians and the Medes so that it may not be altered, that Vashti is to come no more before King Ahasuerus; and let the king give her royal position to another who is better than she. ²⁰So when the decree made by the king is proclaimed throughout all his kingdom, vast as it is, all women will give honour to their husbands, high and low." ²¹This advice pleased the king and the princes, and the king did as Memucan proposed; ²²he sent letters to all the royal provinces, to every province in its own script and to every people in its own language, that every man be lord in his own house and speak according to the language of his people.

Queen Vashti's refusal to enter the king's presence is at least as bold a move as Esther's later entry without permission (5:1). It disturbs the complacent self-congratulation of the court festivities, and becomes the spring of the remarkable series of events which constitute the subject-matter of our book. Two related issues are raised by it which are central in all that follows. The first is the question of authority: whom to obey? The second is the nature of causation: what or who *really* controls what happens in the world?

(i)

The first of these has been introduced in verse 11. Had anyone asked King Xerxes where authority in Persia lay, he might have chosen to regard the question as treason rather than naïvety. The setting, even the language, of the whole chapter is designed to show that the king rules. One or more of the words "king", "queen" or "royal" occur in all but two verses of the chapter. This is partly in the nature of the case, since the scene is at court. Yet at times it looks a deliberate ploy of the author's, as at verse 7 ("the royal wine"), verse 18 ("the king's princes"), verse 22 ("the royal provinces"). Everything in Persia belonged to the king. Everything was *for* the king. One simply did not disobey the king. But Vashti did—and the fact that she was queen was not in principle a mitigating circumstance.

We can almost see Xerxes spluttering into his golden goblet as he is told that the queen will not come (v. 12). His reaction is interesting. He has recourse to the "law" (v. 13). In a sense he thus introduces a locus of authority in Persia which was distinct from himself. The well-known unalterability of the laws of Medes and Persians is proclaimed as a principle in our verses (v. 19). The effect of this was that the king was in a sense subject to laws that had already been made. This put a certain curb on arbitrary power—though of course it was a mixed blessing, because it could prohibit compassionate acts. Conversely, the king could always make *new* laws.

Nevertheless, the revolt of Vashti introduces the system of power in Persia as it will affect the course of events in the story. Because of the unalterability of laws, the decree which Haman later obtains against the Jews cannot be revoked by the mere exposure of Haman; hence the counter-decree of chapter 8. Persia's system of authority, therefore, has all the flaws of a flawed humanity, yet ultimately its human agents cannot control it.

The queen's protest introduces a further, rather different point. The arbitrariness and unreasonableness of the command addressed to her produces in her a divided loyalty: loyalty to the authority system at whose centre stood her demanding husband, and loyalty to her own dignity. She thus prepares for a far greater conflict of loyalties, involving a "law" of which, presumably, neither Xerxes nor Queen Vashti had an inkling.

(ii)

Our remarks about the nature of power in Persia have already suggested that there is an element in what makes things happen that is beyond the king's control. How much the nature of causation is an interest of our author at this point can only emerge fully as the story develops. We shall see, in due course, the huge discrepancy between what the king *thought* he was setting in train by deposing Vashti, and what his action would *actually* produce. He believed that he was striking a blow against an unruliness of women in Persia that might follow Vashti's disobedience (vv. 17–18. Notice also v. 22, where the charge to the men to speak the language of their people reflects the practice, in an Empire which embraced many races and in which intermarriage was common, of adopting the language of the husband in the home.) This is somewhat ironic, given that he himself is about to get Esther, who will soon be the real initiator of action in his *own* household. Nevertheless, to carry out his anti-feminist strike, he mobilizes the efficient Persian postal system to deliver a decree that looks at best foolish and unnecessary, and which in any case bears little relation to the issues that the strange events at his banquet have really raised, i.e. the impending confrontation between the Jews and their detractors. A king may indeed reign over a hundred and twenty-seven provinces and live in a luxury that befits his standing. But his real control over events, even his appreciation of what is going on around him, can be very limited indeed. Earthly authority, alas, leads too readily to pride; those who bear it in wisdom know that it is rightly accompanied by humility.

A FUNNY THING HAPPENED

Esther 2:1–23

¹After these things, when the anger of King Ahasuerus had abated, he remembered Vashti and what she had done and what had been decreed against her. ²Then the king's servants who attended him said, "Let beautiful young virgins be sought out for the king. ³And let the king appoint officers in all the provinces of his kingdom to gather all

the beautiful young virgins to the harem in Susa the capital, under custody of Hegai the king's eunuch who is in charge of the women; let their ointments be given them. ⁴And let the maiden who pleases the king be queen instead of Vashti." This pleased the king, and he did so.

⁵Now there was a Jew in Susa the capital whose name was Mordecai, the son of Jair, son of Shime-i, son of Kish, a Benjaminite, ⁶who had been carried away from Jerusalem among the captives carried away with Jeconiah king of Judah, whom Nebuchadnezzar king of Babylon had carried away. ⁷He had brought up Hadassah, that is Esther, the daughter of his uncle, for she had neither father nor mother; the maiden was beautiful and lovely, and when her father and her mother died, Mordecai adopted her as his own daughter. ⁸So when the king's order and his edict were proclaimed, and when many maidens were gathered in Susa the capital in custody of Hegai, Esther also was taken into the king's palace and put in custody of Hegai who had charge of the women. ⁹And the maiden pleased him and won his favour; and he quickly provided her with her ointments and her portion of food, and with seven chosen maids from the king's palace, and advanced her and her maids to the best place in the harem. ¹⁰Esther had not made known her people or kindred, for Mordecai had charged her not to make it known. ¹¹And every day Mordecai walked in front of the court of the harem, to learn how Esther was and how she fared.

¹²Now when the turn came for each maiden to go in to King Ahasuerus, after being twelve months under the regulations for the women, since this was the regular period of their beautifying, six months with oil of myrrh and six months with spices and ointments for women— ¹³when the maiden went in to the king in this way she was given whatever she desired to take with her from the harem to the king's palace. ¹⁴In the evening she went, and in the morning she came back to the second harem in custody of Sha-ashgaz the king's eunuch who was in charge of the concubines; she did not go in to the king again, unless the king delighted in her and she was summoned by name.

¹⁵When the turn came for Esther the daughter of Abihail the uncle of Mordecai, who had adopted her as his own daughter, to go in to the king, she asked for nothing except what Hegai the king's eunuch, who had charge of the women, advised. Now Esther found favour in the eyes of all who saw her. ¹⁶And when Esther was taken to King Ahasuerus into his royal palace in the tenth month, which is the month of Tebeth, in the seventh year of his reign, ¹⁷the king loved Esther more than all the women, and she found grace and favour in his sight more

than all the virgins, so that he set the royal crown on her head and made her queen instead of Vashti. [18]Then the king gave a great banquet to all his princes and servants; it was Esther's banquet. He also granted a remission of taxes to the provinces, and gave gifts with royal liberality.

[19]When the virgins were gathered together the second time, Mordecai was sitting at the king's gate. [20]Now Esther had not made known her kindred or her people, as Mordecai had charged her; for Esther obeyed Mordecai just as when she was brought up by him. [21]And in those days, as Mordecai was sitting at the king's gate, Bigthan and Teresh, two of the king's eunuchs, who guarded the threshold, became angry and sought to lay hands on King Ahasuerus. [22]And this came to the knowledge of Mordecai, and he told it to Queen Esther, and Esther told the king in the name of Mordecai. [23]When the affair was investigated and found to be so, the men were both hanged on the gallows. And it was recorded in the Book of the Chronicles in the presence of the king.

(i)

The story of Esther is a little like the plots of modern novels or films in which the reader/audience is slowly introduced to the characters, who appear at first to bear no relation to each other, but whose lives are ultimately interwoven in a complex way. The scene having been set in chapter 1, events *might* have unfolded in any number of ways. Their *actual* course is now determined by two coincidental circumstances.

The opening scene (vv. 1–4) follows naturally enough from the disgrace of Vashti. The king's servants, ever watchful for some new idea that would please him, suggest a kind of beauty contest, whose winner—and the king would be sole judge—would be queen. The servants thus cleverly facilitate an important affair of state and at the same time pander to the king's well-known interest in lovely women. (This latter characteristic is suggested not only by chapter 1 but also by non-biblical historical sources.)

There now follows a report of the first coincidental circumstance (vv. 5ff.). It so happened that a Jew named Mordecai and his cousin Esther (whom he had adopted) were living in Susa at the time. Their presence there is explained by the fact that Mordecai's grandfather, Kish, was among those who had been taken into exile in Babylon a century earlier. The family had evidently migrated, at some subsequent stage, to Susa. It so happened that Esther was beautiful, and that she was at just the age which made her a participant in the great royal beauty contest. (Participation was presumably compulsory.)

The author, though he leaves much *un*said in his character portrayals, is at some pains to suggest modesty of behaviour on Esther's part. The Jewish girl could not only please a king but also a, presumably disinterested, eunuch (v. 9). When she went before the king, in her turn (v. 15), she did so without ostentation, taking only what the occasion absolutely demanded and declining the gimmicks of beautification (v. 13). We are told nothing about whether Esther *wanted* to be queen. Such could hardly be the desire of a fastidious Jewish girl, nor indeed her cousin, in the light of the abhorrence with which intermarriage was regarded. (cf. Ezra 9–10. The same considerations would weigh with strict Jews in Susa as in Jerusalem.) Yet our author does not make an issue of this. He is more concerned to show how, in fact, events turned out so that the Jews in the Empire might be saved from their enemies. Esther's qualities were such that, even despite herself, she must become queen. Having done so she enters into that royal sphere (notice the "royal" terminology recurring in vv. 17–18) whose portrayal dominated chapter 1. Here as there we have a banquet (v. 18). This time, however, it is *Esther's* banquet. There is thus just a hint that the *character* of Esther now has some influence on the way things are in Persia.

(ii)

The second coincidental event is related in verses 21–23. Mordecai has been in close proximity to the palace ever since Esther was taken into the harem (v. 11). Verse 21 finds him sitting in the King's Gate. This location presupposes a degree of privilege on Mordecai's part, and suggests that he may have been a royal official of some sort. Again the author lets us speculate on this, as it does not serve the special interests of the story. We do not even know whether it had already been Mordecai's habit to sit at the King's Gate, or whether he has begun to do so only since Esther's entry to the harem. The fact that this location is different from "the court of the harem" (v. 11) suggests the former.

It is here, in any case, that Mordecai picks up an item of information which it was to the king's advantage to know. He thus becomes instrumental, via Esther, in saving the king's life. Xerxes thus "owes him one". At the end of chapter 2, then, even before the entry of Haman to the scene, there are two major factors in the situation which will ultimately stand the Jews in good stead: Esther is queen, and Mordecai, quite independently, is in favour.

(iii)

Even as Esther enters upon her queenly status and privileges the seeds are sown of her own version of the dilemma which faced her predecessor. For Vashti, the conflict of interest simply involved her personal dignity. For Esther it will involve her identity as a Jewess. The importance of this factor is suggested by the two-fold allusion to the fact that, on Mordecai's instructions, Esther suppressed it (vv. 10, 20). Nevertheless, Esther's Jewishness constitutes an alternative loyalty to her loyalty to her husband, which—both as wife and subject—was, in his eyes at least, absolute. It may be because of a hope that the two loyalties would never come into conflict that Mordecai had counselled silence on the matter of racial identity. We on the other hand may well speculate that, had the new queen been more open on the point, the king would never have given way to Haman's genocidal plans in chapter 3. The move was probably intended to protect Esther somehow. But it had the opposite effect. Not even Mordecai has such insight into the hidden things that determine destinies that he plays every card right!

(iv)

The problem of Jewish identity is taken a little further, however. If it implies a loyalty which the king might find incompatible with his interests, our author is at pains to show that that loyalty *need not conflict* with the duties of good citizenship. Mordecai's action on the king's behalf proves that being a Jew in Empire does not imply subversive aspirations. It is interesting that while the Persian Vashti (not to mention Bigthan and Teresh!) should be regarded as posing a threat to good order in Persia, the Jew Mordecai should be a supporter of it. Similarly, the people at large benefit from Esther's accession (v. 18b).

We do not have to approve of classical Asian despotism in order to see that there is a point here for all, at any time, who have ultimate commitments in the religious sense, and yet who must live under governments. Commitment is possible in different spheres. Those who, in modern times, deny any Christian interest in political processes cannot have read with sensitivity the stories not only of Mordecai, but also of Joseph and Daniel. A conflict of interest may indeed come, and *has* come to many. But each of us, until it does, can take to ourselves the exhortation which in God's name the prophet Jeremiah addressed to the exiles in Babylon to "seek the welfare of the city where I have sent you" (Jer. 29:7).

DILEMMA—I: MORDECAI

Esther 3:1–15

¹After these things King Ahasuerus promoted Haman the Agagite, the son of Hammedatha, and advanced him and set his seat above all the princes who were with him. ²And all the king's servants who were at the king's gate bowed down and did obeisance to Haman; for the king had so commanded concerning him. But Mordecai did not bow down or do obeisance. ³Then the king's servants who were at the king's gate said to Mordecai, "Why do you transgress the king's command?" ⁴And when they spoke to him day after day and he would not listen to them, they told Haman, in order to see whether Mordecai's words would avail; for he had told them that he was a Jew. ⁵And when Haman saw that Mordecai did not bow down or do obeisance to him, Haman was filled with fury. ⁶But he disdained to lay hands on Mordecai alone. So, as they had made known to him the people of Mordecai, Haman sought to destroy all the Jews, the people of Mordecai, throughout the whole kingdom of Ahasuerus.

⁷In the first month, which is the month of Nisan, in the twelfth year of King Ahasuerus, they cast Pur, that is the lot, before Haman day after day; and they cast it month after month till the twelfth month, which is

the month of Adar. [8]Then Haman said to King Ahasuerus, "There is a certain people scattered abroad and dispersed among the peoples in all the provinces of your kingdom; their laws are different from those of every other people, and they do not keep the king's laws, so that it is not for the king's profit to tolerate them. [9]If it please the king, let it be decreed that they be destroyed, and I will pay ten thousand talents of silver into the hands of those who have charge of the king's business, that they may put it into the king's treasuries." [10]So the king took his signet ring from his hand and gave it to Haman the Agagite, the son of Hammedatha, the enemy of the Jews. [11]And the king said to Haman, "The money is given to you, the people also, to do with them as it seems good to you."

[12]Then the king's secretaries were summoned on the thirteenth day of the first month, and an edict, according to all that Haman commanded, was written to the king's satraps and to the governors over all the provinces and to the princes of all the peoples, to every province in its own script and every people in its own language; it was written in the name of King Ahasuerus and sealed with the king's ring. [13]Letters were sent by couriers to all the king's provinces, to destroy, to slay, and to annihilate all Jews, young and old, women and children, in one day, the thirteenth day of the twelfth month, which is the month of Adar, and to plunder their goods. [14]A copy of the document was to be issued as a decree in every province by proclamation to all the peoples to be ready for that day. [15]The couriers went in haste by order of the king, and the decree was issued in Susa the capital. And the king and Haman sat down to drink; but the city of Susa was perplexed.

(i)

The character of Haman would be unbelievable had he not been replicated countless times in history and most appallingly in our own century. His introduction is abrupt. We hear of him for the first time even as we hear of his promotion to Prime Minister (v. 1)—and just when we might have expected preferment for Mordecai, following 2:21–23. (We do not know how soon after Mordecai's loyal act Haman caught the king's eye. Verse 7 shows that we have moved on nine years since chapter 1. But the author makes little of the chronology of events, preferring to show how they relate to each other in their meaning. The events of 2:21–23 may have been separated from those of 3:1ff. by years. But this

does not lessen the irony of them, and their proximity in the text
ensures that we shall not miss it.)

Once again the king lacks insight. He would have done better
to leave Haman in obscurity. Yet if the seeds are already sown of
ultimate Jewish triumph, there is a sense too in which opposition
to them—as a people with a supreme loyalty to God—must out.
(Notice the readiness of the king's servants to promote a conflict,
desiring perhaps to test which power is stronger, v. 4.) Suddenly
things are running badly for the Jews. The promotion of Haman
immediately produces the conflict of interest which Mordecai had
hoped to avoid. Everyone was bowing to Haman; Mordecai
could not (v. 2).

Mordecai's inability to bow to Haman can only be attributed to
his Jewishness. Indeed—coming clean now—he says as much to
those who enquire into what must have seemed very injudicious
behaviour (v. 4*b*). It is not immediately clear why his Jewishness
prohibited obeisance to a high official. It has often been pointed
out that Jews (or Israelites) *did* bow on other occasions (e.g. 1
Sam. 24:8). The reason probably is that Haman was an *Agagite*
(v. 1), i.e. a descendant of Agag, king of the Amalekites, who
were among Israel's oldest and bitterest enemies (Exod. 17:8ff.).
Agag himself had met a violent end at the hands of Samuel,
following a commission to King Saul to wipe out Amalek (1 Sam.
15:32–33). Mordecai's action, then, is probably to be explained
by his refusal to be subservient, as a Jew, to the ancient enemy.
The point is, in any case, that he *perceived* obeisance to Haman to
be impossible in view of his higher loyalty. He was thus in the
same position that Daniel was in when an embargo was laid upon
prayer to God (Dan. 6:6–9). Daniel must yet pray (Dan. 6:10);
and Mordecai must be faithful too to the God of his fathers, and
the present generation of his people.

DILEMMA—I: A FINAL SOLUTION?

Esther 3:1–15 (*cont'd*)

(ii)

Haman's furious reaction has nothing to do with principle, but is purely the offended pride of one who sees himself deprived of honour which he thinks is rightly his (v. 5). Perhaps there had been personal rivalry in the past. Perhaps, indeed, Haman knew the other to be no mean adversary. Rather than take him on directly, therefore (v. 6), he chose a response that was both more cunning and frighteningly unscrupulous.

Trusting his cause to the casting of lots (v. 7) (whether to determine the time when he should approach the king or the time of the pogrom is unclear), he brings his accusation (v. 8). Its mixture of truth and untruth, its ruthlessness and above all its ghastly modernness are chilling. It has four parts.

The *first*, namely that there is a certain people (not actually identified by Haman) scattered abroad in his kingdom, is unexceptionable. The *second*, that their laws are different from those of every other people, is a cunning half-truth. The reference is to the Jewish *Torah* (or Pentateuch), the possession of which did indeed, and does still, mark out the Jews from other nations. Furthermore, properly understood and followed, those very laws would have pointed every nation to God. Haman turns this truth against the Jews by using it to arouse the king's suspicions that they are disloyal. His *third* statement, inferring from the second that they do not obey the king's laws, is a direct lie. We the readers already know it to be such from the evidence of Mordecai's interest in the welfare and security of the king. The king, of course, has failed to put together the pieces of the jig-saw which would have enabled him to evaluate Haman's statement critically; and in any case, was not Haman his favourite? The lie, therefore, gains plausibility from the foundation which Haman has laid. Then *fourthly* comes his grim conclusion, with the smell of the gas-chambers about it, namely that it does not *profit* the king to tolerate such a people.

The attack is a masterly propaganda exercise. Haman has persuaded the king of three major untruths: that *he* is best fitted to be Prime Minister, though we know Mordecai is; that the Jews should be destroyed, though we know the queen herself is Jewish; that the Jews do not benefit the king, though we know that they

do. The one who is committed to untruth utterly convinces the
dull and credulous king, who wields the power. Every minority
community, with its own cultural distinctions, is vulnerable to this
kind of attack. For modern believers it may mean that they can
never persuade their secular contemporaries that they are
"reasonable" and responsible people, but may have to endure
unjust opprobrium as a kind of occupational—or rather con-
fessional—hazard. It is well to remember that the danger in which
the Jews now stood stemmed directly from Mordecai's explanation of his refusal to conform in terms of his Jewishness. He thus
sets an example to Christians too that we should be seen and
counted for what we are, and take the consequences.

(iii)
The king is convinced. The fabulous sum of money offered by
Haman in return for permission to wipe out the Jews (v. 9) is
declined (v. 11; the phrase "The money is given to you" effectively means "keep it!"). And Haman is given a free hand.

The remainder of the chapter describes the promulgation of
the decree. Once again the machinery of Empire is put in motion.
The postal couriers (v. 13) operated a system similar to the old
Pony Express, so familiar from "westerns". Riders were stationed at 24-hour intervals and could thus convey messages over
long distances very rapidly. They were used only for affairs of
state; they had a determination similar to that reflected in the
slogan "the mail must get through"; and the orders they bore
would be treated everywhere with the utmost seriousness. Verse
12 shows that no part of Empire would be missed. We can
imagine the glee of a Sanballat or a Geshem at an opportunity
such as this. The writing is thus on the wall for the Jews. The
object is nothing less than annihilation (v. 13*a*). The cold-blood-
edness of the decree becomes the more gruesome by the setting of
a date on which the pogrom is to be carried out (v. 13*b*).

At this point, Haman is on the crest of the wave. Yet he has
already made his fatal error. Unlike Mordecai, he has put his
trust in a "prince"—Ps. 146:3—who may well change again. And

behind his trust in Xerxes lies a deeper faith in a kind of *fate* which governs events; hence his resort to the lot (v. 7). Haman was neither the first nor the last to observe that there is an inscrutability in things which makes a mockery of human plans and strength. Here, in a sense, he recognizes something which the author of Esther is concerned to show. But again, there is a world of difference between recognizing that there is *something* that leads events more surely than men can, and knowing that that something is no blind fate but a personal and loving God.

(iv)

Significantly, the decree is not received with universal rapture. The king and Haman may sit down to drink (recalling the somewhat later unholy alliance of Pilate and Herod on another occasion when the "powers that be" were manipulated by those who hated the Truth; Luke 23:1–12, especially v. 12). But Susa is perplexed (v. 15). The king's people show greater understanding than he. *They* know how to choose between Mordecai and Haman. Haman's ascendancy in Persia is bad not only for the queen but for all Persians. It was right for Mordecai to act as a responsible citizen. But there is a world of difference between doing that and "putting [one's] trust in princes".

DILEMMA—II: ESTHER...

Esther 4:1–17

¹When Mordecai learned all that had been done, Mordecai rent his clothes and put on sackcloth and ashes, and went out into the midst of the city, wailing with a loud and bitter cry; ²he went up to the entrance of the king's gate, for no one might enter the king's gate clothed with sackcloth. ³And in every province, wherever the king's command and his decree came, there was great mourning among the Jews, with fasting and weeping and lamenting, and most of them lay in sackcloth and ashes.

⁴When Esther's maids and her eunuchs came and told her, the queen was deeply distressed; she sent garments to clothe Mordecai, so that he might take off his sackcloth, but he would not accept them. ⁵Then Esther called for Hathach, one of the king's eunuchs, who had been appointed to attend her, and ordered him to go to Mordecai to learn what this was and why it was. ⁶Hathach went out to Mordecai in the open square of the city in front of the king's gate, ⁷and Mordecai told him all that had happened to him, and the exact sum of money that Haman had promised to pay into the king's treasuries for the destruction of the Jews. ⁸Mordecai also gave him a copy of the written decree issued in Susa for their destruction, that he might show it to Esther and explain it to her and charge her to go to the king to make supplication to him and entreat him for her people. ⁹And Hathach went and told Esther what Mordecai had said. ¹⁰Then Esther spoke to Hathach and gave him a message for Mordecai, saying, ¹¹"All the king's servants and the people of the king's provinces know that if any man or woman goes to the king inside the inner court without being called, there is but one law; all alike are to be put to death, except the one to whom the king holds out the golden sceptre that he may live. And I have not been called to come in to the king these thirty days." ¹²And they told Mordecai what Esther had said. ¹³Then Mordecai told them to return answer to Esther, "Think not that in the king's palace you will escape any more than all the other Jews. ¹⁴For if you keep silence at such a time as this, relief and deliverance will rise for the Jews from another quarter, but you and your father's house will perish. And who knows whether you have not come to the kingdom for such a time as this?" ¹⁵Then Esther told them to reply to Mordecai, ¹⁶"Go, gather all the Jews to be found in Susa, and hold a fast on my behalf, and neither eat nor drink for three days, night or day. I and my maids will also fast as you do. Then I will go to the king, though it is against the law; and if I perish, I perish." ¹⁷Mordecai then went away and did everything as Esther had ordered him.

(i)

Superficially the action of chapter 4 can be summed up quite briefly. Mordecai, hearing of the decree, joins Jews everywhere in donning the attire of grief and goes to a point just outside the King's Gate. (He could not enter it in the garb of mourning. This, therefore, was as near to Esther as he could come.)

Esther, when the gravity of the situation has dawned upon her, at first resists Mordecai's instruction to appeal to the king on behalf of her people. Her reasons are given in verse 11. It comes as something of a surprise to us that the new queen who so enraptured Xerxes when he first saw her—and could still do so, as the next chapter will show—has not been called to his presence for a month. Here as in other matters we are not told why. The reasons for Esther's hesitation are clear enough, however. The structure of Persian authority set some store by the inaccessability of the king to any except those whom he chose to call to him. The seven princes of 1:14, who "saw the king's face", occupied a specially privileged position. Infringement of the etiquette by which the king's face was veiled from all others was tantamount to an act of treason. And to enforce the ban upon the over-bold a squad of men armed with axes stood about the throne ready to hack them down—unless the king in his mercy extended the golden sceptre to restrain them.

Esther's anxiety, therefore, was not misplaced. Mordecai responds by reminding her that a higher authority than kings governs in the matter. The issue, he urges, is not the saving of Esther's own skin. She will be as much endangered by her silence as by her intercession. The Jews will be saved whether or not she meets the call of the moment. But her own salvation may depend on whether she accepts the unique opportunity which is hers. Whether Mordecai's words are prophetic or merely rhetorical matters little. Esther takes the point and decides to act. From now on she is the chief initiator of action in the story, already directing Mordecai (v. 17), and soon the king also. The chapter ends on a note of suspense, however. The decisive confrontation has yet to be made.

DILEMMA—II: . . . AND GOD

Esther 4:1–17 (*cont'd*)

(ii)

The story can be told thus with only fleeting reference to the deeper issues which are at stake. These are two. The *first* concerns the reaction of Esther herself to the news of Mordecai's distress. From the start she attempts to close out the possibility that there is a serious issue to confront. Mordecai is in sackcloth and so she sends him clothes! Surely she knew better than that. Her action is what a prophet might have called "healing the wound of my people lightly" (Jer. 6:14). She wished not to know what would have been hurtful and threatening. All this is natural and in it Esther merely resembles most people most of the time. She, moreover, is subject to a king whose whim was law, and felt, no doubt, that responsible action of any sort was out of the question. It is to this feeling that she gives open expression in verse 11. Mordecai's task is to persuade her that just such action is not only not out of the question, but absolutely required of her, and at once.

Esther's ultimate compliance with Mordecai's demand is, therefore, a considerable moral victory. It involves a recognition that she is inescapably involved in a conflict between right and wrong in which she must take one side or the other. Taking the side of right (specifically standing up for the protection and vindication of God's people) will involve ultimate personal risk. This Mordecai has known all along (and no doubt it is with grief that he reveals to Esther the true nature of her situation, for that is arguably all he is doing). When Esther's thoughts turn to fasting, therefore (and implicitly, prayer) Mordecai might well have exclaimed, anticipating Professor Higgins: "By George, she's got it!" She has realized that she is in spritual conflict, and is arming herself as only a child of God can. When Esther utters the solemn words: "If I perish, I perish" (v. 16), we need not read them as the fatalism of one who has no hope, but as the determination which sees that faith permits only one course of action.

(iii)

The *second* issue which lies beneath the surface of chapter 4 is that which we have observed from time to time but which now comes to its climactic statement, namely, who or what disposes over the things that happen in the world, and how does human action relate to it? The whole Book of Esther is carefully designed to throw up this question in an acute form. On one level everything that happens can be directly attributed to some demonstrable cause. Esther becomes queen, for example, because Vashti was deposed. The decree goes out against the Jews because Mordecai would not bow to Haman. Yet we have constantly been aware that these explanations, though in one sense complete, are not exhaustive. There is another level of causality. For Haman this is expressed in his resort to the wretched Pur (3:7). For Mordecai, inheritor of the faith of his fathers, it must imply a belief in the God of Abraham, Isaac and Jacob, the God who had delivered his people from destruction countless times before, and supremely in the exodus, by the frustration of another great empire.

If this is so, the reader may well ask, why is it that the author of Esther so studiously avoids naming God in the book? Here if anywhere (v. 14) we might expect him to be named. Against the background of Israelite history Mordecai *can only* mean (a) that *God* has brought Esther to the present position in order to deliver his people, and (b) that if she will not do it then *God* will arrange it in some other way. Yet the thought is expressed in rather veiled terms. This is deliberate, and the reason, paradoxically, is precisely to *affirm* God's activity behind events.

Any observer of the world, ancient or modern, can in principle discern the immediate and superficial causes of things that happen. He *may*, furthermore, conclude from this that all things can be *sufficiently* explained in a natural way, thus denying that God acts—or exists—at all. The style in which Esther is written *acknowledges* the fact that there is often, or usually, no obvious sign that God is at work in the world. But the whole series of coincidences in the book are made to show very clearly that, nevertheless, natural explanations are never enough. There is a purposefulness behind events which the pagan acknowledges by his recourse to lots, but which the godly know to belong to the nature of their Creator and Redeemer (Prov. 16:4—which even suggests a place in God's purposes for Haman. Who knows whether, at some later stage in history, things might not have

turned out much worse for the Jews had they not come to a head
in the time of Esther?)

The Book of Esther, in its very tone, has much to say to a
modern world which has become accustomed to explaining things
apart from God. We in the 20th century are good at tracing causes
and effects, but poor at understanding the meaning of reality. For
the Christian the beginning of that pilgrimage is at the cross of
Christ, the supreme act of redemption by the very God whom
Mordecai trusted to deliver his people from the tyranny of
Haman.

(iv)

It remains to point out that the idea that God inevitably achieves
his purposes for his people in no way diminishes the need for
them to be fully and responsibly involved as he does so. This is
really just to remind the reader of what we said (at the beginning
of this section) about the need for Esther to come to terms with
reality and meet the need of the hour. The knowledge that God is
in control should not lead to resigned inactivity, but to the recognition that he commands, and the faith to follow wherever he
leads.

HALF MY KINGDOM

Esther 5:1–14

¹On the third day Esther put on her royal robes and stood in the inner
court of the king's palace, opposite the king's hall. The king was sitting
on his royal throne inside the palace opposite the entrance to the
palace; ²and when the king saw Queen Esther standing in the court,
she found favour in his sight and he held out to Esther the golden
sceptre that was in his hand. Then Esther approached and touched the
top of the sceptre. ³And the king said to her, "What is it, Queen
Esther? What is your request? It shall be given you, even to the half of
my kingdom." ⁴And Esther said, "If it please the king, let the king and
Haman come this day to a dinner that I have prepared for the king."
⁵Then said the king, "Bring Haman quickly, that we may do as Esther
desires." So the king and Haman came to the dinner that Esther had

prepared. ⁶And as they were drinking wine, the king said to Esther, "What is your petition? It shall be granted you. And what is your request? Even to the half of my kingdom, it shall be fulfilled." ⁷But Esther said, "My petition and my request is: ⁸If I have found favour in the sight of the king, and if it please the king to grant my petition and fulfil my request, let the king and Haman come tomorrow to the dinner which I will prepare for them, and tomorrow I will do as the king has said."

⁹And Haman went out that day joyful and glad of heart. But when Haman saw Mordecai in the king's gate, that he neither rose nor trembled before him, he was filled with wrath against Mordecai. ¹⁰Nevertheless Haman restrained himself, and went home; and he sent and fetched his friends and his wife Zeresh. ¹¹And Haman recounted to them the splendour of his riches, the number of his sons, all the promotions with which the king had honoured him, and how he had advanced him above the princes and the servants of the king. ¹²And Haman added, "Even Queen Esther let no one come with the king to the banquet she prepared but myself. And tomorrow also I am invited by her together with the king. ¹³Yet all this does me no good, so long as I see Mordecai the Jew sitting at the king's gate." ¹⁴Then his wife Zeresh and all his friends said to him, "Let a gallows fifty cubits high be made, and in the morning tell the king to have Mordecai hanged upon it; then go merrily with the king to the dinner." This counsel pleased Haman, and he had the gallows made.

(i)

Once Esther has made up her mind to risk all for her people, our author does not linger over the sequel. The tacit implication of the preceding chapter has been that faithful action on behalf of the Jews will meet its due reward. And sure enough, when Esther appears before the king in her royal splendour the beauty which first impressed him wins him again, and the golden sceptre is duly extended. The drama of this moment is passed over with little ado. In an important sense it has already been resolved in Esther's decision.

The opening verses of chapter 5 move quickly, rather, towards new drama. From the moment of Esther's entry into the inner court she has the air, not of a sacrificial victim, but of a queen. The phrase "put on royal robes" (v. 1) is literally "put on

royalty". And in the very act of extending to Esther the golden
sceptre we find the king offering her half the kingdom also (v. 3).
There is unquestionably an element of oriental exaggeration in
this. Kings were wont to make extravagant offers at such moments, more or less by way of a compliment, and without the
intention that they be taken literally. Both the offerer and the one
favoured knew that the real limits were less than what was
named. In a similar situation King Herod would later be embarrassed when pushed to his real limits by Herodias' daughter;
Mark 6:22ff. Xerxes himself, according to Herodotus, wriggled
in vain to extricate himself from a promise to a mistress which cost
him a beautiful robe made for him by Queen Amestris. (On
Amestris see Introduction.) Esther, therefore, knows the score
well. Xerxes can be fickle. Even as she enters more and more into
the royal sphere, she must ensure that she has the king's favour to
the extent of making her petition successful. For it might come
closer to the *letter* of Xerxes' offer than he either intended or
would grant.

This explains Esther's failure to come to the point straight
away. Why, we ask, does she not strike while the iron is hot and
secure the Jews' reprieve while the king is in a good mood? To
dally over a dinner party seems irrelevant. To do it *twice*—while
Jews throughout the Empire suffer agonies of alarm—seems
reckless and irresponsible.

Two important things are achieved, however, by Esther's tactics (for tactics they are, rather than a crisis of confidence). The
first is that those of us who are enjoying the story are well served,
for dramatic tension is piled on by the delay in confronting the
king with the truth. This is more than just a literary device,
however. For on the psychological level, secondly, the tactics
have their own plausibility. Esther, in fact, is plotting to produce
the circumstances which will ensure the desired outcome to her
request. She does this by introducing Haman to the scene. The
king had certainly not bargained for this. Haman may be his
favourite, but he can hardly want him around just at the moment.
Esther's introduction of Haman, therefore, serves not only to
have him conveniently placed for exposure when the propitious

moment comes, but to begin to provoke frustration in the king against him. Notice, furthermore, how Esther's *first* dinner is *for the king* (v. 4). Her second, however, is *for the king and Haman* (v. 8). There is just a hint here that Esther's purpose is to sow a resentment in the king's mind, and have him think that this Haman was staking too big a claim both in the kingdom and in his wife's esteem.

(ii)

Haman, fool that he is, sees none of the dark clouds gathering on the horizon. He is impressed only with the fact that he is getting his feet further under the table than he had ever hoped (vv. 11–12), and that his bliss is sullied by Mordecai's continued refusal to do him honour—an offence that seems all the greater to him in the light of his increased standing in his *own* eyes (vv. 9, 13).

There is something of a comic element in Haman's sudden transitions from rapture to black anger in these verses—an element which will be more pronounced in the next chapter. The comedy is not there for its own sake, however. It serves to emphasize how much Haman is divorced from the realities of his situation. Esther has contrived to make him appear over-arrogant in the king's eyes, and he falls right into the trap. He exults in the high honours which are so charged with danger. The two-fold dinner invitation—with a 24-hour interval between the two occasions—allows time for Haman's misguided self-confidence to mature. Blinded by his hunger for power and his hatred of Mordecai he forms a plan: to build a gallows for his rival and then tell the king (! v. 14) to hang him on it, an audacity which shows how much his reason is impaired. The Book of Proverbs comments admirably on Haman's folly when it says: "Pride goes before destruction" (Prov. 16:18) and again: "There is a way which seems right to a man, but its end is the way to death" (Prov. 16:25). Haman is the perfect fool. At what seems to him the height of his glory, he devises the petard with which he will himself be hoist.

Chapter 5 brings Esther and Haman—the two people in Persia who above all others can influence the king—together in his presence. When it comes to a conflict, as it must, we know that the very *human* allurements of Esther are undergirded by a Power that governs all things.

DECLINE...

Esther 6:1–14

¹On that night the king could not sleep; and he gave orders to bring the book of memorable deeds, the chronicles, and they were read before the king. ²And it was found written how Mordecai had told about Bigthana and Teresh, two of the king's eunuchs, who guarded the threshold, and who had sought to lay hands upon King Ahasuerus. ³And the king said, "What honour or dignity has been bestowed on Mordecai for this?" The king's servants who attended him said, "Nothing has been done for him." ⁴And the king said, "Who is in the court?" Now Haman had just entered the outer court of the king's palace to speak to the king about having Mordecai hanged on the gallows that he had prepared for him. ⁵So the king's servants told him, "Haman is there, standing in the court." And the king said, "Let him come in." ⁶So Haman came in, and the king said to him, "What shall be done to the man whom the king delights to honour?" And Haman said to himself, "Whom would the king delight to honour more than me?" ⁷And Haman said to the king, "For the man whom the king delights to honour, ⁸let royal robes be brought, which the king has worn, and the horse which the king has ridden, and on whose head a royal crown is set; ⁹and let the robes and the horse be handed over to one of the king's most noble princes; let him array the man whom the king delights to honour, and let him conduct the man on horseback through the open square of the city, proclaiming before him: 'Thus shall it be done to the man whom the king delights to honour.'" ¹⁰Then the king said to Haman, "Make haste, take the robes and the horse, as you have said, and do so to Mordecai the Jew who sits at the king's gate. Leave out nothing that you have mentioned." ¹¹So Haman took the robes and the horse, and he arrayed Mordecai and made him ride through the open square of the city, proclaiming, "Thus shall it be done to the man whom the king delights to honour."

¹²Then Mordecai returned to the king's gate. But Haman hurried to his house, mourning and with his head covered. ¹³And Haman told his wife Zeresh and all his friends everything that had befallen him. Then

his wise men and his wife Zeresh said to him, "If Mordecai, before whom you have begun to fall, is of the Jewish people, you will not prevail against him but will surely fall before him."

¹⁴While they were yet talking with him, the king's eunuchs arrived and brought Haman in haste to the banquet that Esther had prepared.

In this passage the themes of apparent coincidence and underlying purposefulness come together with tremendous comic irony. Look at the coincidences which rush to secure Mordecai's vindication and Haman's doom. The king cannot sleep; he orders the official book of memorable deeds to be read—an ancient king's version of the late-night film; the reader stumbles on the account of Mordecai's loyal deed, recorded for us in 2:21–23; he looks about for a suitable bearer of the dignities which he has resolved to confer upon his benefactor, and lo and behold, his Prime Minister has just called—what better man for the job! Here is comedy already. Each of the characters on stage is ignorant of the motives and plans of the other. The king knows as little of Haman's passion to be rid of Mordecai as Haman knows of the king's plan to elevate him. Only the reader can savour the exquisite irony and suspense. Which of the two will speak first and disillusion the other?

The king speaks (v. 6) and does so in such a way as to sustain the delicious misunderstanding. His reference to "the man whom the king delights to honour" permits the vain Haman to believe that he himself is meant. (His words in verse 6 would make a perfect pantomime stage-whisper!) Under this delusion he describes the fabulous rewards which in his fantasies he has devised for himself. Haman, in his blindness, must have jumped at the opportunity to speak thus, without apparently seeking the honours for himself. Any man who did that would immediately have aroused a king's suspicion. To wear robes the king has worn and ride a horse the king has ridden was tantamount to being another king. (The crowned horse, incidentally, is known from reliefs, and is another royal emblem.) If Xerxes saw through Haman it was certainly another black mark against his name, a memory that would return in the moment of his exposure. Yet he does not hesitate to heap all these things on Mordecai.

Haman's recklessly hopeful speech produces the best comic moment in the tale; though for the pretender himself it is pure tragedy. The naming of Mordecai (v. 10) as the recipient of the honours is a hammer blow to Haman's perfect but fragile confidence. The blow is the more devastating because the honours were of his own concoction, and designed to be as glittering as he could imagine. Now he is instructed to "leave out nothing that you have mentioned". And he is himself to be the mediator of the king's goodwill to this hated enemy. Little wonder that the once-voluble Haman is now silent. He is struck dumb. We are left to imagine the numb shock slowly giving way to bitter shame and self-recrimination.

We have already spoken of Haman as the proverbial fool. His fate now reminds us further of that other bane of the righteous, the "prosperous wicked". This is the subject of the lament of the Psalmist (Ps. 73), to whom it appears that the innocent too often suffer in the world, while the wicked enjoy its fatness (vv. 4ff., 13–14). The Psalmist's conclusion there is that appearances have deceived him, for the true condition of the wicked is one of appalling danger and horror (vv. 17–20). Haman has appeared to have achieved everything that was available to a man in the Persian Empire. Yet we have observed that his advantages— even when they appeared greatest—could not procure him satisfaction ("all this does me no good", 5:13). And now it becomes clear that he *never could* have ultimately succeeded in his tilt for power against Mordecai and the Jews, because the divine controlling hand would not permit it.

The author of Esther shows how, under that hand, events conspire to do justice in the end. If, according to the proverb, "honour is not fitting for a fool" (Prov. 26:1), then Haman shall not enjoy his honour long. It is right that, as Mordecai is lifted from his sackcloth and ashes, Haman should be thus reduced (v. 12). The world is at any time full of "Hamans" who still appear to enjoy the advantages so resented by the Psalmist. Psalm 73 and the fate of Haman himself, however, counsel against the Christian's thoughts straying to injustice on the part of God. The New Testament, stretching to eternity the canvas on which human lives are played out, allows for the redress of *all* injustices in the end.

The *inevitable* ascendancy of the Jewish people, having by this stage been all but demonstrated by events, is now given open expression by Haman's wife Zeresh and his friends (v. 13). These very people, oddly, had incited him not long before to build the fateful gallows for Mordecai (5:14). Perhaps the truth dawns only now that Haman has received his first setback. Their sudden insight sends him disconsolate to the second of Esther's banquets, that which is for the king *and Haman*, but which can now be at best no more than a mockery of his grand designs.

A further oddity in the chapter is that the king, in honouring Mordecai, seems aware that he is a Jew (v. 10), yet the fact remains unrelated in his mind to the sentence of death which he himself has passed upon all Jews. Did he intend secretly to exempt Mordecai?—or neutralize the decree? What were Mordecai's thoughts as he accepted his honour, yet without having heard the word of reprieve that meant infinitely more? The author lets us guess. For the moment, we are allowed to reflect on the incongruity of the fact that a Jew has been found worthy of the highest honour while, with his fellow-Jews, fated to extinction because "it is not for the king's profit to tolerate them" (3:8). There is something here—though grotesquely portrayed—of the ambiguity of the presence in the world of all believers: applauded and accepted for the benefits they bring (one thinks of Mother Teresa), yet suspected and despised for their separate identity and rejection of the world's standards. Whatever honours the world awards, the Christian's ambitions can only be fulfilled and satisfaction won if they are centred on the good of God's people which is eternally assured.

. . . AND FALL

Esther 7:1–10

¹So the king and Haman went in to feast with Queen Esther. ²And on

the second day, as they were drinking wine, the king again said to Esther, "What is your petition, Queen Esther? It shall be granted you. And what is your request? Even to the half of my kingdom, it shall be fulfilled." ³Then Queen Esther answered, "If I have found favour in your sight, O king, and if it please the king, let my life be given me at my petition, and my people at my request. ⁴For we are sold, I and my people, to be destroyed, to be slain, and to be annihilated. If we had been sold merely as slaves, men and women, I would have held my peace; for our affliction is not to be compared with the loss to the king." ⁵Then King Ahasuerus said to Queen Esther, "Who is he, and where is he, that would presume to do this?" ⁶And Esther said, "A foe and enemy! This wicked Haman!" Then Haman was in terror before the king and the queen. ⁷And the king rose from the feast in wrath and went into the palace garden; but Haman stayed to beg his life from Queen Esther, for he saw that evil was determined against him by the king. ⁸And the king returned from the palace garden to the place where they were drinking wine, as Haman was falling on the couch where Esther was; and the king said, "Will he even assault the queen in my presence, in my own house?" As the words left the mouth of the king, they covered Haman's face. ⁹Then said Harbona, one of the eunuchs in attendance on the king, "Moreover, the gallows which Haman has prepared for Mordecai, whose word saved the king, is standing in Haman's house, fifty cubits high." ¹⁰And the king said, "Hang him on that." So they hanged Haman on the gallows which he had prepared for Mordecai. Then the anger of the king abated.

(i)

The demise of Haman now quickly ensues. The fatal blows have been struck, and the reader awaits the villain's exposure and come-uppance. Once again, of course, the characters involved know less than we do. The king still does not know that his queen is a Jewess, and Esther cannot know how he will take the news. Nor is she aware, it seems, of Mordecai's advancement and therefore of the turning tide. Haman remains as oblivious as the king, presumably, both to Esther's Jewishness and her close relationship with Mordecai. He may yet have hopes, therefore, of salvaging some honour for himself following his humiliation—which was known to be such only to himself and his closest associates—in the Mordecai affair. The stage is set for revelations.

The first revelation comes from the queen, taking her cue from the king's repeated offer of whatever she wished. It must have come as a shock to both her companions. For Esther it is the moment when her courage is finally tested. In revealing Haman's villainy she must also disclose that she belongs to a people under sentence of death. Esther has been accused of callousness in her attack upon Haman, and in her silence as he seeks her mercy. Could she not have spoken less damningly against him?—even attempted to mitigate his crime? As soon as we try to penetrate the minds of our characters, however (which here as so often the author does not encourage us to do), it is clear that we cannot readily condemn. Esther's own safety and that of her people is at stake. Her only hope lies in displaying the villainy of her antagonist in all its hideousness.

With this in view she makes reference to the sordid financial transaction that had accompanied the decree (perhaps the king had taken the money after all, despite his disclaimer, 3:11, which would then have to be seen as conventional eastern politeness). The same concern explains her uncompromising words in verse 6*a*, which imply that Haman is an enemy, not only of herself, which is obvious, but of *the king*. The story neither at this point nor anywhere else presents Esther as a model of piety in every respect. Her action here is commended nevertheless as the logical consequence of her decision to place her own life at risk for the greater good of saving her people. This she now does in the only way she knows. She leaves us an example of courage, backed up by a resolute use of all her resources. (These include, alongside her femininity, a God-given astuteness. On "sanctified cunning" see the commentary on Neh. 2:1–8.)

As for Haman, our last picture of him is of his terror before what he knows to be the swift vengeance of kings, appealing in desperation to Esther for a mercy which he himself had never shown. If an appeal to Xerxes seemed to be ruled out because the king had already "determined" evil against him (v. 7), his approach to Esther could hardly avail more. His foolish prostration before one of those whose death he had attempted to engineer serves only to increase his guilt in the king's eyes by what looks like an attack upon her virtue. His downfall is merely hastened by it. Once again, a proverb seems to comment (see Prov. 26:27).

(ii)

Xerxes himself is no "knight in shining armour". His actions need not be interpreted as based on any fineness of feeling. He is merely a king who is obsessed with the preservation of a tyrannous *status quo* and, more especially, his own interests. It is not Haman's attempted genocide that angers him; had he not connived at that himself? It would be possible too to overstress his noble feelings for Esther; we must keep romantic or chivalrous notions at arm's length here. Ultimately it is the revelation that *Haman is his enemy* that determines Xerxes' condemnation of him.

The action in the little scene brings this out nicely. The king's first instinct in the wrath that he feels following the accusation of his Prime Minister is to take a walk in his garden! Is this a likely response? He may well have been somewhat confused, of course. Certainly, he was involved in a far more complicated situation that he had anticipated when the party began the day before. Who was more dispensable, queen or Prime Minister? If these questions were in his mind when he went off for his stroll they were quickly answered on his return. The sight of Haman "falling on the couch where Esther was"—no doubt reclining—looked like the kind of advance towards *his* queen which under the harem (understood as an abstract idea, namely the prohibition of all approach to the king's wives) was absolutely taboo. (The word used by the king and translated "assault", v. 8, has the overtones of a sexual attack.) As if this were not enough (though the immediate covering of Haman's face, v. 8, as of a criminal, suggests that it was), Xerxes discovers in the next moment that the villain also harbours hostility against *his* benefactor, Mordecai. The only offences which King Xerxes recognizes, therefore, are offences against himself.

It is possible for peoples to survive under such kings. But there is no salvation in *trusting* them. This is why the Jews—though they be loyal citizens and even enjoy such honours as come their way—could never *assimilate* in such a way as to recognize *only* the temporal authority. Rather, they must keep their separate identity (which despite the momentary victory recounted in the Book of Esther will be a trouble to them yet) and they must submit above all to the authority of their God, in whom alone is real salvation. The Christian lives with a similar hierarchy of allegiances. If they never conflict, let him praise God; and let him pray for the grace to put God first should he have to choose.

TURNABOUT

Esther 8:1–17

¹On that day King Ahasuerus gave to Queen Esther the house of Haman, the enemy of the Jews. And Mordecai came before the king, for Esther had told what he was to her; ²and the king took off his signet ring, which he had taken from Haman, and gave it to Mordecai. And Esther set Mordecai over the house of Haman.

³Then Esther spoke again to the king; she fell at his feet and besought him with tears to avert the evil design of Haman the Agagite and the plot which he had devised against the Jews. ⁴And the king held out the golden sceptre to Esther, ⁵and Esther rose and stood before the king. And she said, "If it please the king, and if I have found favour in his sight, and if the thing seem right before the king, and I be pleasing in his eyes, let an order be written to revoke the letters devised by Haman the Agagite, the son of Hammedatha, which he wrote to destroy the Jews who are in all the provinces of the king. ⁶For how can I endure to see the calamity that is coming to my people? Or how can I endure to see the destruction of my kindred?" ⁷Then King Ahasuerus said to Queen Esther and to Mordecai the Jew, "Behold, I have given Esther the house of Haman, and they have hanged him on the gallows, because he would lay hands on the Jews. ⁸And you may write as you please with regard to the Jews, in the name of the king, and seal it with the king's ring; for an edict written in the name of the king and sealed with the king's ring cannot be revoked."

⁹The king's secretaries were summoned at that time, in the third month, which is the month of Sivan, on the twenty-third day; and an edict was written according to all that Mordecai commanded concerning the Jews to the satraps and the governors and the princes of the provinces from India to Ethiopia, a hundred and twenty-seven provinces, to every province in its own script and to every people in its own language, and also to the Jews in their script and their language. ¹⁰The writing was in the name of King Ahasuerus and sealed with the king's ring, and letters were sent by mounted couriers riding on swift horses that were used in the king's service, bred from the royal stud. ¹¹By these the king allowed the Jews who were in every city to gather and defend their lives, to destroy, to slay, and to annihilate any armed force of any people or province that might attack them, with their children and women, and to plunder their goods, ¹²upon one day throughout all the provinces of King Ahasuerus, on the thirteenth day of the twelfth month, which is the month of Adar. ¹³A copy of what was written was to be issued as a decree in every province, and by proclamation to all peoples, and the Jews were to be ready on that day to avenge themselves upon their enemies. ¹⁴So the couriers, mounted on their swift horses that were used in the king's service, rode out in haste, urged by the king's command; and the decree was issued in Susa the capital.

¹⁵Then Mordecai went out from the presence of the king in royal robes of blue and white, with a great golden crown and a mantle of fine linen and purple, while the city of Susa shouted and rejoiced. ¹⁶The Jews had light and gladness and joy and honour. ¹⁷And in every province and in every city, wherever the king's command and his edict came, there was gladness and joy among the Jews, a feast and a holiday. And many from the peoples of the country declared themselves Jews, for the fear of the Jews had fallen upon them.

(i)

The issue in chapter 8 is how to obtain a reversal of the decree against the Jews (chapter 3) in the light of the fact that decrees are irreversible (v. 8*b*). Haman himself is dead, but his malign influence lives and is still a major threat. Esther's intercession for her people is not yet complete.

The first two verses make a transition from the events of chapter 7. The king makes a present of Haman's estate to Esther, perhaps thinking now that the whole matter is at an end. He seems content to know that his queen and new favourite are safe, and shows little interest in the Jews as a people. Esther prepares for a last-minute assault on his indifference. With this in view, she arranges for Mordecai to be brought to her side, probably not only by revealing his relationship to her, but also by extolling his qualities (this being suggested by the words "what he was to her", v. 1). Mordecai now gains the promotion which had earlier come to Haman; the present of the signet ring (v. 2) makes him the new Prime Minister (cf. 3:10). As if to emphasize his new status Esther proceeds to bestow on him the estate which the king has just given her. It is important to notice that though it is technically the king who advances Mordecai it is really Esther who is in control. She has arranged the matter so that when she comes to make her plea she will be seen to have the support of the most powerful man in the kingdom, next to Xerxes himself. The king would have to be firm of purpose to resist the charms of the woman who has never yet failed to move him, and in addition the silent strength of the man whom he has lately honoured and but moments ago made his Prime Minister.

Esther now pleads as only she can. The king shows that he is basically well disposed to whatever she might ask by extending the sceptre, perhaps simply indicating this time that she need not prostrate herself to address him (as she has done, v. 3). Yet, knowing that she asks the unaskable, she goes on to stir a mix of flattery and coyness (v. 5) which must have been irresistible. (Notice the alternation of phrases which emphasize the king's right to do as he wishes with phrases which draw attention to Esther's desire to please him, v. 5*a*.) She then comes to the point (vv. 5*b*, 6) and secures what the king evidently regards as the best deal he can offer. The decree cannot be revoked. Esther and Mordecai—now recognized as a "team", since the "you" in verse 8 is plural and thus addressed to them both—may devise a further decree "as they please". (This sweeping permission corresponds to that originally given to Haman, 3:11.) And so the stage is set for a great turning of the tables.

(ii)
The writing, the terms and the dissemination of the new decree

parallel the first in a detailed way (8:8ff.; 3:8ff.). We have noticed how in each case there is a giving of the signet ring (to Haman and Mordecai) and how the freedom to draw up the decree is delegated to the interested party (Haman and Mordecai/Esther). In addition the decree is addressed once more to the satraps, governors and princes in all the provinces of the Empire, in the language of all the nations, sealed with the king's ring, sent by "Pony Express" and promulgated in every place. As to the terms , just as the king's subjects everywhere were permitted to "destroy, to slay, and to annihilate all Jews, young and old, women and children, in one day . . . and to plunder their goods" (3:13), so now the Jews are allowed to "destroy, to slay, and to annihilate any armed force . . . that might attack them, with their children and women, and to plunder their goods, upon one day" (8:11–12).

There is a correspondence also and naturally enough in the reactions to the two decrees. Following the former, the Jews mourn (4:1–3); following the latter, they rejoice (8:16–17). Mordecai himself exchanges humiliation and grief (4:1) for honour and celebration (8:15). Similarly, whereas the people of Susa— i.e. the non-Jewish population—were formerly perplexed (3:15), they now join the Jews in rejoicing (8:15). We recall our comment on the earlier passage, that the people at large knew better what was good for the kingdom than the king did. The triumph of the Jews would be good news for most of the country.

A final element in the mirror-image which these verses form with things that have gone before is that non-Jews (presumably those who have been hostile and now feel endangered) *pretend to be Jews*. This is the likeliest understanding of verse 17*b*. Where once Esther, inspired by Mordecai, had hidden her Jewish identity and thus effectively made herself like a non-Jew, non-Jews now contrive to be mistaken for Jews. The new royal standing of Esther and Mordecai (for Mordecai is hardly less "royal" now than his cousin, v. 15) is matched by an ascendancy of the Jews in general in Persia. The people that seemed doomed has not only escaped destruction, but come to occupy a place of privilege, the envy of the Empire. All this has happened because of their

reliance on God alone and because of their willingness (exemplified by Esther and Mordecai) to make it known.

(iii)

It remains to consider the *morality* of the decree for which Esther
and Mordecai have such direct responsibility. It has smacked so
much of ignoble vengefulness to many readers that they have
been embarrassed to own the book at all. The passage is not a
pretty one, but this is probably an over-hasty verdict.

It has been argued in defence of Esther and Mordecai that their
intention was to follow the so-called law of talion (Exod. 21:24)
which established for Israel a principle of just penalties in legal
proceedings ("eye for eye, tooth for tooth" etc.) that was for its
day advanced and enlightened. In other words, they set out to
exact of their enemies *only* what these had first planned to inflict
on them and theirs. However, these enemies had not yet done
anything to the Jews. It is doubtful, therefore, whether the law of
talion was relevant to this situation.

Were Esther and Mordecai then simply giving way to a desire
for vengeance? All that we can say is that a *careful* reading of the
terms does not suggest so. It is not peoples as such against whom
the Jews in the Empire are empowered to act, but "armed
forces"; similarly, they are given no warrant to attack, but only to
gather for self-defence and to inflict any casualties which occurred as they exercised that right (v. 11). The words "with their
children and women" are important here. Scholars are divided on
the question whether this means that the Jews might destroy the
women and children of the peoples who took up arms against
them, or whether it means that they might destroy those who took
up arms against *them* (i.e. the Jews) along with *their* (i.e. the
Jews') women and children. Since the only legitimate target in
view is actually "armed forces"—which, as such, do not *have*
women and children—the latter interpretation is to be preferred.
The decree can then be understood purely as a defensive
measure, envisaging no more force than was necessary in order
to neutralize the first decree.

If, then, there is a *justice*, even a poetic justice, in the new turn of events, it is a justice conceived in the mind of the One who has, unseen and unnamed, governed all that has led us to this point. Once again, it is his reliability in the cause of his faithful people that constitutes the real point of the narrative. The motives and qualities of the Jews themselves are not the author's chief interest, and indeed are, according to his wont, left veiled by him. The central thing, for Jews then as for believers now, is that God does not ultimately abandon his people to the tender mercies of fortune or of wicked men.

PURIM

Esther 9:1–28

[1]Now in the twelfth month, which is the month of Adar, on the thirteenth day of the same, when the king's command and edict were about to be executed, on the very day when the enemies of the Jews hoped to get the mastery over them, but which had been changed to a day when the Jews should get the mastery over their foes, [2]the Jews gathered in their cities throughout all the provinces of King Ahasuerus to lay hands on such as sought their hurt. And no one could make a stand against them, for the fear of them had fallen upon all peoples. [3]All the princes of the provinces and the satraps and the governors and the royal officials also helped the Jews, for the fear of Mordecai had fallen upon them. [4]For Mordecai was great in the king's house, and his fame spread throughout all the provinces; for the man Mordecai grew more and more powerful. [5]So the Jews smote all their enemies with the sword, slaughtering, and destroying them, and did as they pleased to those who hated them. [6]In Susa the capital itself the Jews slew and destroyed five hundred men, [7]and also slew Par-shan-datha and Dalphon and Aspatha [8]and Poratha and Adalia and Aridatha [9]and Parmashta and Arisai and Aridai and Vaizatha, [10]the ten sons of Haman the son of Hammedatha, the enemy of the Jews; but they laid no hand on the plunder.

[11]That very day the number of those slain in Susa the capital was reported to the king. [12]And the king said to Queen Esther, "In Susa the capital the Jews have slain five hundred men and also the ten sons of Haman. What then have they done in the rest of the king's

provinces! Now what is your petition? It shall be granted you. And what further is your request? It shall be fulfilled." ¹³And Esther said, "If it please the king, let the Jews who are in Susa be allowed tomorrow also to do according to this day's edict. And let the ten sons of Haman be hanged on the gallows." ¹⁴So the king commanded this to be done; a decree was issued in Susa, and the ten sons of Haman were hanged. ¹⁵The Jews who were in Susa gathered also on the fourteenth day of the month of Adar and they slew three hundred men in Susa; but they laid no hands on the plunder.

¹⁶Now the other Jews who were in the king's provinces also gathered to defend their lives, and got relief from their enemies, and slew seventy-five thousand of those who hated them; but they laid no hands on the plunder. ¹⁷This was on the thirteenth day of the month of Adar, and on the fourteenth day they rested and made that a day of feasting and gladness. ¹⁸But the Jews who were in Susa gathered on the thirteenth day and on the fourteenth, and rested on the fifteenth day, making that a day of feasting and gladness. ¹⁹Therefore the Jews of the villages, who live in the open towns, hold the fourteenth day of the month of Adar as a day for gladness and feasting and holiday-making, and a day on which they send choice portions to one another.

²⁰And Mordecai recorded these things, and sent letters to all the Jews who were in all the provinces of King Ahasuerus, both near and far, ²¹enjoining them that they should keep the fourteenth day of the month Adar and also the fifteenth day of the same, year by year, ²²as the days on which the Jews got relief from their enemies, and as the month that had been turned for them from sorrow into gladness and from mourning into a holiday; that they should make them days of feasting and gladness, days for sending choice portions to one another and gifts to the poor.

²³So the Jews undertook to do as they had begun, and as Mordecai had written to them. ²⁴For Haman the Agagite, the son of Hammedatha, the enemy of all the Jews, had plotted against the Jews to destroy them, and had cast Pur, that is the lot, to crush and destroy them; ²⁵but when Esther came before the king, he gave orders in writing that his wicked plot which he had devised against the Jews should come upon his own head, and that he and his sons should be hanged on the gallows. ²⁶Therefore they called these days Purim, after the term Pur. And therefore, because of all that was written in this letter, and of what they had faced in this matter, and of what had befallen them, ²⁷the Jews ordained and took it upon themselves and

their descendants and all who joined them, that without fail they would keep these two days according to what was written and at the time appointed every year, 28that these days should be remembered and kept throughout every generation, in every family, province, and city, and that these days of Purim should never fall into disuse among the Jews, nor should the commemoration of these days cease among their descendants.

(i)

The last two chapters of Esther record the longed-for deliverance and its aftermath. The fateful day of the pogrom, named in the original decree (3:13), has arrived (v. 1). The Jews brace themselves for attack, and implement the terms of the *second* decree by gathering to fight. We are given no details either about the extent of bitterness against them or the cause of the fighting. Clearly there were many who dared to do the work of Haman, who had always counted, presumably, on a degree of anti-Semitism in the Empire. The fighting appears to have been bitter, even spreading to the acropolis at Susa (v. 6, where again "capital" implies the royal and administrative complex). This suggests that the Jews had enemies besides Haman in high places, even if the provincial governors were tending to favour the Jews because of the influence of Mordecai (vv. 3–4). The hostility against the sons of Haman (v. 10) could mean that they were active in promoting the anti-Jewish cause, rather than that they were killed purely for revenge.

Here as in the terms of the decree the author is careful to give the impression that the Jews acted honourably. Only men are killed, which is consistent with a situation in which organized fighting forces are initiating the hostilities. The fact that no plunder is taken (vv. 10, 15) shows that the Jews are not exploiting their advantage for illicit gain. Details like these are intended to show that the defensive action was free from wrong motivation. The reason for Esther's request that the permission for hostilities be extended into the second day (v. 13) is not given. We may infer that she knew of those who were determined to carry the attack on the Jews further and therefore that the need for self-defence was not yet past.

(ii)

Considerable stress is laid on the fact that the plan to destroy the Jews has produced precisely opposite results to those intended by the plotters. Verse 1 states the point explicitly. The enemies had hoped to "get the mastery", but had been mastered. Similarly, Adar is described as "the month that had been *turned* for them from sorrow into gladness and from mourning into a holiday" (v. 22); cf. also verses 24–26, where Haman's casting of Pur to destroy the Jews is said to have "come upon his own head". In the same connection mention may be made of the phrase "they *did as they pleased* to those who hated them" (v. 5). This does not necessarily mean that they acted bloodthirstily and without restraint. The point is about authority. Whereas all the power of the Empire had formerly stood against their very existence, now they were licensed to live.

It is consistent with the style of writing throughout the book that these things are said without explicit reference to God. We read in verse 1 that the day "had been changed", not "God had changed it". Verse 22 is similarly phrased. The reasons for this apparently deliberate policy have been mentioned before. In a world from which God *appears* to be absent he is nonetheless present. There are several hints in the chapter, however (as if they were really needed) that it is God who has brought about the change of circumstances. The first relates to the phrase just noted, viz. the Jews "did as they pleased". A similar statement appears in Neh. 9:24 where *the Lord* is said to have sent the ancient people of Israel into the land of Canaan to do with its inhabitants "as they would". There is no question *there* about where the people's authority came from. The full meaning of the phrase in our passage, then, seems to be that, the restraining authority of Persia being temporarily lifted, the Jews are subject only to God. The second hint is in the expression "the fear of Mordecai" (v. 3). Scholars have pointed to the similarity between this and the phrase "fear of Isaac" (Gen. 31:42) which in that context is a way of speaking about God. This becomes, then, one of the most suggestive allusions to God in the book.

Finally, God's agency in the *turning* which the events of chapter 9 represent is indicated in the theme of Purim. The Pur, or lot, (cf. 3:7) has played a very minor role in the narrative up to now. In the final section it comes to prominence, though in such a way as to prompt some scholars to think that it fits ill with the rest of the story. However, the references to Pur do have a theological function here. We mentioned in relation to Haman's casting of Pur that it signified his pagan belief that beyond the scope of human power there were other factors that governed events. Verses 24–26 take up this idea to show the wretched folly of an appeal to any superhuman power *which lacks the understanding that that power is none other than the God of Israel.* Events are not governed by chance. Rather they are guided by the God who has delivered his people from hostile empires in the past and will do so again.

(iii)

It is thus that the closing events in the Book of Esther become— for all their talk of slaying—very directly an appeal to have faith in God. The "lot" of the faithful is, in the end, *not* to be destroyed, but to have life. In a world in which hostility to the household of faith seems to flourish naturally, and indeed in which atheistic explanations of the universe grow more strident, "scientific" and apparently convincing, it belongs to faith to "hold fast" *nevertheless* to our hope—now specifically in Christ— "for he who promised is faithful" (Heb. 10:23). Christians believe that God showed his faithfulness, in a way that was infinitely more profound and consequential than the deliverance in the provinces of Persia, when Jesus Christ "turned the tables" on opprobrium and death *not* by using violence to defend himself and thus *avoid* it, but by laying down his power and *submitting* to it. His resurrection is the greatest turning-point in history, that which bears life for a *new* Israel (cf. Rom. 9:6) and permits a deep underlying hope in the face of everything which in this world conspires to rob us of it.

FINALE

Esther 9:29–10:3

²⁹Then Queen Esther, the daughter of Abihail, and Mordecai the Jew gave full written authority, confirming this second letter about Purim. ³⁰Letters were sent to all the Jews, to the hundred and twenty-seven provinces of the kingdom of Ahasuerus, in words of peace and truth, ³¹that these days of Purim should be observed at their appointed seasons, as Mordecai the Jew and Queen Esther enjoined upon the Jews, and as they had laid down for themselves and for their descendants, with regard to their fasts and their lamenting. ³²The command of Queen Esther fixed these practices of Purim, and it was recorded in writing.

¹King Ahasuerus laid tribute on the land and on the coastlands of the sea. ²And all the acts of his power and might, and the full account of the high honour of Mordecai, to which the king advanced him, are they not written in the Book of the Chronicles of the kings of Media and Persia? ³For Mordecai the Jew was next in rank to King Ahasuerus, and he was great among the Jews and popular with the multitude of his brethren, for he sought the welfare of his people and spoke peace to all his people.

(i)

For Esther and Mordecai the exercise of faith issues in feasting and joy: a common Old Testament response to the experience of deliverance (cf. Neh. 12:27). Nor is it a matter of private celebration. Mordecai's "circular" to all the Jews in the Empire establishes a holiday, to be marked by feasting, gladness and the exchange of presents. As the fighting had been spread over two days, so now would be the festivities. Verse 19 testifies to some variation in practice which may have developed in the wake of the events, reflecting the fact that the Jews in Susa had to wait a day longer than those in the provinces before they felt sufficiently secure to celebrate. Mordecai's letter, however, requires two days of celebration to be observed by all Jews wherever they live. Esther's own authority is subsequently added to that of her cousin (vv. 29–32). The holiday is to be called Purim because events had proved what was the true "lot" of the Hamans and of the faithful.

The letters of Mordecai and Esther continue to exercise their authority upon Jews. Despite speculation that Purim was originally a pagan Persian festival merely adopted, and adapted, by Jews, the Book of Esther remains our only source of knowledge about it. This has the effect of bestowing on the book an important role in the Jewish cultic year. Since Purim is the only major Jewish festival not actually authorized by the Pentateuch, Esther comes to have an honour in the eyes of many Jews second only to that, their most respected body of writings.

In this way, therefore, the Jews have ensured that the acts of God on their behalf should not simply pass into oblivion. The very writing of the Book of Esther recognized the ever-present danger that people—even those of the household of faith—would look upon the world and conclude that there was no God. But that perception—along with the perceptions of all the biblical writers who have recorded for us the story of salvation—will have served no purpose if it is not preserved among those who look to God. Corporate remembrance, solemn and joyful, is essential to the healthy life of the Church. It is not necessary to imitate the practices of Purim. (Celebrants are permitted—even encouraged—by a later Jewish writing to give themselves enthusiastically to revelry until they cease to be able to distinguish between cries of "Cursed be Haman!" and "Blessed be Mordecai!" The modern celebration of Christmas is not always far removed from this, unfortunately.) Nevertheless there is a true joy among the people of God when they remind each other of his deliverance, which Christians know to have been supremely and definitively accomplished in Christ.

(ii)

The short final chapter is hardly more than a summarizing footnote. We are reminded of the greatness of Xerxes, with which the book opened, in order to impress upon us not only the accuracy of the things recorded, but also the extent of the honour which the king was able to confer upon Mordecai. The final picture of Mordecai is, however, of one who, far from exploiting his power for personal ends, was motivated only by love of his people and desire for their good. The principle of endowment with gifts *for the benefit of God's people* is thus exemplified by Mordecai as by other Old Testament figures (e.g. Nehemiah); the same principle is enunciated theologically in the New Testament (Eph. 4:11ff.). It is such, i.e. those who put themselves and their resources at the disposal of other people, and particularly the people of God, who receive an honour which is not contingent upon the whim of an earthly tyrant.

FURTHER READING

General

P. R. Ackroyd, *Israel under Babylon and Persia* (Oxford University Press, 1970)

R. N. Frye, *The Heritage of Persia* (Weidenfeld & Nicholson, 1962)

Ezra and Nehemiah

L. H. Brockington, *Ezra, Nehemiah and Esther* (New Century Bible) (Oliphants, 1969)

F. C. Fensham, *The Books of Ezra and Nehemiah* (The New International Commentary) (Eerdmans, 1982)

D. F.Kidner, *Ezra and Nehemiah* (Tyndale Old Testament Commentaries) (Inter-Varsity Press, 1979)

J. M. Myers, *Ezra–Nehemiah* (The Anchor Bible) (Doubleday, 1965)

Esther

J. G. Baldwin, *Esther* (Tyndale Old Testament Commentaries) (Inter-Varsity Press, 1984)

S. B. Berg, *The Book of Esther: Motifs, Themes and Structures* (Scholars' Press, 1979)

R. Gordis, *Megillat Esther* (New York, KTAV, 1982)

C. A. Moore, *Esther* (The Anchor Bible) (Doubleday, 1971)